YOUNG CHILDREN'S COMMUNITY BUILDING IN ACTION

Rethinking the concepts of citizenship and community in relation to young children, this groundbreaking text examines the ways in which indigenous understandings and practices applied in early childhood settings in Australia and New Zealand encourage young children to demonstrate their care and concern for others and so, in turn, perceive themselves as part of a larger community.

Young Children's Community Building in Action acknowledges global variations in the meanings of early childhood education, of citizenship and community building, and challenges widespread invisibility and disregard of Indigenous communities. Through close observation and examination of early years settings in Australia and New Zealand, chapters demonstrate how practices guided by Aboriginal and Māori values support and nurture children's personal and social development as individuals, and as citizens in a wider community. Exploring what young children's citizenship learning and action looks like in practice, and how this may vary within and across communities, the book provides a powerful account of effective pedagogical approaches which have been long excluded from mainstream dialogues.

Written for researchers and students of early childhood education and care, this book provides insight into what citizenship can be for young children, and how Indigenous cultural values shape ways of knowing, being, doing and relating.

Louise Gwenneth Phillips is an early childhood and arts education academic at the School of Education, The University of Queensland, Australia.

Jenny Ritchie is an Associate Professor in Te Puna Akopai, the School of Education, at Te Whare Wananga o te Upoko o te Ika a Maui, Victoria University of Wellington, New Zealand.

Lavina Dynevor is a proud Wakka Wakka woman and passionate Aboriginal early childhood educator and mentor in Australia.

Jared Lambert is Head Teacher at Berhampore Kindergarten, He Whanau Manaaki o Tararua, Wellington, New Zealand.

Kerryn Moroney is a proud Luritja woman who promotes equitable early childhood education systems in Australia.

CONTESTING EARLY CHILDHOOD

Series Editors: Liselott Mariett Olsson and Michel Vandenbroeck

This ground-breaking series questions the current dominant discourses surrounding early childhood, and offers instead alternative narratives of an area that is now made up of a multitude of perspectives and debates.

The series examines the possibilities and risks arising from the accelerated development of early childhood services and policies, and illustrates how it has become increasingly steeped in regulation and control. Insightfully, this collection of books shows how early childhood services can in fact contribute to ethical and democratic practices. The authors explore new ideas taken from alternative working practices in both the western and developing world, and from other academic disciplines such as developmental psychology. Current theories and best practice are placed in relation to the major processes of political, social, economic, cultural and technological change occurring in the world today.

Loris Malaguzzi and the Schools of Reggio Emilia
A Selection of his Writings and Speeches, 1945 – 1993
Paola Cagliari, Marina Castagnetti, Claudia Giudici, Carlina Rinaldi, Vea Vecchi and Peter Moss

The Posthuman Child
Educational Transformation Through Philosophy with Picturebooks
Karin Murris

Constructions of Neuroscience in Early Childhood Education
Michel Vandenbroeck, Jan De Vos, Wim Fias, Liselott Mariett Olsson, Helen Penn, Dave Wastell and Sue White

Alternative Narratives in Early Childhood
An Introduction for Students and Practitioners
Peter Moss

'Be Realistic, Demand the Impossible'
A Memoir of Work in Childcare and Education
Helen Penn

Young Children's Community Building in Action
Embodied, Emplaced and Relational Citizenship
Louise Gwenneth Phillips, Jenny Ritchie, Lavina Dynevor, Jared Lambert and Kerryn Moroney

For more information about this series, please visit: www.routledge.com/Contesting-Early-Childhood/book-series/SE0623

YOUNG CHILDREN'S COMMUNITY BUILDING IN ACTION

Embodied, Emplaced and Relational Citizenship

Louise Gwenneth Phillips, Jenny Ritchie,
Lavina Dynevor, Jared Lambert
and Kerryn Moroney

Routledge
Taylor & Francis Group

LONDON AND NEW YORK

First published 2020
by Routledge
2 Park Square, Milton Park, Abingdon, Oxon OX14 4RN

and by Routledge
52 Vanderbilt Avenue, New York, NY 10017

Routledge is an imprint of the Taylor & Francis Group, an informa business

© 2020 Louise Gwenneth Phillips, Jenny Ritchie, Lavina Dynevor, Jared Lambert and Kerryn Moroney

The right of Louise Gwenneth Phillips, Jenny Ritchie, Lavina Dynevor, Jared Lambert and Kerryn Moroney to be identified as authors of this work has been asserted by them in accordance with sections 77 and 78 of the Copyright, Designs and Patents Act 1988.

British Library Cataloguing-in-Publication Data
A catalogue record for this book is available from the British Library

Library of Congress Cataloging-in-Publication Data
Names: Phillips, Louise Gwenneth, author. | Ritchie, Jenny (Jenny Ruth), author. | Dynevor, Lavina, author.
Title: Young children's community building in action : embodied, emplaced and relational citizenship / Louise Gwenneth Phillips, Jenny Ritchie, Lavina Dynevor, Jared Lambert and Kerryn Mornoney.
Description: Abingdon, Oxon ; New York, NY : Routledge, [2019] | Includes bibliographical references and index.
Identifiers: LCCN 2019007273| ISBN 9781138369658 (hb : alk. paper) | ISBN 9781138369665 (pb : alk. paper) | ISBN 9780429428531 (eb)
Subjects: LCSH: Citizenship--Study and teaching (Early childhood)--Australia. | Citizenship--Study and teaching (Early childhood)--New Zealand. | Children, Aboriginal Australian--Education (Early childhood) | Children, Maori--Education (Early childhood) | Community and school--Australia. | Community and school--New Zealand.
Classification: LCC LC1091 .P485 2019 | DDC 372.830994--dc23
LC record available at https://lccn.loc.gov/2019007273

ISBN: 978-1-138-36965-8 (hbk)
ISBN: 978-1-138-36966-5 (pbk)
ISBN: 978-0-429-42853-1 (ebk)

Typeset in Bembo
by Taylor & Francis Books
Printed and bound by CPI Group (UK) Ltd, Croydon, CR0 4YY

To the children, educators, Elders and ancestors of the land on which we meet, we are humbly indebted for your collective wisdom on community building.

CONTENTS

ILLUSTRATIONS

Figures

Tables

A NOTE ABOUT THE COVER

Centre circle

'Bunya tree' by Samuel Murray (II) Community artist (Lavina Dynevor's father)
Bunya trees and their nuts have a long Aboriginal Australian history of bringing people together from all over Australia for their rich food source – we draw from this history and symbolism.

Left and right

Circle designs by Nadya Akengata Karakia

ACKNOWLEDGEMENTS

We gratefully acknowledge the communities with whom we worked to create this book. Thank you for welcoming us in and trusting us with what we know is special and dear to you – your children and your wisdom. We are humbled by this precious gift and ask readers to continue to handle with care. Special gratitude goes to Jacqui Tapau, Director of Gundoo Early Learning Centre for seeing value in the study, welcoming us and standing by us all the way through. Our sincere appreciation also to He Whānau Manaaki Kindergarten Association and the teachers of Katoa Kindergarten for your trust in our project. We also are deeply appreciative of the thoughtful critique of drafts by our dear colleagues and friends Tracey Bunda and Mere Skerrett. And this work would not have been possible without the support of the Spencer Foundation New Civics Initiative Major Grant for our *Civic Action and Learning with Young Children: Comparing Approaches in New Zealand, Australia and the United States* project led by Dr Jennifer Keys Adair (University of Texas).

FOREWORD

Michel Vandenbroeck

Respect for diversity and for human dignity is not about tolerance for those who deviate from the norm. It is about the deconstruction of the norm that creates the idea of deviation. And that is precisely what this book does and why it is so much needed in the groundbreaking 'Contesting Early Childhood' series. It cannot be denied that the physical, spiritual and emotional violence of colonisation has left serious marks both in the colonised and the coloniser. Among the colonial heritage is the implicit assumption that the Northern hemisphere is the cradle of civilisation and enlightenment and that the knowledge that science has produced in this hemisphere is universally valid. Among these implicit assumptions, the ideal of the autonomous, self-sufficient and productive citizen is hegemonic. And that hegemonic image constructs an image of the child as an actor that needs socialisation by the adult, on its way to achieve the status of autonomy and self-sufficiency. Education, in this vein, is the process by which this ideal image can be achieved. And that process can be observed, measured and translated in data. PISA, PIRLS, IELS and so many other global testings are but operationalisations of how education serves a predefined outcome and how that outcome is reduced to the global citizen, the productive adult that needs to strive for the same individual achievement, independent of where he or she lives; an achievement that can in turn be measured in terms of the return on the educational investments. As Harry Hendrick (2016: 17–18) observed: 'Gramsci famously noted that ideology aspires to be "common sense" (…) through a social-scientifically informed sleight of hand, its proponents transform what is fundamentally a particular political notion into a norm of cultural consensus.'

Louise Gwenneth Phillips, Jenny Ritchie, Lavina Dynevor, Jared Lambert and Kerryn Moroney show that other discourses are possible and sustainable. Through their collaborative work with indigenous peoples in Australia and New Zealand, they show that other conceptualisations of citizenship are possible and feasible and that a shift of perspective generates other forms of knowledge on children and on early childhood education. Early childhood education is a particularly interesting site of studies, as it is a site where the intimacy of family life intersects with public concerns about inequality, education, gender policies, labour policies et cetera. What the authors of this book eloquently illustrate is that, therefore, early childhood education cannot but be a political site, as it is permeated with conceptions of what is the good life, what is the society we would wish to live in and would wish our children to live in, what is the individual and what is the collective, what is public and what is private. And since these notions may vary according to history and geography, depending on the social, cultural and political contexts they are embedded in, it becomes clear that they are man-made (or woman-made) and therefore can be changed by men and women. Most importantly, the authors of this book show us that – as fundamental notions that underpin our educational systems are not invariant and universal – choice is possible. And where choice is possible, it becomes impossible not to choose. Confronted with the knowledge that somehow, somewhere, meanings of early childhood education, of citizenship and community building, of the individual and the collective, of the private and the public may be different, compels us to debate and legitimize the choices we make. And thus to dialogue about these choices with those who are first and foremost concerned: children, families and local communities. In that dialogue, one could bear in mind what Paulo Freire (1970: 78) taught us: 'Dialogue cannot exist without humility [...] How can I dialogue if I always project ignorance onto others and never perceive my own?' In that sense, the present book is truly decolonizing: it has the power to liberate our heart and minds from preconceived ideas about the meaning of early childhood education and the place of the child in the community. Liberation, in that sense, can undoubtedly make room for new debates, dialogues, disagreements and yet untested feasibilities.

References

Freire, P. (1970). *Pedagogy of the Oppressed*. New York: Herder and Herder.
Hendrick, H. (2016). *Narcissistic Parenting in an Insecure World: A History of Parenting Culture 1920s to Present*. Bristol: Policy Press.

PREFACE – LOCATING OURSELVES

Before commencing the content of this book, we introduce ourselves and our connection to notions of young children's rights and citizenship – what we come to refer to as community building. In both Aboriginal and Māori cultures it is an important practice to introduce yourself and where you are from. As NgugiWakka Wakka country woman Tracey Bunda explains: 'In Aboriginal communities, naming oneself through defining, in Aboriginal vernacular, who is your mob and where does your mob come from, what country, is protocol' (Phillips & Bunda, 2018, p. xi).

In Māori contexts, any gathering, or hui, of people who do not already know each other is likely to start with a whakawhanaungatanga, which is a round whereby each person takes it in turn to introduce themselves. This introduction will usually include a tribal pepeha, a statement that identifies the local geographical features and key ancestors of the person's tribal home marae, or village. This sharing of geographical and genealogical contexts enables immediate connections to be made, generating a sense of community.

Louise's story

I am a fifth generation white Australian of English, Irish and German convict and settler ancestry. After independently travelling around India when I was 18 I became very troubled about my Australian identity and returned determined to listen to and learn from Aboriginal Australian ontologies and experiences of colonisation and the Australian nation-building project. I also decided to study become an early childhood teacher. In this degree, I chose to complete every elective on Aboriginal studies available, an internship with an Aboriginal child care centre and a study tour to Wilcannia and Arrernte country. During my undergraduate early childhood study I became a passionate advocate for Aboriginal knowledges in education and children's rights. I recall in 1989 coming to know about the United Nations Convention on the Rights of the Child through Foster Parents Plan Australia and meeting with the Head of the School of Early Childhood to see what the school was going to do to address and implement this international instrument.

In 2000, when Prime Minister John Howard refused to apologise to Indigenous Australians for the past government policy of forced removal of children from their families, contrary to the recommendation of the Bringing Them Home Report (Human Rights & Equal Opportunity Commission, 1997), was a key moment when I was alerted to young children's activism which ignited my inquiries into children's citizenship. I had told a story to a group of four- to five-year-olds at community child care centre in inner-city Sydney about a young Indigenous Australian woman named Elsie, which drew from the childhood experiences of Aboriginal Australian women documented in the book *Murawina: Australian Women of High Achievement* (Sykes, 1993). On completing the story, two boys, aged five, expressed their outrage at the acts of the government officials with these comments 'Put them in a brown bear cage' and 'Hang them upside down'. I then asked the children, 'Well what do you do here when something unfair happens?' to which one child replied, 'You say sorry'. Then suddenly another boy leapt to his feet with urgency and blurted out, 'John Howard did not say sorry'. It seemed he had identified a connection between the story I had just told, possible discussions with his teacher and family, and a recurring feature in the media that year. The boy continued with, 'Get John Howard to come here and say sorry to the Aborigines!'

I wanted to support the children's enthusiasm to take action, but it was unlikely that John Howard would visit their childcare centre. As a compromise I suggested that the children could write letters to the government expressing their thoughts and feelings regarding the forced removal of Aboriginal and Torres Strait Islander children from their families. This suggestion had barely left my mouth when they all moved from the gathering on the carpet to the writing area of the room. Their letters revealed their earnest desires to rectify the situation.

The next day we wrote a group letter to the government to accompany the individual letters, which included the children's drawings and messages. The group decided collectively upon the following words:

> To the Government,
>   Could you please say sorry to the Aborigines for stealing children from their families and home, and invading their land? Please find enclosed our drawings and messages. From…

Immediately on completing this script the children moved spontaneously towards the poster-size letter and signed their names on the bottom. This needed no prompting; they were proud to have their names associated with their social act of writing this letter to the government.

There were three points in this encounter at which I marvelled at the enthusiasm and capacity of young children to engage with social justice issues. The first point was when one child identified a connection between the Stolen Generation story that I had shared and John Howard's refusal to apologise for the practice of removing Aboriginal and Torres Strait Islander children from their families. The second point was when the whole group of children moved to the writing table to write their letters to the government without explicit instructions. The third point was when the children self-initiated signing their names on the group covering letter to the government.

These moments have resonated with me for years, and I have shared this account at many of my storytelling workshops and conference presentations with early childhood educators and academics. My frequent sharing of this experience has been motivated by celebration, a celebration of the capacity of young children to engage in dialogue on injustice and demonstrate self-motivation to redress the injustice. When able to undertake postgraduate research some five years later, this encounter framed my doctoral study into young children's active citizenship through social-justice storytelling as pedagogy, which then later motivated the Spencer Foundation study 'Civic action and learning with young children: Comparing approaches in New Zealand, Australia and the United States' from which this book draws.

Lavina's (Bena) story

I'm a strong proud family Wakka Wakka woman from the Aboriginal community of Cherbourg, where I was born and raised by my parents with the help of my grandparents and close knitted extended families, who've all taught me and my siblings the same strong values and beliefs that they were once taught as a child or have learnt from experiences throughout their lives. Because of my upbringing I carry scars of my family's: the wounds of the mistreatments, acts and barriers of significant past events that mainly my Elders have faced. I may not have been there in the time of their events, but we all have to learn to live with the wounds that it made.

My passion is working with children, either in my local community or workplace of Gundoo Early Childhood Learning Centre. I've worked in our local childcare centre for nine years. It wasn't until I started my studies at the childcare centre that I learnt about UN's conventional rights of a child, it all just made sense to me because it had been taught to me all along from generation through generation. My parents or caregivers didn't have knowledge of children's rights it was just our cultural ways.

My motivation to be part of the study and co-author of this book is:

- To give people a sense of how I feel on the many different topics that are raised through the connections and experienced practices, of the first nation children not just in my community, but other in countries as well.
- For children and families to know their rights and for educators to think deeper when Aboriginal children act or react to certain subjects of learning.

- To share my community values – of looking out for one another: sharing and caring.
- To encourage and support families, letting them know about children's rights.
- To respond to the children's actions and concerns. I've learnt so much by looking and listening to the children.

Through this book I hope people stop, look and listen to our children, acknowledge and respect community values and that children's rights and agency are embedded into their everyday lives.

Kerryn's story

I'm first and foremost Luritja, a proud Aboriginal woman. With a proud Aboriginal family and country, part of me will always be in Luritja country and now I live on the Queensland coast. I feel my country calling me back and something inside me knows that's my kin. And introducing who I am, rather than Kerryn Moroney my name, my identity in civic space and work space is generally what people want to know who I am. With Aboriginal people we want to know where we are from. It's not where I'm residing but the country to which I belong. We also question around family to see connections that we can make – a connection to kin, because we are all connected to country and to every living being and thing so you try and find your connection to that through country.

I have known from a young age that there is inequity in our society and in particular the agency of civic rights. As a child I knew that I would have to wait as the white people in the local store would be served first. I have felt first-hand the racism in this nation and as a child it is confronting and awakens and silences ways of knowing that help you navigate your way. My early childhood experiences have informed my own interest in civic agency as an early childhood teacher. As a teacher, I was told from a very young age that was what my role was – to look after our little ones. In a cultural context there are roles and having held those roles of looking after little people and being told that is my role culturally but also I'm taking that on in professional spaces to ensure that Aboriginal and Torres Strait Islander culture is seen as a strength in children and we don't view children as deficit in our education spaces and we see that Aboriginal and Torres Strait Islander knowledge and our ways of understanding walking this place and country and caring for country can enrich all Australians. That is part of all Australians' history and until we recognise that history goes beyond white history in this nation and we honour that. And not only the history but to value Aboriginal and Torres Strait Islander knowledge and ways of living in this land, only then I believe we can have some true understandings and we can walk together into the future but until we start caring for country the way it's meant to be cared for. Because for thousands of years of caring for this country ensured that this country continued to be. I think there is a big responsibility in today's education systems to be looking at place based learning and connection of knowledge to the land. We can ensure that not only for agency for its citizens but there's agency for the Country and the Kin. And to be all connected as it should and was. I think having members of my family with a large interest in social justice, education and art, and more than education – my kin has helped me understand the agency that isn't there and to fight for those civic rights. I do that in my work in the education daily. I try and ensure that Aboriginal and Torres Strait Islander perspectives are seen as an integral part of learning and not as a tack on or add on resource kit that we buy online or that we get consulted on by an outside body to come in and talk around our cultural capability or children's understanding of Aboriginal culture seen from a traditional position where culture is seen as static. We still hold our Aboriginality and I think back to Linda Burney's quote: 'it's not the colour of your skin or the shape of your nose, it's what comes from within'. We still like to equate Aboriginal and Torres Strait Islander people's identities to percentages. We still don't have an under-standing of what culture is, what First Nation culture is across this nation. And how we all can learn from it to build a shared history. I think that we're not sup-porting the rights of all children to understand and hear the stories of an old land and connect to the many nations that we now call Australia.

My first wondering about children's civic agency was on university study during my Bachelor of teaching degree. I had the opportunity to travel to New Zealand and visit early childhood education settings on the North Island in 2001. At one of the settings we were asked to sing ourselves into the environment. As a group of Aboriginal Australians we felt honoured to be a part of this rich cultural experience and a proud Wiradjurri man in our group sang a song about fishing for bream as we walked in to meet the children and teachers. On entering the traditional building we were met by children coming over to us and putting their faces for-ward for us to exchange the same sit and meet in Māori culture. During the visit we witnessed children actively engage in their civic rights and one such learning experience was being led down to the beach in the afternoon by Elders to collect pipis and read the tides. I asked the teacher how can they be so close to the beach with no fences and how does government regulating allow this. The teacher said, 'our government doesn't tell us what our children need, we tell the government what our children need and they listen'. This was a moment that has stuck with me and has assisted formulation of my thinking about children civic agency.

Time for the voices that have walked this land since time memorial to be heard and felt in our nation as we all walk daily.

Jenny's story

Born in Wellington in 1959, of Cornish, Lithuanian Jewish, Scottish and Irish ancestry, I identify as Pākehā. Even as a young child I had a keen sense of injustice. I was sceptical about the rights of adults to speak on behalf of children. The authoritarian style of my schooling back in the 1960s and early 1970s in Well-ington and Hamilton, New Zealand often felt oppressive and depressing. After leaving school at 16 in 1975 I progressed through a number of different jobs which included working as a laboratory assistant in a medical laboratory; a factory hand in a peach canning factory in Mooroopna in Victoria, Australia; a library assistant; a childcare worker; and a postie. In 1980–1981 I completed a kindergarten teaching diploma, during which time I was convicted for protesting the 1981 rugby Springbok Tour of the apartheid era South African team. Kindergarten teaching affirmed my commitment to the importance of respecting and valuing young children and their families, their creativity and their struggles. Working in predominantly Māori communities in Rotorua and Huntly attuned me to different worlds and ways of being, knowing, doing and relating. My radar for injustice was often triggered by the mismatch between the offerings of well-intentioned Pākehā teachers and the realities of the children and families in these communities. Māori mothers often hung out on the footpath just outside of the kindergarten after bringing their children only as far as the entrance gate. Donna Awatere's (1984) book *Māori Sovereignty* resonated. She spoke of the invisible sign outside of educational institutions that only Māori could see that read 'Maoris keep out'. I remain disturbed by the memory of a mother telling me that her four-year-old son had been repeatedly telling her he was sick of life.

I heard Louise present on her PhD work about storytelling and social justice at a conference in 2010, and meeting up afterwards she presented her idea of a research project on young children's civic action. In my previous research I had been fortunate to work with early childhood teachers and teacher educators on ways they were giving expression to the commitments within our early childhood curriculum, Te Whāriki, related to Te Tiriti o Waitangi, the 1840 agreement between Māori and settlers which in particular affirmed Māori tino rangatiratanga, their right to collective self-determination. Very experienced teachers had observed that they had often found it challenging to engage in dialogue with children about these matters. During one of our projects, my colleague Cheryl Rau and I had a realisation that as researchers we had been unrealistically requiring our teachers to deliver on this thing we called 'child voice' – we had been coming from a very adultist perspective. Reflecting on a photo teachers had taken of children playing with stones beside the Waikato River, whilst waiting for the call to join a pōwhiri (greeting ceremony) at Tūrangawaewae Marae, we realised that children's voices were not just their 'voices'. They were expressing themselves through their embodied interactions with each other, with the earth, with the river stones, within their own frames of reference.

So when Louise suggested a project that would focus on young children's civic action, I felt an immediate sense of possibility …

I want to gratefully acknowledge the generosity, humour and all-round good-heartedness of the wonderful teachers of Katoa Kindergarten who all fully supported our study: Trinity, Katrina, Garth, Sonya, Scott, Maddie, Jessica, Jared, Cinnamon and Jesse. Also, I express my absolute appreciation to Elisabeth Jacob, who, as part of her doctoral studies internship at the University of Quebec, spent many months during 2015–2016 as a research assistant for this project: collecting ethics consent forms; gathering vast quantities of video footage; carefully coding this using qualitative software; and brilliantly producing the 'day in the life video'. Her warmth, enthusiasm, efficiency and technical expertise were incredibly valuable contributions to the project. My appreciation also to Rolene Watson, an anthropology student at Victoria University of Wellington, who recorded detailed anthropological field-notes for four months from May until August 2016. I would also like to acknowledge and thank my dear friend and colleague Mere Skerrett for many, many critical conversations and for feedback on key parts of this book. Ehara taku toa i te toa takitahi, engari he toa takitini.

Jared's Story

> To my twin brother Nicholas,
> Thank you for always believing in me and pushing me to succeed. I'm rising up for you, Rest In Peace.

For me it all began when I started at Katoa Kindergarten back in 2016. My whole teaching career I had found what truly inspired me to teach was social development, by this point I knew that my assessment for children's learning always had a social lens, and emphasised social justice. So when Jenny showed up to kindergarten to conduct observations for her research I was curious. She approached me and began to explain a little bit about the project. I was immediately drawn in because through our philosophical conversations what kept resonating for me was what it looked like in practice. For me, that was children working together, supporting one another for a shared purpose. It was about children developing their own peer culture and hidden curriculum and the ways they went about including each other in that. Essentially they were creating their own sense of citizenship within our kindergarten. I loved everything about it because it related so strongly to my own passion and interest in social development. But what Jenny did for me was extend my thinking and show me how my own assessment for children's learning aligned with civic action. A term in all honesty when we first began I wasn't very familiar with, or struggled to see applicable to children within an early childhood education context. But Jenny walked me through it, showed me videos she had taken and identified citizenship in action. At this moment I fell in love with the whole idea, I started to see it everyday throughout routines and I started to design learning experiences around it. As I stepped into a leadership role I even worked with the team to create whole programme plans based in the idea of civic action.

One special moment was when we had created a plan around Rangatiratanga (leadership) we had invited a series of local community members into kindergarten to talk to our children about the different leadership roles that are out there in our community. As part of this our local MP visited, he talked to the children about working together to make a difference and how this allows their voice to be heard. He even practised voting with them by asking them 'who likes ice-cream' the whole kindergarten raised their hands. He asked 'who likes strawberry flavour?'

some children raised their hands, he then asked 'who likes chocolate flavour?' and lots of children raised their hands. He smiled and said 'you all just voted, you have all just shared your opinions and voice with me'. It was such a fantastic golden moment.

References

Awatere, D. (1984). *Maori Sovereignty*. Auckland, NZ: Broadsheet.

Human Rights & Equal Opportunity Commission. (1997). *Bringing Them Home: Report of the National Inquiry into the Separation of Aboriginal and Torres Strait Islander Children from Their Families*. Sydney: HREOC. Retrieved from http://www.austlii.edu.au/au/journals/AILR/1997/36.html.

Phillips, L.G. & Bunda, T. (2018). *Research Through, With and as Storying*. Abingdon, UK: Routledge.

Sykes, R. (1993). *Murawina: Australian Women of High Achievement*. Sydney: Doubleday.

1

COMMUNITY BUILDING, CITIZENSHIP, COLONISATION AND GLOBALISATION

Recognition of young children as active citizens is relatively new in theory, policy and practice, and so there is a paucity of research and writing that examines early childhood experiences pertaining to young children's civic learning and action. Whilst there is increasing recognition in early childhood education curricula of young children's competence and capacity, little is known of what young children's citizenship learning and action looks like in practice. This book discusses findings from a comparative, ethnographic study within two early childhood settings, one in an Aboriginal Australian community in Queensland, Australia and the other in a predominately Māori and Pacific Island peoples' community in Porirua, New Zealand. Based on extensive ethnographic data we explore how children, educators, environments and communities construct children as citizens and the scope of civic action initiated by children. We describe the pedagogies and environments that foster children's capacities for civic participation and engagement, and the structural impediments to young children's civic learning and action. We have not sought to demonstrate any equivalences between the two nations and their Indigenous peoples and ontologies, but instead to invite enhanced awareness of the very different historical, colonisation and contemporary contexts.

By working with Indigenous collectivist communities and young children, citizenship is redefined in relational and embodied ways as reflecting community values and customary processes. We argue, firstly, that recognition and application of civic teaching and learning as a life continua commencing in early childhood education will produce informed global active citizens, and secondly, that the world can learn significantly from Indigenous communities about foundational principles of living and working with others for the common good of both humanity and the planet. We communicate these arguments through decolonised readings of the landscape of citizenship; analysing how national and cultural conceptualisations of young children mediate children's, families' and teachers' participation in civic action; illustrating how cultural values shape and define young children's civic action; and foregrounding Indigenous children's ways of enacting community rights and responsibilities (civic action).

But first what is 'citizenship' and is it the term that we want to use? The word citizen stems from the Latin word *civitas* with the idea emerging in the Greek city states between about 700–600 BC and located in Aristotle's *Politics*, being defined as a person that is both ruled and rules (Chesterman & Galligan, 2009) as a concept for societal organisation. However, Indigenous societies existed for many thousands of years before this …

Aboriginal Australian ways of knowing, being, doing and relating

Aboriginal Australian peoples have always been here, on the land now known as Australia (Pascoe, 2014). Scientific thinking has sought to measure and trace origins; to date archaeological evidence dates back to 65,000 years ago, with the out-of-Africa theory disputed (Clarkson et al., 2017). Aboriginal people have always lived here. Listen to the old people, they know. What we share here is knowledge that is in the public domain. To know, be, do and relate in Aboriginal Australian ways can really only be known through the lived experience of Aboriginality.

KERRYN: It's hard to be explicit and speak about what it is to be Aboriginal in just one context and it's difficult. It's much more and includes actions and connections and more than can be isolated to words on paper. It's doing. Because we don't give enough time to let other things speak – like to the wind and the Country. The stories that have guided my being remind me to think about how we can throw a lot of words around all the time … I feel I can yarn here now with Louise in a culturally safe space as we have taken the time walking, listening and learning from the voices and stories of the Country and its people.

> Pursuant to Aboriginal worldviews, published texts, archival material, images in art, digital mediums, artefacts or otherwise are not lifeless data waiting to be collected, interpreted and reconstituted by perceptions … Aboriginal stories, however expressed or embodied, hold power, spirit and agency. Knowledge can never be truly separated from the diverse Countries that shaped the ancient epistemologies of Aboriginal people, and the many voices of Country speak through the embodiment of story into text, object, symbol or design.
>
> (Kwaymullina, Kwaymullina & Butterfly, 2013, p. 5)

Aboriginal societal ways of knowing, being, doing and relating are grounded in the spirituality of what is named in English as 'Dreaming', though many Aboriginal peoples feel 'Dreaming' provides a poor description of a complex belief system embedded in tens of thousands of years of tradition, story, ceremony and lore which honour spiritual connection to country (as in earth, not Western construction of nation) and kinship rules. The spirituality of Aboriginality is communicated through traditional stories, art and ceremony, which:

describe that to people you know, what it is to be you. What it is to be you, you've got to follow that colour. And that fits into the Land, of what it is, your relationship, your close guidedness, and also close memories. You've got that memory of those people in you, the colours of those, who they are, ala-kenhe. You've got to know it, you've got to know that to be really you.

(Turner, 2010, p. 60)

Aboriginal lore is taught through story; knowledge is known through story.

On Quandamooka (North Stradbroke Island, Moreton Island and Bay and part of the coast of Brisbane), according to Karen Martin (2003): 'We believe that country is not only the Land and People, but is also the Entities of Waterways, Animals, Plants, Climate, Skies and Spirits' (purposefully honouring all of these entities full respect through proper nouns) (p. 2017). As Kerryn explains, we don't own country, country owns us. From an Aboriginal perspective, responsibility to country:

is grave; there is no hiding in a conscious universe … the exercise of will in a situation where the choice to deny moral action is to turn one's back on the cosmos and ultimately on one's self. The choice to assume responsibility is a multivalent one involving self-interest, reverence, morality, and mysticism.

(Rose, 1987, p. 264)

Spiritual connection to country, Bunurong man Bruce Pascoe explains, runs deep through all actions: 'there is no separation between the sacred and non-sacred' (Pascoe, 2014, p. 127).

Through such an ontology 'Aboriginal people constructed a system of pan-continental government that generated peace and prosperity' (Pascoe, 2014, p. 129) for tens of thousands of years. Perhaps it is the complex system of kinship that enabled peaceful co-existence with others. With kin classifications, as 'the very basis of social structure' (Yengyoyan, 1987, p. 212), complex genealogical and status relationships to others are known and enacted. Aboriginal kinship rules are laws spiritually ascribed by sacred ancestors and are extraordinarily more sophisticated than European kinship systems, with most defining 28 kinship roles (Langton, 2018). Aboriginal kinship system is based on a collectivist ontology in which people think of themselves in terms of their relationship to others and their community (Yeo, 2003). The kinship system, and a shared set of values determines how Aboriginal people work together (Lohoar, Butera & Kennedy, 2014). Children learn their kinship relations, behaviours, rights and responsibilities progressively from a very young age (Daylight & Johnstone, 1986). 'We as Aboriginal people, we always relate to other people, connect with them, no matter who we are. If I see an Aboriginal person … I'll always say "that person is one of us, he's part of us"' (Turner, 2010, p. 7). An outsider with no identified kinship link is allocated a kinship role, so that a kinship relationship is defined and authorised. For example, Kerryn and Louise, as outsiders to the Gundoo community, were referred to as Aunty by the children and Sis(ter) by educators. The kinship system is not only about human relationships, but also relationships with land, water, flora and fauna, and spiritual beings, understood through totemic and skin systems. Any encounter with another is enacted from a premise of relationality and respect. For example, Aboriginal people worked in partnership with dolphins in bays to drive fish in to catch (Pascoe, 2014, p. 143), supporting an ethos of living with all living beings sustainably: *only take what you need – so we can come back*. As Uncle Bob Anderson (1998) shares 'All living things, be they mammals, birds, reptiles, insects or trees are our sisters and brothers and therefore we must protect them. We are their custodians. We not only share with them; we also guard them' (p. 8).

Further,

> The songlines [spiritual routes of connection to country] of Aboriginal and Torres Strait Islander people connected clans from one side of the country to another. The cultural, economic, genetic and artistic conduits of the songlines brought goods, art, news, ideas, technology and marriage partners to centres of exchange.
>
> *(Pascoe, 2014, p. 129)*

There were/are agreed shared values and norms, intergenerationally passed on through Ancestral Law and enacted through ritual practices and deference to Elders (Keen, 2004). Some of this law is reflected in Kakadu Elder, Bill Neidjie's (1986) poem – 'Law of the land':[1] Our story is in the land…

It is written in those sacred places.
My children will look after those places,
That's the law.

Dreaming place…
You can't change it, no matter who you are.
No matter you rich man, no matter you king
You can't change it.

I feel it in my body
With my blood.
Feeling all these trees,
All this country
When this wind blow you can feel it.

Same for country…
You feel it.
You can look, but feeling…
That make you.

While you sleeping
you dream something.
Tree and grass same thing.
They grow with your body,

With your feeling.

You brought up with earth, tree and water.

Karen Martin (2003) explains further:

> Ways of Knowing are specific to ontology and Entities of Land, Animals, Plants, Waterways, Skies, Climate and the Spiritual systems of Aboriginal groups ... We are part of the world as much as it is part of us, existing within a network of relations amongst Entities that are reciprocal and occur in certain contexts. This determines and defines for us rights to be earned and bestowed as we carry out rites to country, self and others – our Ways of Being ... Our Ways of Doing are a synthesis and an articulation of our Ways of Knowing and Ways of Being. These are seen in our languages, art, imagery, technology, traditions and ceremonies, land management practices, social organisation and social control ... these are life stage, gender and role specific.
>
> *(pp. 209–210)*

Leadership for governance was/is enacted through Elders elevated through gradual and complex initiation processes, and earnt respect (not because of force or inheritance) (Pascoe, 2014). Though the elderly are highly respected as important community contributors, Elders are not always elderly, but are rather selected for maturity (not necessarily biological), cultural knowledge and leadership abilities (Lohoar, Butera & Kennedy, 2014; McIntyre, 2001). They impart the law to their clans, tribes and communities. Each group has rights and responsibilities for different pieces of the:

> epic integrity of the land ... They had to imagine how the whole picture looked and they had absolute confidence in the coherence of the accretive construction of their law over thousands of years and knew that the jigsaw would make sense and their responsibility was to ensure it continued to make sense.
>
> *(Pascoe, 2014, p. 138)*

Aboriginal Australian peoples work for the collective good rather than individual achievement. Focus is on what the group can achieve collectively (Martin, 2008, p. 44). Justice, peace protection, management of social roles and the division of the land's wealth were/are defined by ancestral law and interpreted by those chosen as the senior Elders (Pascoe, 2014). Bruce Pascoe, from the Bunurong clan of the Kulin nation, claims that Aboriginal government is the most democratic model of all the systems humans have devised, as it worked across a large land mass for diverse populations surviving thousands of years, and that isolation from vastly different cultures and worldviews may well have enabled the conditions for long-standing peace (p. 132). This claim by Pascoe is substantiated by recognition that across all the archaeological investigations carried out in Australia there has been no evidence found of wars between Aboriginal tribes or clans. Individual acts of violence are evident in ancient Aboriginal art, but 'there is no trace of imperial warfare' (p. 130). This is extraordinarily significant through its rarity in the history of humanity, and as Pascoe asserts 'demands respect' and 'must be investigated' (p. 130). Yet, colonisers foolishly ignored and continue to ignore this profound wisdom regarding peaceful societal organisation.

Tikanga Māori: ways of knowing, being, doing and relating

Māori cosmology and worldviews are recognised as deriving from the 'mythical and original homeland of Maori called Hawaiki, a place distant in time and space, which is the link with the spirit world' and source of the Atua, or Gods from whom Māori and all plants, animals and other living creatures are descended (Henare, 2001, p. 202). Their arrival in the land now called Aotearoa was the culmination of many, many journeys over an extended period of time:

> Scientific discovery shows that the deep history of Māori and Moriori goes back to the last Ice Age, when the first modern humans reached the Pacific coasts of Asia around 60,000 years ago. The sea was then about 60 metres below the present level, and some people, ultimately of the same African origin as all modern people, came around the coastal rim of the Indian Ocean and crossed the 100-kilometre-wide channel separating Southeast Asia from the Australasian continent of Australia and New Guinea – one landmass at that time. Others came through the continental interior, filtering down the forested river valleys to the coasts of Indochina and China – then joined to Taiwan. When the seas rose again, 10,000 years ago, human populations flourished on the tropical margins and islands of Southeast Asia and the western Pacific … [And] with the advent, between 4,000 and 5,000 years ago, of the vital technology of sail … thereafter began the era of migrations into the remote Pacific.
>
> *(Anderson, 2016, p. 18)*

Archeological data such as radio-carbon dating indicate that this migration reached Aotearoa sometime between 1200 and 1300 AD (Anderson, 2016).

Traditionally the term 'Māori' referred to something considered normal, usual or natural. Māori social structure includes whānau (families, extended both horizontally and vertically), hapū (larger kinship grouping of related whānau, primary political group in traditional society) and iwi (tribes, groupings with shared ancestry and mana whenua, that is, links to a particular geographical area). It should be noted that 'iwi, hapū and whānau were not hermetically discrete social, cultural, and political entities inhabiting exclusively maintained bordered territories. Rather, they were complex constellations of lineages woven together by intermarriage, political alliance, and by migration and resettlement' (Poata-Smith, 2013, p. 51).

Mana is the power, prestige and authority conferred at birth and derived from the Atua (gods).

Weaving across and throughout Māori kinship groupings is a shared whakapapa, the genealogical layerings of interconnections. This worldview is collectivist, anchored by a value of unity or kotahitanga, and spiritually sustained through deep practices that recognise and uphold the fundamental overarching interplay of mauri, hau, wairua, tapu and noa in securing wellbeing. An individual has membership to a community and place via their whakapapa which confers their status of tūrangawaewae, or belonging. Leadership, or rangatiratanga, was demonstrated through supporting the wellbeing of the group by protecting and maintaining the spiritual wellbeing of people and place, and securing peaceful relationships. In a recent Waitangi Tribunal hearing, claimants from Te Paparahi o Te Raki (the great land of the north) made it clear that the exercise of rangatiratanga, chieftainship, included managing the 'interplay of belonging, nurturing, chiefly responsibilities, mana, and peace' (Waitangi Tribunal, 2014, p. 173).

As repositories and continuities of whakapapa, children in pre-colonial times were accorded mana (respect) and some were assigned particular roles from birth (Pere, 1982; Makereti, 1938). They were allowed a great deal of freedom to participate within everyday activities of their whānau and hapū, and often accompanied their Elders. In fact, the bonds between grandparents and mokopuna (grandchildren) were particularly strong. According to the imminent anthropologist Te Rangi Hiroa (Sir Peter Buck):

> Much, if not most of the personal instruction in the early years, was received from grandparents ... The able-bodied parents were freed to devote full time and attention to the work which needed physical energy. The grandparents, who were too old for hard work, attended to the lighter tasks and the care of the grandchildren ... They told them stories and simple versions of various myths and legends ... The elements of a classical education in family and tribal history, mythology and folklore were thus imparted by male and female tipuna [Elders] at an early age ...
>
> *(Te Rangi Hiroa, 1950, p. 358)*

When issues arose, a rūnanga or discussion and decision-making forum would be called, and children were included in the discussions:

> Ta te maori, me hui katoa, te iti te ruhi, tane te wahine, te koroheke te ruruhi me te tamariki, te mohio me te kuare, te mea e ata whakaaro ana me te hikaka; e uru katoa ana ki nga Runanga maori, me o ratou whakaaro me o ratou korero; e whakatika una tenei wahine me ana korero ano, e whakatika ana hoki tenei taitamariki ma ana ano ...
>
> All must assemble together, the small and the great, the husband, the wife, the old man, the old woman and the children, the knowing and the foolish, the thoughtful and the presumptuous; these all obtain admittance to the

Runanga Maori, with all their thoughts and speeches: this woman gets up and has her talk, and that youth gets up and has his [or hers] …

(Te Manuhiri Tuarangi And Maori Intelligencer, No. 10, 1 August 1861, p. 11, as cited in Benton et al., 2013, p. 318)

In her most recent book, the imminent anthropologist Dame Anne Salmond offers the narrative of an early Western observer of Māori communities, the trader Joel Polack, writing in the 1830s that he had observed children participating as equals with adults during meetings of the community. He described how:

[The children] also asked questions in the most numerously attended assemblies of chiefs, who answer them with an air of respect, as if they were of a corresponding age to themselves. I do not remember a request of an infant being treated with neglect, or a demand from one of them being slighted.

(Polack, as cited in Salmond, 2017, p. 386)

According to a Mr J. Watson speaking in 1838 to a British House of Lords Select Committee inquiry into 'New Zealand affairs':

The Customs and Laws appear to be very much alike, and they seem to be remarkably tenacious of them, and they initiate their children into them in very early Days. It is very amusing to see them teaching their Children; they will teach their Children as if they were old persons and in return hear them as patiently as if they were old People speaking, allowing the Child to ask any questions.

(Watson, 1838, as cited in Benton et al., 2013, p. 393)

Early western accounts characterised the freedom and autonomy of Māori children as 'indulgence', and noted that tamariki were seldom 'disciplined', in contrast with the often brutal treatment of children in the West (Smith, 1995; Salmond, 1991). Yet very few of the early western observers, nor the mainly British settlers who were to follow, bothered to learn the Māori language or to understand the traditional Māori worldview which is guided by deeply embedded, spiritually grounded ethics, one version of which is outlined by Manuka Henare (2001) and summarised as follows:

- ethic of wholeness, cosmos (te ao mārama)
- ethic of life essences, vitalism, reverence for life (mauri)[2]
- ethic of being and potentiality, the sacred (tapu)
- ethic of power, authority and common good (mana)
- ethic of spiritual power of obligatory reciprocity in relationships with nature (hau)
- ethic of the spirit and spirituality (wairuatanga)
- ethic of care and support, reverence for humanity (manaakitanga)

- ethic of belonging, reverence for the human person (whanaungatanga)
- ethic of change and tradition (te ao hurihuri)
- ethic of solidarity (kotahitanga)
- ethic of guardianship of creation (kaitiakitanga) (pp. 213–214).

In this worldview, Māori children were very much included as repositories of the Atua and ancestors, and of the future descendants in the genealogical progression. Spiritual protections required regular and frequent rituals to ensure wellbeing, invoking a collectivity of care and reciprocal obligation.

We will pick up these ethical threads later in the book as we examine young children's community building in our two research communities. Māori societal organisation like Aboriginal Australian societal organisation is based on complex kinship systems, which honour connections to all living beings and place, spiritually guided through sacred law. We see value in learning from the wisdom of these ontologies that have sustained across eras and survived the violent onslaught of colonisation.

Western constructs of citizenship

The Ancient Greek notions of a citizen as person that is both ruled and rules (Chesterman & Galligan, 2009) were a logical consequence of the development of the *polis*, or the political system of the Greek city state (Clarke, 1994, p. 6). Women and children were not counted as citizens in the origins of western citizenship and democracy, according to Aristotle, 'the citizen must be a male of known genealogy, a patriarch, a warrior, and the master of the labour of others (normally slaves)' (Pocock, 1998, p. 33). The private realm (oikos) was where women and children were considered to inhabit only and the public sphere (polis) was the domain of public affairs determined by active citizens, aka men of wealth and 'status' (Pattie, Seyd & Whiteley, 2009). Citizenship rights to take part in the conduct of public affairs (e.g., through right to vote, to run for public office), and the right to freedom of expression (e.g., to express opinion, and receive and impart information) were ascribed only to male property owners in Britain (and its colonies) until the early 1900s (Pattie, Seyd & Whiteley, 2009).

The long association of **property ownership** with citizenship began too in Ancient Greece with the patriarch of a household owning more than a home, but 'the house was the basic component of the economy' with 'the term "economy"' deriving 'from the Greek words for household (oikos) and rules (nomos)' (Bellamy, 2008, p. 54). Home ownership indicated economic independence, which was important for politics because it meant, as Bellamy explains, that a) they could devote time to civic duties, because they were free from earning a livelihood, b) they were not dependent on others, and c) they had a stake in the political community. 'Public good, independence, and possession of a stake in the political community remain important for thinking about politics' (p. 55). By politics Bellamy is referring to political participation as a citizen, though on these terms children are not positioned as independent, and without property ownership they are not considered to possess a stake in the political community. Civic duty for public good is accessible, though is often defined by adults, with children experiencing citizenship as obedience.

A notion of being loyal to the state as a faithful subject was informed by the ideas of Rousseau (1762/1968) about citizenship as devotion to civic duty and obedience to laws (Dagger, 1997). These ideas have swelled into a metanarrative of the **good citizen**, whereby citizens work hard and obey the laws (Batstone & Mendieta, 1999). Such an ideology has had a strong presence in children's stories with Tatar (1987/2003) noting that the fairy tales of Wilhelm Grimm are imbued with this message, as he manipulated the tales he heard with the values of the time. Further, these lyrics that were sung by school children in Germany in the 1800s typified such values: 'Hard work and obedience: Those are the qualities to which all good citizens must aspire' (p. 29). With Grimm's fairy tales permeating Anglophone popular culture, Stephens and McCallum (1998) claimed that these tales contribute to the cultivation of metanarratives of the values that they espouse. Whalley (1996) concurred that the equation of obedience with good citizenship has continued to be a strong message in children's stories. The ideology of the good citizen has had a strong impact on narratives and discourses for both adults and children. For example, the media portrayal of terrorists as assailants of extreme evil is seen to attack the metanarrative of good citizen (Seymour, 2006). The metanarrative of good citizen continues to bear weight in discussion and practice of citizenship.

The notion of citizenship as **membership** of a political community, in ancient Greece, was defined as a city or township. With the formation of nations in the late 18th century this became based on nationhood (Heater, 1999). A view of citizenship simply as a legal status of nation-state membership, which is granted through birthright or naturalisation (Faulks, 1998; Gilbert, 1996), has since become what is commonly understood as citizenship. The active participation permitted in a nationhood view is that of the legislated convention of voting. Such a view of citizenship overemphasises the purpose of legislation in defining the scope of citizenship. For children, nationhood citizenship is being a citizen with no rights, as children are recognised as citizens (through birthright), yet they cannot participate as they do not have the right to vote.

Wrapped up in nationhood citizenship is civic duty to your nation, as is declared in citizenship pledges. In Australia, the wording of the secular pledge is:

> From this time forward I pledge my loyalty to Australia and its people, whose democratic beliefs I share, whose rights and liberties I respect, and whose laws I will uphold and obey.
>
> *(Australian Government, 2018)*

And in New Zealand the affirmation of allegiance wording is:

I (say your name) affirm that I will be faithful and bear true allegiance to Her Majesty Queen Elizabeth the Second, Queen of New Zealand, her heirs and successors according to law, and that I will faithfully observe the laws of New Zealand and fulfil my duties as a New Zealand citizen.

(New Zealand Government, 2018)

Both reek of loyalty and obedience to the state.

The creation of 'national, democratic, welfare states as the main context for citizenship has allowed the criteria for membership to become progressively more inclusive internally, while remaining externally exclusive' (Bellamy, 2008, p. 54). For example, the scrutinising of who is entitled to become an Australian or New Zealander is enforced through extensive border protection and immigration legislation and policies. Residency and citizenship exclusions, as we have witnessed in Australia through the indefinite offshore detention of asylum seekers including children, are in breach of international human rights protocols. Many thus argue that citizenship should thus be defined in terms of universal human rights (Bellamy, 2008).

An emphasis on citizenship as **rights** possession draws from what is understood as the first sociological theory of citizenship: *Citizenship and social class* by Marshall (1950). In this essay, Marshall defined a typology of citizenship rights for citizens in a developmental order that was balanced against obligations. The categories of rights included civil, political and social rights. To Marshall, civil rights of the right to own property, the right to work in your choice of profession and freedom of speech or assembly were the first to be established through the legal system. Political rights were the second phase of growth of citizenship, as per Marshall, through the right to exercise political participation in institutions, such as parliament and local councils. And Marshall saw social rights as the focus of the 20th century defined as the right to economic welfare and security provided through institutions, such as educational systems and social services (Pattie, Seyd & Whiteley, 2004). Based on these definitions of civil, political and social rights, children only have access to social rights. In this regard, it is worth noting that Marshall viewed children and young people as future citizens and not as citizens of today. Citizenship defined as rights possession is understood as a liberalist approach, which constructs citizens 'not as "members of the community" but as strangers to each other' with assumed expectations of each other through universalised rights and obligations enforceable by the state (Yuval-Davis, 1997, p. 6). A vast difference to the kinship system of Aboriginal Australian and Māori societies, in which your relation to one another is known.

The western construct of citizenship is exclusionary. 'The divide between citizens and non-citizens has often depended not so much on geography as on the fact of belonging to a particular race, religion or class, or some combination of these' (Chesterman & Galligan, 2009, p. 4). The colonisation of Australia and New Zealand violently played out such exclusionary thinking and practice.

Colonisation and citizenship construction in Australian and New Zealand

Australia as a nation was built on a perception of the continent as empty (terra nullius) by the British who saw their 'successes in industry accorded their colonial ambition a natural authority' (Pascoe, 2014, p. 12). The Aboriginal and Torres Strait Islanders' existence, livelihood, dignity and sovereignty was denied through genocide, violation, theft of peoples and lands, and denial of human rights. Australia is the only British settler society without a history of treaty making or constitutional recognition of its Indigenous peoples (MacDonald & Muldoon, 2006). The making of Australia began as a dumping ground for Britain's unwanted citizens (the poor and the felonious), through isolated penal colonies placed around the continent. In contrast, the birth of Aotearoa New Zealand was as a Māori nation, with the 1835 'He Whakaputanga o te Rangatiratanga o Nu Tireni' (the Declaration of Independence), proclaiming Māori sovereignty over the country. This status thus necessitated the 1840 Tiriti o Waitangi/Treaty of Waitangi to legitimate British settlement. Despite the assurance of protections of Māori rights and authority over their lands and resources contained in Te Tiriti o Waitangi, the British Crown and settlers immediately assumed sovereignty and proceeded to pass a raft of legislation effectively alienating Māori from these promised rights, and enforcing land and cultural alienation with discriminatory policies, force and imprisonment (Orange, 1987; Walker, 2004).

In stark contrast to such violent beginnings in which the colonial authorities enforced by the British redcoats assumed and exercised power (assuming these rights through their imported socially constructed status), Australia and New Zealand soon became world leaders in democratic politics (Chesterman & Galligan, 2009). However, the application of the concept of citizenship in the nation-building of Australia and New Zealand did not readily confer the same rights to the nations' Indigenous peoples.

Determination of civilised/civilisation

The concept of biological determinism drawn from social Darwinism prevailed in Western thinking at the time of colonisation of the land now known as Australia. This hierarchically positioned Aboriginal Australians and African Hottentots on the lowest place on the scale of civilisation with white peoples assigned the highest position (Sabbioni, 1998). Such thinking provided colonisers with a rationale to define Aboriginal Australians as 'primitive, uncivilized, childlike, and doomed to extinction' (Sabbioni, 1998 p. xxv), and thereby treat Aboriginal peoples as less than human, devoid of any rights, enacted through genocide, violation and theft of and from Aboriginal peoples. Before colonisation there was an estimated population of 750,000 Aboriginal people and approximately 700 languages spoken across Australia (Mooney, 2018). More than 15,000 deaths of Aboriginal peoples through massacres were recorded from 1788 to 1930 (Ryan et al., 2017). Australian census data from the 1920s indicates that only about 58,000 'full-blood' Aboriginal people survived (Harris, 2003). As early as 1845, Catholic Archbishop John Bede Polding provided the following evidence on the declining population of Aboriginal peoples to Governor Gipps' Enquiry:

> The aggressive mode of taking possession of their country, which necessarily involves a great loss to the natives.
>
> The horrible extent to which sensual indulgence is carried by the whites, in the abuse of females in an early period of life – mere children – who are thus made incapable of becoming mothers of healthy offspring.
>
> The introduction of diseases for which they have no proper remedy.
>
> *(West Australian Record 5 October 1893 cited by Harris, 2003, p. 82)*

Polding drew attention to what Harris acknowledges as the 'least discussed, most hidden, and most sinister cause of death and depopulation, [the] sexual abuse of women and children' which 'at times ... outnumbered all other causes of Aboriginal death' (p. 94). The chilling trauma of being used and poisoned for white male gratification permeates psyches across generations. White male pioneers fabricated doctrine to meet their bodily desires, such as Willshire (1896) who believed that God intended Aboriginal women to be used by white men as he placed them wherever pioneers went. The sexual objectification and violation of Aboriginal women became a common game for white colonisers illustrated through widespread colloquia of 'gin hunts', 'black velvet', 'gin sprees', and so on. The brutal irony of the supposed 'most civilised' peoples per-petrating the most *uncivilised* (i.e. 'not suitable for a well developed, peaceful society where people are treated fairly', Cambridge University Press, 2019) acts. White colo-nisers did not develop a peaceful society nor did they treat people fairly.

> Colonial Australia sought to forget the advanced nature of Aboriginal society and economy ... Villages were burnt, the foundations stolen for other build-ings, the occupants killed by warfare, murder and disease, and the country usurped. It is no wonder that after 1860 most people saw no evidence of a complex prior civilisation.
>
> *(Pascoe, 2014, pp. 17, 18)*

A sobering reflection on the empire-building and perpetual trajectory of growth agenda of colonisation and western civilisation reveals that past ascendant civilisa-tions, such as those of the Romans, Phoenicians and Egyptians, eventually ran into dead ends (Pascoe, 2014, p. 128).

The late, pre-eminent Māori education academic Dr Ranginui Walker has pro-vided many insights into the supposed 'civilising' of Māori by British settlement. He writes:

> Like its Greek and Roman predecessors, the British Empire portrayed itself as civilised and painted the people it encountered in the New World as savage,

uncivilised and inferior ... Although the culture of New Zealand's tangata whenua [Indigenous peoples], with its hunting, fishing, gathering and gardening economy, was a sustainable design for living, it was almost destroyed by the colonial enterprise of converting the natives from barbarism to Christianity and civilisation.

(Walker, 2016, p. 19)

The first missionaries, who had arrived in Aotearoa in 1814, were described by Walker as:

the advance party of cultural invasion [whose] mission of converting Māori from 'barbarism to civilisation' was predicated on notions of racial and cultural superiority. They believed in a divine right to impose their world view on those whose culture they were displacing.

(Walker, 2016, p. 20)

Important, however, in the colonisation history for Aotearoa is the early recognition by the British Crown of Māori rights and of New Zealand as a Māori sovereign nation. Leading up to the legitimation of British settlement, their Colonial Office recognised Māori as rights holders in their own nation. Here is an extract from the 1839 instructions from Lord Normanby of the British Colonial Office provided to Captain William Hobson who was being sent to secure a treaty to allow for British settlement of New Zealand:

I have already stated that we acknowledge New Zealand as a sovereign and independent state so far at least as it is possible to make that statement in favour of a people composed of numerous dispersed and petty tribes ... But the admission of their rights, though inevitably qualified by this consideration, is binding on the faith of the British Crown.

The Queen disclaims for herself and for her subjects, every pretention to seize on the islands of New Zealand, or to govern them as a part of the dominion of Great Britain, unless the free and intelligent consent of the natives, expressed according to their established usages, shall first be obtained.

(Normanby, 1839, as cited in Salmond, 2017, p. 259)

These recognitions of Māori rights indicate a respect for Māori that was not evident in the early dealings of Britain with Australia's Indigenous peoples.

Britain here acknowledged the independent status of New Zealand as a Māori sovereign nation, as per the 1835 He Whakaputanga/Declaration of Independence of the United Tribes of New Zealand. Article Three of Te Tiriti o Waitangi/The Treaty of Waitangi of 1840 affirmed Māori as citizens with equal rights to those of England. Despite these seemingly progressive proclamations, discourses pertaining to the need for the 'civilising of savages' were nonetheless fundamental to colonisation, and particularly prevalent in education. According to Ranginui Walker, the

'Government's motives for funding mission schools included civilising the natives and pacifying the country', whilst assigning them to an underclass of unskilled labour and domestic service (Walker, 2016, p. 23).

'Citizenship' as fencing

The concept of individual property rights as a marker of citizenship was imposed on Indigenous peoples through colonisation. Fences became a marker of property ownership (as exemplified in Joan Ross' artist work in Figure 1.1). Citizenship as property ownership colonised Australian land and Aboriginal Australians with fences (Power & Somerville, 2015). As noted earlier, Aboriginal peoples' relationship with country is spiritually entangled and honoured through collective rights and responsibilities enacted through epic integrity (Pascoe, 2014). In Aboriginal ontology, fences divide, cut and block. 'Fences on the ground make fences in the mind' (Gammage, 2011, p. 321). They demarcate Black/white contact zone, claimed land and enforced incarceration. The Queensland Aboriginals Protection and Restriction of the Sale of Opium Act, 1897 (and similar acts for the other colonies of Australia) fenced Aboriginal people in reserves and missions and legislated the removal of Aboriginal children and young people. All of which was part of a grand colonising master plan to erase a dying race (Power & Somerville, 2015). The fence resounds 'as a powerful signifier for Aboriginal people of the regulation of their and their children's lives in the making of the Australian nation'. They 'represent deep experiences of incarceration and exclusion from fundamental human rights, including the right to bring up one's children, to land ownership, to speak one's language, and to basic freedom of movement' (Power & Somerville, 2015, p. 67).

In the early years of the colonisation of Aotearoa, the British settlers found themselves in the invidious position of relying on Māori for their provisions, since

FIGURE 1.1 Joan Ross (2012) Landscaping (still from digital animation *The claiming of things* – duration 7.37)

Māori initially retained their control over their lands, as had been promised in Article Two of Te Tiriti o Waitangi/The Treaty of Waitangi. In 1852 the settlers assumed the role of government, excluding Māori from the franchise, and proceeded to pass a myriad of laws aimed at alienating Māori lands. Māori fencing to protect their lands and crops was disrespected and demolished by settlers as in the following example:

> I found that the white settlers did just as they liked pulled down the fences and drove the cattle on the potatoes, this is the systematic robbery by which the ... settlers deprived the natives of the plantations and all this while they have borne it patiently and not even once attempted to avenge their wrongs
>
> *(Clarke, 1843, as cited in Waitangi Tribunal, 2003, p. 136)*

In the 1870s the peaceful Māori community of Parihaka installed fences around their crops in order to resist settler attempts to claim their land. However, the constabulary repeatedly dismantled these destroying Māori crops and property, and eventually invading the village. Under the spiritual guidance of the pacifist prophets Te Whiti o Rongomai and Tohu Kakahi, the community responded quietly, an early example of non-violent passive resistance, the children singing and offering the invaders baskets of food. Nonetheless, the village was plundered, and the leaders and other men of the community were shipped away from their families to the South Island (Waitangi Tribunal, 1996; Cameron et al., 2017). The New Zealand parliament subsequently passed a law to suspend the right of habeas corpus and thus retain Māori prisoners indefinitely without trial, despite the Tiriti/Treaty Article Three undertaking that Māori would be equal citizens.

The colonising forces of citizenship and fencing continues in Australia and New Zealand, as whitefella/Pākehā laws of citizenship dominate. This is starkly evident in incarceration rates in both nations. In Australia 27% of prisoners are Aboriginal or Torres Strait Islander, yet only 2% of the entire Australian population (Australian Bureau of Statistics, 2017). And in terms of citizenship as property ownership, in 2011 68% of non-Indigenous Australians owned their home, whereas 59% of Indigenous Australians rented (Australian Bureau of Statistics, 2012). In Aotearoa New Zealand, Māori comprise 14.9% of the population (Statistics New Zealand, 2014) yet make up 51% of the prison population (New Zealand Department of Corrections, 2018). Neoliberal social and economic policies of the past three decades have seen a major decline in Māori home ownership: 'In 1986, around half of Pacific and Māori children lived in an owner-occupied dwelling. By 2013, the proportions were 38.5 percent of Māori children and 28.4 percent of Pacific children' (Statistics New Zealand, 2016).

Citizens without rights

The colonisation projects of Australia and New Zealand positioned each nation's Indigenous peoples as citizens without rights. Their nationhood birthright to citizenship was acknowledged, but rights were denied.

Under introduced British rule, Aboriginal peoples were, by virtue of being born in Australia, British subjects, since it had been claimed under British colonial rule (Chesterman & Galligan, 2009). Then with the federation of Australia in 1901, the only references to Aboriginal Australians in the Commonwealth of Australia Constitution Act (1901) were to exclude them from: race restrictions to be brought to Australia as indentured labourers; and being counted as people of the Commonwealth. There is no mention of citizens or citizenship in the Constitution. The intent of the exclusion from being counted was to do with proportioning state revenue (Chesterman & Galligan, 2009). Then when Commonwealth legislation created the legal entity of 'Australian citizen' in 1948, Aboriginal Australians, along with other Australians, automatically became citizens. Though the 'law' now stated Aboriginal Australians were citizens of Australia, they were denied a share in the ruling by Commonwealth and State governments. 'They had no say about being subjected to such rule, which was imposed by force, and no share in the rights and entitlements that ordinary citizens enjoyed' (Chesterman & Galligan, 2009, pp. 2–3).

Aboriginal Australians have been positioned as citizens without rights throughout much of Australian political history. As Kerryn's mother recalls of her youth, 'we had the rights of cow and we were herded like cattle'. Chesterman and Galligan (2009) relate that 'however rich Australia's democratic tradition and political culture may have been, Australian citizenship was empty and barren at its core and blatantly discriminatory in its parts' (p. 4). The Commonwealth Franchise Act (1902), though famously recognised for granting (white) women the right to vote, barred Aboriginal Australians from voting. This Act then set the legislative scene for excluding 'aboriginal natives' from subsequent citizenship rights and entitlements (Chesterman & Galligan, 2009). After Federation, the states became increasingly authoritarian in managing Aboriginal peoples, as it was realised that as a 'race' they were not going to die out, and therefore the policy shifted from so-called protection of ancient peoples to regulation of an undesirable racial minority. The civic status of all Aboriginal people was akin to that of children, the emphasis being on protection with no civic or political rights – they were wards of the state (McGrath, 2010). It was not until 1962 that Aboriginal peoples in every state were granted the right to vote through amendments to the successor Electoral Act (Chesterman & Galligan, 2009). And in 1967 the two discriminatory points in the Constitution noted above were deleted following a Referendum. Recognition of this discrimination and exclusion had to be judged by others – those sitting comfortably with their existing citizenship rights. Images of young Aboriginal children featured in posters appealing for the 'yes' votes, perhaps based on thinking that public appeal would be more likely for a 'vulnerable' baby (see Figure 1.2).

The results of the 1967 referendum saw 90% of Australian voters vote for the two exclusionary points to be deleted from the Constitution. It symbolised a shift in attitude to Aboriginal peoples and a move toward Aboriginal sovereignty. Public recognition of Aboriginal peoples' lack of citizenship rights began after this referendum result (McGrath, 2010). The constitutional changes from the referendum

FIGURE 1.2 Write YES for Aborigines in the Lower Square May 27th, authorised by Faith Bandler, Sydney: Witton Press, [1967] nla.obj-136875607

now meant that 'the Commonwealth had the power to pass laws specifically for Aborigines' and required 'Aborigines to be counted in census statistics' (Galligan & Chesterman, 2009, p. 9). Though recognition of citizenship, when it finally was granted, was a bittersweet pill. 'It released indigenous people from the intrusive systems of "protection" to which they had been subject', but it also 'conferred legitimacy upon the colonial state that had been the agent of their dispossession' (Kingsbury & Gover, 2005).

For non-Indigenous Australians, citizenship is taken for granted, whereas for Aboriginal and Torres Strait Islander People as Indigenous Leader Pat Dodson explained in a speech as Social Justice Commissioner in 1993: 'it may be suggested that we have two citizenships; one in relation to our indigenous nations, and one in relation to the Australian nation ... [So] ... "Citizenship within which society?" and secondly, "recognition by which political system?"' (as cited in Tudbull & Andersen, 2017).

In New Zealand, the early settler nation-building began later than that of Australia and was framed as the 'colonising crusaders' sought to compete with other potential countries for the desired, financially well-off British migrants and focussed on the motifs of 'progress', 'paradise' and 'Britishness' (Belich, 1996, p. 287), in an attempt to create the 'Britain of the South' (Sinclair, 1986, p. 16). Subsequently, New Zealand has prided itself on its progressiveness and egalitarianism (social-liberalism), with frequent reference made to being the first nation to give women the vote, to having positive race relations and to a social welfare system that provided for its citizens 'from the cradle to the grave'. All of these motifs could and should also be questioned as myths, yet their power even as myths has had significant influence in shaping each nation. Whilst the history of race relations in New Zealand is not pretty, ongoing Māori activism has eventually shaped the nation's identity in distinctive ways. Much of this activism has focussed on the promises of Te Tiriti o Waitangi/The Treaty of Waitangi, to equal citizenship rights.

New Zealand's status of being the first nation to grant women's suffrage belied the oppression of Māori women perpetuated from the early days of settler contact. Women Rangatira (Chiefs) were turned away when they went to sign the 1840 Tiriti o Waitangi. And despite the assurances to Māori written in the treaty, once the settlers assumed government in 1852, Māori were disenfranchised by the adoption of the Westminster parliamentary system in which only males with property held in individual title were eligible to vote. This assumption of sovereignty and exclusion of Māori from the fundamental rights of citizens to influence the laws and policies of their nation was to have devastating consequences. Legal scholar Moana Jackson (1992) describes the impact thus:

> In so doing, it dismissed the Maori wisdom of thought and the meanings which that gave to life itself. It began to capture and redefine the very processes of Maori thought. It began the colonization of Maori philosophy. The process thereby induced an agony in the Maori soul as this sought to survive under an increasing Pakeha domination which mocked it. Maori began to develop an internalized state of alienation in which they rejected themselves because the meanings which their philosophy gave to their existence were being removed. In their place an alien philosophy was being erected, an all-pervasive foreign word which gave meaning to all that henceforth was to be regarded as good – and it was all White.
>
> *(p. 4)*

The nation-building of 'New Zealand', originally named by a Dutch seaman who claimed 'discovery' of lands long occupied by Māori, upon which he didn't actually set foot, thus perpetuated the colonisation pattern established earlier elsewhere around the world, as various Western powers competed for power, wealth and glory, at the expense of the citizenship rights of the original inhabitants of the territories they accrued.

Globalisation and citizenship

As colonised nations, both Australia and New Zealand have built increasingly diverse population bases through waves of immigration from varying countries of origin (Forrest & Dunn, 2006), building multicultural identities in citizenship (Spoonley, 2017). From the 1980s, a global outlook to citizenship and democratic civic participation has been advocated in Australia (e.g., see Castles et al., 1988), and though generally there is support for multiculturalism, the increasing cultural diversity has also been met with fear, suspicion of the unfamiliar and leaders feeling less certain of speaking for all Australians (Moran, 2005). Conservative governments across recent decades have strengthened border control, playing 'to the darkest fears in the Australian psyche' (McMaster, 2002, p.288) relating to invasion (Glendenning, 2015) and 'the floodgate' (McMaster, 2002, p. 288). In New Zealand, the historical recognition of Indigenous rights of Māori, and consequent late 20th century policies of 'biculturalism' have more recently been overlaid with a major increase in ethnic diversity emanating from changes to immigration policy in the 1980s. This has resulted in the current situation of superdiversity (Royal Society of New Zealand, 2013), whereby this 'significantly enhanced diversity has altered debates about identity, nationalism and citizenship' (Spoonley, 2017, p. 209), to the extent that constructs of citizenship as nationhood have begun to lose relevance (Smith, 2004).

During recent decades, the force of the global economy has grown in strength, so that multinationals wield more power than governments. The free market has 'extended to every part of our public and personal worlds' and the state is no longer 'a provider of public welfare' but 'a promoter of markets and competition', aka neoliberalism (Birch, 2017). This has transformed citizenship. Democratic principles of equality are in tension with the inequalities of wealth and income in the 'marketplace' resulting in further disenfranchisement of the working class. Through neoliberalism, citizens have been reconstructed from holders of social rights to consumers in the market, and recognition of collectivist rights have been replaced with a focus on individual responsibility, whereby citizenship has been redefined as 'a contract rather than a status' (Humpage, 2015, p. 31) that is embroiled with economic standing (Kymlicka & Norman, 1995). And so globalised neoliberalism has witnessed the privileging of the protection of the rights of property owners on a global scale through the rise of power of multinationals (Smith, 2004). Only a very small elite minority are benefitting, with the wealth gap exponentially magnified. 'The situation of indigenous people, often the most vulnerable sector in terms of its labour market position and reliance upon social welfare, inevitably became especially precarious' (MacDonald & Muldoon, 2006, p. 211). Property ownership rights hold sway over participatory rights of citizens. The entangled roots of western citizenship with economic independence, in a hothouse of the (so-called) free market on steroids has resulted in those with the most wealth having the greatest airplay. It is these conditions that supported billionaire Donald Trump to claim presidency of the United States of America and daily dominate international media with what many read as sound bites of dangerous insanity.

The greed of neoliberalism has further exacerbated the global order of national identities, with wealthy nations holding higher status and power (Beck, 2000). Though globalisation has blurred boundaries for markets, determination of citizenship remains the sovereign privilege of nation states feeding border conflict and ethno-religious wars amidst tension of the market transgressing national borders (Benhabib, 2015). With the state no longer providing as much public welfare, there is ambiguity as to who is responsible for protecting social rights. Indigenous peoples have been further undermined (MacDonald & Muldoon, 2006). Deference to the United Nations' human rights instruments, committees and treaties bodies and international non-government groups such as Amnesty International and Human Rights Watch for the promotion and protection of human rights has grown since the 1960s, to assert inequalities in access to citizenship rights for marginalised groups – women, children and Indigenous peoples (Lister, 2003; Tsutsui & Wotipka, 2005). However, it is important to note that in all the UN human rights instruments there is no human right to citizenship. Though the establishment of these human rights organisations may have commenced in economically rich nations, 'as human rights become institutionalized in global politics, participation by citizens of developing countries has grown ... to establish racial equality in the postcolonial world order' (Tsutsui & Wotipka, 2005, pp. 589–590). The International Decade for World Indigenous Peoples (1995–2004) and the UN adoption of the Declaration of the Rights of Indigenous Peoples (UNDRIP) in 2007 have strengthened the rights of Indigenous peoples in the global landscape witnessing Indigenous activists utilising these international forums and instruments to press claims for a distinct Indigenous citizenship honouring collective rights and sovereignty (MacDonald & Muldoon, 2006). Though it is worth noting that when the UNDRIP was adopted by the UN, Australian and New Zealand were two of the four votes against it (United Nations – Indigenous Peoples Department of Economic and Social Affairs, nd) and were amidst the last nations to be signatories.

Globalisation has both enabled and constrained Aboriginal Australian and Māori citizenship. Global platforms, networks and mechanisms offer enhanced means to assert Indigenous rights, though the exacerbated wealth gap has negatively impacted Indigenous peoples dependent on welfare, as state social policy has been redesigned for consuming liberal individuals, eroding state welfare towards redundancy.

Feminist approaches to citizenship

'Behind the cloak of gender-neutrality' there lurks in much of the citizenship literature a clearly male citizen whose interests and concerns have dictated the citizenship agenda (Lister, 2003, p. 4). Feminist social policy scholar and British parliamentarian Ruth Lister thus argues for a feminist citizenship project that is about giving 'due accord to women's agency' both individually and collectively, recognising and countering deep-seated discrimination and male oppression and domination but not dwelling on it (p. 6). Lister proposes reformulating liberalist and civic republican approaches to citizenship to straddle the two key elements of citizenship of status and practice with 'human agency ... mediated by structure and culture ... informed by the principle of inclusiveness' arguing that 'a feminist reconstruction of citizenship has to be internationalist and multi-layered in its thinking' (p. 196). Another feminist scholar Nira Yuval-Davis (1997) argued for a non-sexist, non-racist and non-Westocentric theory of citizenship to be a multi-tiered construct, acknowledging people's membership in a range of local, ethnic, national and trans-national collectivities. Citizenship enacted through diverse collectivities is especially necessary in neoliberal times, Yuval-Davis contends, utilising multi-tiered mechanisms to work in and around how states redefine and re-privatize their tasks and obligations. Bonds with nation-state citizenship are loosened and global citizenship which links human rights and responsibilities discussed above are foregrounded. Discrimination and exclusion are countered and redressed through redistribution of resources and institutions of global governance.

Both Lister and feminist political theorist Iris Marion Young (1989) acknowledge the flaws of universal rights and citizenship and argue for 'differentiated universalism'. The principle of equal rights has not translated into social justice and equality for all citizens. This is visibly evident in our earlier discussion in which Aboriginal Australians and Māori have been positioned as citizens without rights or second-class citizens. Young proposes 'differentiated citizenship as the best way to realize the inclusion and participation of everyone in full citizenship' (p. 251). She explains that universal citizenship expressed as a 'general will has tended to enforce a homogeneity of citizens' (p. 251). This is not the case, as metaphorically illustrated in the most important commandment of Animalism of George Orwell's (1945) *Animal Farm* – 'all animals are equal, except some are more equal than others'. This 'commandment' prophetically highlighted the privileging of a few to the disadvantage of many.

Differentiated citizenship requires mechanisms for group representation. That we recognise that there are differences in capacities, culture, values and practices among groups, and that some of these groups are privileged (more equal than others), so 'strict adherence to a principle of equal treatment tends to perpetuate oppression or disadvantage' (Young, 1989, p. 251). Young thus proposes that special rights are necessary to address group differences to erode oppression and disadvantage and enable inclusion and participation for everyone, such as the United Nations Convention on the Rights of the Child (1989) and United Nations Declaration of Rights for Indigenous Peoples (2007). We agree with Young's assertion that special treatment is necessary for oppressed groups to ensure their full participation in paramount decision-making processes as citizens.

Following on from Lister's principle of inclusiveness, feminists argue for citizenship that is relational. For example, Werbner and Yuval-Davis (1999) contend that citizenship is understood 'as a more total relationship, inflected by identity, social positioning, cultural assumptions, institutional practices and a sense of belonging' (p. 4). The focus is on relationships between citizens and responsibilities towards the wider community, more akin to communitarian approaches to citizenship (Lister, 2007). With the western construct of citizenship being built on a notion of a system for affairs in the public sphere, and the legacy of women and children being relegated to the private domain, feminists have sought a reconstruction of citizenship that serves both spheres, and blurs the binary: 'to shift the dynamic of the interaction between public and private from a vicious circle that undermines women's citizenship to a virtuous circle that promotes it' (Lister, 2007, p. 200). And Yuval-Davis (1997) proposes that familial/kinship, civil and state domains are all equally part of the assurance of the social, political and civil rights of citizens, dismantling demarcation of:

the private with the family domain and the political with the public domain ... The various sub-, cross- and supra-national and state collectivities of which people are formally and informally citizens can exist in a variety of co-operative and connecting relationships which would differentially determine the positionings and the access to resources of different people at different times.

(p. 22)

Feminist critiques of western citizenship and proposed approaches hold weight and meaning for inclusion of children as political beings; for the differentiation of children's and Indigenous rights; and the necessity for citizenry as relational across societal domains.

Replacing 'citizenship' with 'community building'

In recent research, efforts to understand children's standpoints and treat them as knowledgeable actors in the community suggest that children come to understand citizenship in the rich and varying social and political contexts of their everyday lives. If children are positioned as partners in building safe, humane, and responsive communities and not merely as vulnerable dependents and objects of concern, they have the potential to strengthen communities.

(Smith, 2010, p. 6)

In this chapter, we have highlighted the colonising and exclusionary impact of the Western construct of citizenship. Drawing from the emphasis on relationships in Aboriginal Australian and Māori ontologies we are opting to instead refer to 'community building' throughout this book. 'Community building' is what you do to work out how to co-exist with others. During the study, the Gundoo educators chose to refer to the project as 'Our children, our community'. Arendt (1958/1998) describes the polis or structure of a community as the organisation of people that 'arises out of acting and speaking together' (p. 198). So, we are interested to explore how young children build community through acting and speaking together. The way citizenship is defined is intimately linked to the kind of society and political community desired (Mouffe, 1991). We see the greatest scope for peaceful co-existence if the focus is on community building with 'recognition of children as politically relevant beings' (Kulynych, 2001, p. 242). Such an approach sustains the ontological threads of Aboriginal Australian and Māori ways of knowing, being and relating: to foreground relationships and the inclusion of children.

Please note, we are not idealistic in the proposal of community building, we recognise collectivities and communities as ideological and material constructions, who are engaged in ongoing negotiated processes to define their form, boundaries, structures and rules (see Anthias and Yuval-Davis, 1992).

Book overview

From here we move to Chapter Two to discuss how prevalent discourses have influenced Indigenous childhood experience in the nation-building projects of

Australia and New Zealand. National stories of the Aboriginal Australian child citizen and Aotearoa child citizen provoke contextual thinking. The ongoing influence of prevalent discourses of colonialism, progressivism, counter-colonialism, neoliberalism, and racism on children, childhood and early childhood education curriculum and policy in the nation-building projects of Australia and New Zealand are analysed.

In Chapter Three we then critically reflect on approaches that aim to decolonise research methodologies with Indigenous children and other children who are from communities not represented in the dominant cultural group, to inquire into young children's civic learning and action in early childhood settings. Stories of entering Indigenous communities and building life-long relationships for mutually beneficial inquiries are shared. We story our accounts of working to co-construct the research agenda and practices with the communities of the inquiry. We transparently share our experiences of responsive methodologies of listening, waiting and being open to what emerges.

Then in Chapter Four we introduce the Gundoo early learning centre and its community, a rural Australian community in which predominantly Indigenous Australians live, to see what young Aboriginal children's community building in action can be. The chapter opens by introducing the history and values of the community in which Gundoo is located, along with scene setting of Gundoo's structure and philosophy. Then Bena, Kerryn and Louise story evidence of young Aboriginal children's community building, co-interpreted through conversational writing. Our stories are interwoven with cultural readings, theory and literature.

Katoa Kindergarten is introduced in Chapter Five, located in Elsden, Porirua, a community which represents the changing cultural demographics in Aotearoa New Zealand towards Māori, Pacific Island and Asian heritage predominance. Jenny and Jared discuss the ways in which the teachers at this kindergarten supported children to enact their rangatiratanga (chieftainship, or, as translated by the educators, their leadership) through rich portraits of 2–5-year-olds enacting civic action. Māori values of an ethic of collectivism are illustrated.

In Chapter Six, researchers and educators from both Gundoo and Katoa are in dialogue about the thinking and values that inform the pedagogies and environments they use to support children's community building in action. Educator and site practices, cultural values, national curriculum and policy are identified as influential factors. Notions of embodied, emplaced and relational citizenship and conscious, pro-active articulation and modelling of community values that enhance children's empowerment and collective action are explored as transferrable ideas for civic learning with young children globally.

We close the book with a series of challenges that our study and writing on young children's community building with Indigenous communities has stirred. From listening deeply to collectivist ontologies in action we propose alternatives to individualistic approaches in both education and citizenship. We invite readers to take up the challenges, and suggest that to build foundations for citizenship with young children, educators nurture and sustain relationships with Indigenous communities to incorporate Indigenous worldviews and local ecological knowledges to offer hope in rehabilitating the planet from anthropogenic devastation.

Notes

1 Louise has carried her handwritten copy of this with her since she first read it in 1987.
2 Mauri, hau, wairua, tapu and noa: Mauri is the life force or spiritual essence of a person, place or object. Hau is the vital essence associated with vitality and fertility of people and the natural world. Wairua is spirit, and wairuatanga is spiritual interconnectedness. Tapu is a state of heightened mana which is a very powerful force and may require restrictions to protect people. Noa is the state of being normalised, with tapu having been removed.

References

Anderson, A. (2016). *The First Migration. Māori Origins 3000BC – AD1450*. Wellington: Bridget Williams Books.

Anderson, B. (1998). No application forms. *Arts Nexus*. Brisbane: Queensland Community Arts Networks.

Anthias, F. & Yuval-Davis, N. (1992). *Racialised Boundaries: Race, Nation, Gender, Colour and Class and the Anti-Racist Struggle*. London: Routledge.

Arendt, H. (1958/1998). *The Human Condition* (2nd edn). Chicago: The University of Chicago Press.

Australian Bureau of Statistics (2012). *Census of Population and Housing: Characteristics of Aboriginal and Torres Strait Islander Australians, 2011*. Retrieved from http://www.abs.gov.au/ausstats/abs@.nsf/lookup/2076.0main+features502011

Australian Bureau of Statistics (2017). *4517.0 – Prisoners in Australia, 2017, Aboriginal and Torres Strait Islander Prisoner Characteristics*. Retrieved from http://www.abs.gov.au/ausstats/abs@.nsf/Lookup/by%20Subject/4517.0~2017~Main%20Features~Aboriginal%20and%20Torres%20Strait%20Islander%20prisoner%20characteristics~5

Australian Government, Department of Home Affairs (2018). *Australian Citizenship Pledge*. Retrieved from https://www.homeaffairs.gov.au/trav/citi/pathways-processes/citi/austra lian-citizenship-pledge

Batstone, D. & Mendieta, E. (1999). What does it mean to be an American? In D. Batstone & E. Mendieta (Eds), *The Good Citizen* (pp. 1–4). New York: Routledge.

Beck, U. (2000). *What Is Globalization?* Cambridge: Polity Press.

Belich, J. (1996). *Making Peoples. A History of the New Zealanders from Polynesian Settlement to the End of the Nineteenth Century*. Auckland: Penguin.

Bellamy, R. (2008). *Citizenship: A Very Short Introduction*. Oxford, UK: Oxford University Press.

Benhabib, S. (2015, 16 March). Citizenship lecture. Centre of Contemporary Culture of Barcelona. Retrieved from http://www.tttdebates.org/citizenship-a-lecture-by-seyla -benhabib/

Benton, R., Frame, A. & Meredith, P. (Eds). (2013). *Te Mātāpunenga: A Compendium of References to the Concepts and Institutions of Māori Customary Law*. Wellington, NZ: Victoria University Press.

Birch, K. (2017, November 3). What exactly is neoliberalism? *The Conversation*. Retrieved from https://theconversation.com/what-exactly-is-neoliberalism-84755

Cambridge University Press (2019). Cambridge Dictionary: Uncivilised. Retrieved from https://dictionary.cambridge.org/dictionary/english/uncivilized?q=uncivilised

Cameron, N., Pihama, L., Millard, J., Cameron, A. & Kopu, B. (2017). He waipuna koropupū: Taranaki Māori wellbeing and suicide prevention. *Journal of Indigenous wellbeing. Te Mauri – Pimatisiwin*, 2(2), 105–115.

Castles, S.*et al.* (1988). *Mistaken Identity: Multiculturalism and the Demise of Nationalism in Australia.* Sydney: Pluto Press.

Chesterman, J. H. & Galligan, B. (2009). *Citizens Without Rights: Aborigines and Australian Citizenship.* Cambridge: Cambridge University Press.

Clarke, P. B. (1994). *Citizenship.* London: Pluto Press.

Clarkson, C.*et al.* (2017). Human occupation of Northern Australia by 65,000 years ago. *Nature*, 547, 306–310.

Dagger, R. (1997). *Rights, Citizenship, and Republican Liberalism.* Oxford, UK: Oxford University Press.

Daylight, P. & Johnstone, M. (1986). *Women's Business, the Aboriginal Women's Task Force Report.* Canberra: AGPS.

Faulks, K. (1998). *Citizenship in Modern Britain.* Edinburgh: Edinburgh University Press.

Forrest, J. & Dunn, K. (2006) 'Core' culture hegemony and multiculturalism: Perceptions of the privileged position of Australians with British backgrounds. *Ethnicities*, 6, 237–264.

Gammage, B. (2011). *The Biggest Estate on Earth.* Sydney: Allen & Unwin.

Gilbert, R. (1996). Education for active and informed citizenship. In R. Gilbert (Ed.), *Studying Society and Environment: A Handbook for Teachers.* Melbourne: MacMillan.

Glendenning, P. (2015). Asylum seekers, refugees and human dignity. *Social Alternatives*, 34(1), 27–33.

Harris, J. (2003). Hiding the bodies: the myth of the humane colonisation of Aboriginal Australia. *Aboriginal History Journal*, 27, 79–104. Retrieved from http://press-files.anu.edu. au/downloads/press/p73641/pdf/ch0550.pdf

Heater, D. (1999). *What Is Citizenship.* Cambridge: Polity Press.

Henare, M. (2001). Tapu, mana, mauri, hau, wairua: A Māori philosophy of vitalism and cosmos. In J. A. Grim (Ed.), *Indigenous Traditions and Ecology. The Interbeing of Cosmology and Community* (pp. 197–221). Cambridge, MA: Harvard University Press.

Humpage, L. (2015). *Policy Change, Public Attitudes and Social Citizenship: Does Neoliberalism Matter?*Bristol: Policy Press.

Jackson, M. (1992). The treaty and the word: The colonisation of Māori philosophy. In G. Oddie & R. Perrett (Eds), *Justice, Ethics, and New Zealand Society* (pp. 1–10). Auckland: Oxford University Press.

Keen, I. (2004). *Aboriginal Economy and Society.* Melbourne: OUP.

Kingsbury, B. & Gover, K. (2005). Embedded pluralism: globalization and the reappearance of Indigenous peoples' cartographies. Paper read at International Conference for the Study of Political Thought: Conference on the State, 8–10 April 2005 at Columbia University, New York.

Kulynych, J. (2001). No playing the public sphere: democratic theory and the exclusion of children. *Social Theory and Practice*, 27(2), 231–265.

Kwaymullina, A., Kwaymullina, B. & Butterly, L. (2013). Living texts: a perspective on published sources, Indigenous research methodologies and Indigenous worldviews. *International Journal of Critical Indigenous Studies*, 6(1), 1–13.

Kymlicka, W. & Norman, W. (1995). Return of the citizen: a survey of recent work on citizenship theory. In R. Beiner (Ed.), *Theorizing Citizenship* (pp. 283–232). Albany: State University of New York.

Langton, M. (2018). *Welcome to Country: A Travel Guide to Indigenous Australia.* Melbourne: Hardie Grant Publishing.

Lister, R. (2003). *Citizenship: Feminist Perspectives* (2nd edn). Basingstoke: Macmillan.

Lister, R. (2007). Why citizenship: where, when and how children? *Theoretical Inquiries in Law*, 8(2), 693–718.

Lohoar, S., Butera, N. & Kennedy, E. (2014). Strengths of Australian Aboriginal cultural practices in family life and child rearing. *Child Family Community Australia Paper* No. 25. Retrieved from https://aifs.gov.au/cfca/sites/default/files/publication-documents/cfca25.pdf

MacDonald, L. T. A. O. T. & Muldoon, P. (2006). Globalisation, neo liberalism and the struggle for indigenous citizenship. *Australian Journal of Political Science*, 41(2), 209–223. doi:10.1080/10361140600672477

McGrath, A. (2010). 'Bad' history, good intentions and Australia's national apology. In H. Ramsey-Kurz & U. Ratheiser (Eds), *Antipodean Childhood: Growing Up in Australia and New Zealand* (pp. 47–67). Newcastle upon Tyne, UK: Cambridge Scholars Publishing.

McIntyre, P. (2001). Some reflections on the role of Elders in decision making in indigenous communities. *ADR Bulletin*, 3(9), Article 2. Retrieved from https://epublications.bond.edu.au/adr/vol3/iss9/2

McMaster, D. (2002). Asylum-seekers and the insecurity of a nation. *Australian Journal of International Affairs*, 56(2), 279–290.

Makereti [Maggie Papakura]. (1938). *The Old-time Maori*. London: Victor Gollancz Ltd.

Marshall, T. H. (1950). *Citizenship and Social Class and Other Essays* (2nd edn). Cambridge, UK: Cambridge University Press.

Martin, K. (2003). Ways of knowing being and doing: a theoretical framework and methods for Indigenous and Indigenist re-search. *Journal of Australian Studies*, 27(76), 203–214.

Martin, K. (2008). Targeting the divide. *Koori Mail*, 424, 44.

Mooney, N. (2018). *Introduction to Indigenous Australia. Australian Museum*. Retrieved from https://australianmuseum.net.au/indigenous-australia-introduction

Moran, A. (2005). *Australia: Nation, Belonging and Globalization*. New York: Routledge.

Mouffe, C. (1991). Democratic citizenship and the political community. In Miami Theory Collective (Ed.), *Community at Loose Ends* (pp. 70–82). Minneapolis: University of Minnesota Press.

Neidjie, B. (1986). *Australia's Kakadu Man: Bill Neidjie*. Darwin: Resource Managers.

New Zealand Department of Corrections. (2018). Prison facts and statistics – September 2018. Retrieved from https://www.corrections.govt.nz/resources/research_and_statistics/quarterly_prison_statistics/prison_stats_september_2018.html

New Zealand Government (2018). Citizenship ceremonies. Retrieved from https://www.govt.nz/browse/passports-citizenship-and-identity/nz-citizenship/how-to-apply-for-nz-citizenship/citizenship-ceremonies/

Orange, C. (1987). *The Treaty of Waitangi*. Wellington: Allen and Unwin/Port Nicholson Press.

Orwell, G. (1945). *Animal Farm: A Fairy Story*. London: Secker & Warburg.

Pascoe, B. (2014). *Dark Emu Black Seeds: Agriculture or Accident*. Broome, WA: Magabala Books.

Pattie, C.Seyd, P. & Whiteley, P. (2004). *Citizenship in Britain: Values, Participation and Democracy*. Cambridge: Cambridge University Press.

Pere, R. R. (1983/1994). *Ako. Concepts and Learning in the Maori Tradition*. Hamilton: Department of Sociology, University of Waikato. Reprinted by Te Kohanga Reo National Trust Board.

Petersen, N. & Sanders, W. (Eds.). (2009). *Citizenship and Indigenous Australians: Changing Conceptions and Possibilities*. Cambridge: Cambridge University Press.

Poata-Smith, E. S. (2013). Emergent identities: the changing contours of Indigenous identities in Aotearoa/New Zealand. In M. Nakata, M. Harris and B. Carlson (Eds), *The Politics of Identity: Emerging Indigeneity* (pp. 24–59). Sydney: University of Technology Sydney E-Press.

Pocock, J. G. A. (1998). *The Ideal of Citizenship Since Classical Times*. In R. Biener (Ed.) *Theorising Citizenship* (pp. 31–41). Albany: State University of New York Press.

Power, K. & Somerville, M. (2015). The fence as technology of (post-) colonial childhood in contemporary Australia. In V. Pacini-Ketchabaw and A. Taylor (Eds), *Unsettling the Colonial Places and Spaces of Early Childhood Education* (pp. 63–77). New York: Routledge.

Rose, D. B. (1987). Consciousness and responsibility in Aboriginal religion. In W. H. Edwards (Ed.) *Traditional Aboriginal Society: A Reader* (pp. 257–269). South Melbourne: MacMillan.

Rousseau, J. (1762/1968). *The Social Contract*. London, UK: Penguin Books.

Royal Society of New Zealand (2013). *Languages in Aotearoa New Zealand*. Retrieved from https://royalsociety.org.nz/what-we-do/our-expert-advice/all-expert-advice-papers/la nguages-in-aotearoa-new-zealand/

Ryan, L., Pascoe, W., Debenham, J., Brown, M., Smith, R., Price, D. & Newley, J. (2017). *Colonial Frontier Massacres in Central and Eastern Australia 1788–1930*. Retrieved from http s://c21ch.newcastle.edu.au/colonialmassacres/introduction.php

Sabbioni, J. (1998). Preface. In J. Sabbioni, K. Schaffer & S. Smith (Eds.) *Indigenous Australian Voices: A Reader* (p. xxv). Piscataway: Rutgers University Press.

Salmond, A. (1991). *Two Worlds: First Meetings Between Māori and Europeans, 1642–1772*. Auckland: Viking.

Salmond, A. (2017). *Tears of Rangi. Experiments Across Worlds*. Auckland: Auckland University Press.

Seymour, B. (2006). Mutiny in the mainstream. *Journal of Visual Culture*, 5(1), 112–114.

Sinclair, K. (1986). *A Destiny Apart. New Zealand's Search for National Identity*. Wellington: Allen & Unwin in Association with the Port Nicholson Press.

Smith, A. B. (2010). Children as citizens and partners in strengthening communities. *American Journal of Orthopsychiatry*, 80(1), 103–108.

Smith, L. T. (1995). The colonisation of Māori children. *Youth Law Review*, August/September/ October, 8–11.

Smith, P. J. (2004). The impact of globalisation on citizenship: decline or renaissance. InP. L. C. Boyer & D. Headon (Eds), *From Subjects to Citizens: A Hundred Years of Citizenship in Australia and Canada* (pp. 301–328). Ottawa: University of Ottawa Press.

Spoonley, P. (2017). Renegotiating citizenship: Indigeneity and superdiversity in contemporary Aotearoa/New Zealand. In J. Mann (Ed.), *Citizenship in Transnational Perspective. Politics of Citizenship and Migration* (pp. 209–222). Cham: Palgrave Macmillan.

Statistics New Zealand (2014). 2013 Census QuickStats about culture and identity. Ethnic groups in New Zealand. Retrieved from http://archive.stats.govt.nz/Census/2013-cen sus/profile-and-summary-reports/quickstats-culture-identity/ethnic-groups-NZ.aspx

Statistics New Zealand (2016). Changes in home-ownership patterns 1986–2013: focus on Māori and Pacific people. Retrieved from http://archive.stats.govt.nz/browse_for_stats/p eople_and_communities/housing/changing-maori-pacific-housing-tenure.aspx

Stephens, J. & McCallum, R. (1998). *Retelling Stories, Framing Culture: Traditional Story and Metanarratives in Children's Literature*. New York: Garland Publishing Inc.

Tatar, M. (1987/2003). *The Hard Facts of the Grimms' Fairy Tales* (2nd ed.). Princeton, NJ: Princeton University Press.

Te Rangi Hiroa (Sir Peter Buck)(1950). *The Coming of the Maori*. Wellington, NZ: Maori Purposes Fund Board. Whitcomb and Tombs.

Tsutsui, K. & Wotipka, C.M. (2005). Global civil society and international human rights movement: citizen participation in international nongovernmental human rights organisations. *Social Forces*, 83(2), 587–620.

Tudball, L. & Andersen, P.J. (2017). Recognizing Aboriginal and Torres Strait Islander peoples' rights and perspectives through civics and citizenships. In L. Tudball & A. Peterson (Eds). *Civics and Citizenship Education in Australia: Challenges, Practices and International Perspectives* (pp. 61–80). Sydney: Bloomsbury Press.

Turner, M. K., with McDonald, B. & Dobson, V. P. (Trans.) (2010). *Iwenhe Tyerrtye: What It Means to Be an Aboriginal Person*. Alice Springs: IAD Press.

United Nations- Indigenous Peoples Department of Social and Economic Affairs (n.d) *United Nations Declaration on the Rights of Indigenous Peoples*. Retrieved from https://www.un.org/development/desa/indigenouspeoples/declaration-on-the-rights-of-indigenous-peoples.html

Waitangi Tribunal (1996). The Taranaki report: Kaupapa tuatahi, muru me te raupatu: the muru and raupatu of the Taranaki land and people (Wai 143). Retrieved from https://www.waitangitribunal.govt.nz/

Waitangi Tribunal (2003). Te Whanganui a Tara me ōna Takiwa. Report on the Wellington District. WAI 145. Retrieved from https://www.waitangitribunal.govt.nz/

Waitangi Tribunal. (2014). *He Whakaputanga me te Tiriti. The Declaration and the Treaty. Wai 1040. Vol 1.* Retrieved from https://forms.justice.govt.nz/search/Documents/WT/wt_DOC_85648980/Te%20RakiW_1.pdf

Walker, R. (2004). *Ka Whawhai Tonu Matou. Struggle Without End* (revised edn). Auckland: Penguin.

Walker, R. (2016). Reclaiming Māori education. In J. Hutchings & J. Lee-Morgan (Eds), *Decolonisation in Aotearoa: Education, Research and Practice* (pp. 19–38). Wellington: NZCER.

Werbner, P. & Yuval-Davis, N. (1999). Introduction: women and the new discourse of citizenship. In P. Werbner & N. Yuval-Davis (Eds) *Women Citizenship and Difference (Postcolonial Encounters)* (pp. 1–38). London: Zed Books.

Whalley, J. (1996). The development of illustrated texts and picture books. In P. Hunt & S. Bannister Ray (Eds), *The International Companion Encyclopedia of Children's Literature* (pp. 220–230). London: Routledge.

Willshire, W.H. (1896). *The Land of the Dawning: Being Facts Gleaned from Cannibals in the Australian Stone Age*. Adelaide: WK Thomas and Co.

Yengyoyan, A. (1987). Economy. Society and myth in Aboriginal Australia. In W. H. Edwards (Ed.), *Traditional Aboriginal Society: A Reader* (pp. 203–224). South Melbourne: MacMillan.

Yeo, S. S. (2003). Bonding and attachment of Australian Aboriginal children. *Child Abuse Review*, 12(3), 292–304.

Young, I.M. (1989). Polity and group difference: a critique of the ideal universal citizenship. *Ethics*, 99(2), 250–274.

Yuval-Davis, N. (1997). *Gender and Nation*. Thousand Oaks, CA: Sage Publications.

2

CHILDREN AND CHILDHOOD IN DISCOURSES AT PLAY IN AUSTRALIA AND NEW ZEALAND

The construction of child and childhood in public imaginaries is 'a deeply ambivalent attempt to harness, capture and control the movements of the future and the meanings of life-itself' (Sheldon 2010, iv). Discourses regarding children define, inhibit and exclude children in citizenship theory, policy and practices. In western societies, social policy on, for or about children typically focuses on protection (Wyness, 2000) with children typically seen to belong to the '"private" worlds of play, domesticity and school' (Roche, 1999, p. 479), whereas adults generally have full access to all domains of society. Further, different socio-cultural histories inform and shape discourses of children and childhood. Childhood is read as a life stage dedicated to the indoctrination of socio-specific citizenship (see McGillivray 1997). We look to the specific socio-cultural histories in the creation of the colonised nations (Australia, New Zealand), noting influential national tropes and discourses that construct meanings of children and childhood and citizenship and participation. In doing so we identify both similarities and differences within these national discourses of children and childhood. This is advisedly a very brief overview of hundreds of years of constructions of children and childhood reducing scope to interrogate fully the complexity of tensions from varying cultural and social positions, but with the intention being rather to identify the tropes and discourses that linger in public imaginaries.

A story of Aboriginal Australian child citizens

Aboriginal Australian sovereignty has been devastatingly violated by colonisation, so a story of Aboriginal Australian child citizens is a story of resistance, resilience and survival. The story of Molly, Gracie and Daisy's resistance, resilience and survival became internationally known through the film *Rabbit Proof Fence* (2002) based on the book titled *Follow the Rabbit Proof Fence* written by Doris Pilkington

(1996) – that tells her mother's and her mother's cousins' story that happened in the 1930s. Molly, Gracie and Daisy were born of Aboriginal mothers and white fathers, the first mixed race children of the Martu people of central Western Australia at Jigalong. Molly's father worked on the rabbit-proof fence. These biracial children created an unfamiliar disruption to the kinship system and fodder for the enactment of the Aborigines Act WA (Western Australia Government, 1905) in which the Chief Protector of Aborigines was the legal guardian of every Aboriginal child to the age of 16 years, with the authority to remove Aboriginal children from family and detain them in institutions and domestic labour. The WA Chief Protector of Aborigines ordered for Molly, Gracie and Daisy to be taken from their mothers to be institutionalised at Moore River Settlement, 1500 kilometres away. 'The removal policy focused on half-castes, in the belief that they were more likely to lose their connection to family, community and country' (Behrendt, 2014). But Molly, Gracie and Daisy's desire to return to country and kin was 'instinctive, primal and urgent' (Behrendt, 2014). They escaped from Moore River Settlement and with knowledge of country and the white fella's rabbit-proof fence they walked for nine weeks to return to family and Jigalong. To gain some sense of the distance walked view the Cultural Atlas of Australia (2012).

Molly, Daisy and Gracie worked together as a group looking out for each other, with Molly as the eldest taking responsibility for the younger two. Their kinship roles and practices were core. They worked together with the environment to read the land and only take what was needed. The extraordinary endurance of walking more than 2400 kilometres (as they followed another rabbit-proof fence for some time) (Cultural Atlas of Australia, 2012) as children without supplies speaks volumes of the unrelenting perseverance and the embodied calling to kin and country. Resistance, resilience and survival are ongoing themes in Aboriginal children's citizenry. The fence is the haunting presence of citizenship as ownership; citizenship as controlled. It cuts and divides the land and symbolically reflects the divisive two worlds that Aboriginal peoples in colonised Australia are forced to traverse through a careful dance of code-switching.

A story of Aotearoa New Zealand child citizens

When I (Jenny) think of the 'child as citizen' in the context of Aotearoa, the first image that springs to mind is that of the late Dame Whina Cooper, a legendary Māori activist, who in 1975, at the age of 80, led a land march from the far north or tail of Te Ika a Māui, the North Island of New Zealand, to the capital city at the mouth or south of the island (see Figure 2.1). This image for me signals the intergenerational commitment of Māori to upholding their rights as citizens of their land, as promised to them in the 1840 Tiriti o Waitangi, and for which in 1975 they were still actively struggling to uphold, after the devastating loss of their lands, languages, and much much more. In Figure 2.2 we see 'Chief Veili' placing a coin in a collection by missionaries, whilst holding the arm of a mokopuna, demonstrating the intrinsic involvement of Māori children in the day-to-day politics of their tribe:

FIGURE 2.1 Dame Whina Cooper and her mokopuna (https://teara.govt.nz/en/photo graph/29689/whina-cooper-and-her-moko)

Both of these images illustrate the integral involvement of mokopuna in the citizenship struggles of their whānau (extended families), hapū (sub-tribes) and iwi (tribes), the focus of which have predominantly been the recovery of their lands and languages.

Tamariki (children) are highly valued in te ao Māori, the Māori world. Oriori were poetic chants sung to infants which contained sophisticated complex genealogical and ancestral knowledges, ensuring intergenerational transmission. According to the Māori scholar and leader Sir Apirana Ngata, 'It is a well known fact that there is much Maori lore, the lore of the *Whare Wananga* – *House* of Learning, of the priests of the various tribes, contained in these poems' (1951, p. 1).

The depth of knowledge contained in oriori signifies the esteem with which young children were held and that they were viewed as repositories of tribal histories. Furthermore, 'Oriori referenced the main goals that were to bring up children to be bold, brave and independent of thought and action within the whanau/ hapu' (Jenkins & Harte, 2011, p. 20).

FIGURE 2.2 Artist unknown: Missionary meeting (Alexander Turnbull Library, 1856)

Māori children were thus highly respected and valued, and involved in a community context of struggle to reinvigorate their language and traditional knowledges.

Colonialism

Barbaric acts of genocide, violation and theft of and from the Indigenous peoples formed the nations of Australia (see Roberts, 1981) and New Zealand (see Walker, 2004). Children were not immune to these violent histories. Impoverished, Indigenous and enslaved children were viewed by many colonisers as needing harsh discipline and control, operationalised through missionary schooling (Loos, 2007; May, 2001; Walker, 2004). Schooling was seen as a means of containing, controlling and remediating social problems. Generations of Indigenous children in each country were forcibly removed from their families, communities and homelands to inculcate them into European culture and values as white-legislated nation-building practice intended to eliminate Indigenous culture and society (Human Rights and Equal Opportunity Commission 1997; Walker, 2004).

However, the eras of colonisation for the two countries were different. Australia was founded on a notion of Terra Nullius and as a dumping ground for Britain's poor and felonious (Pascoe, 2014). In contrast, the British settlement of New Zealand was legitimised with the 6 February 1840 signing of Te Tiriti o Waitangi/ the Treaty of Waitangi, which was necessitated by the pre-existing (by five years) He Whakaputanga o te Rangatiratanga o Nu Tirene/Declaration of Independence (see Chapter One for more background on these documents). At this same time the transportation of convicts from Britain to New South Wales, Australia ended through an Order-in-Council dated 22 May 1840 (NSW Migration Heritage

Centre, 2010).[1] Progressive ideas were apparent in the instructions given to Captain Hobson by the colonial office, that were then partially transferred into the wording of the New Zealand Treaty of Waitangi, and which affirmed that Māori were to be treated as equal citizens. This progressivism can be seen in some other aspects of New Zealand legislation, policy and practice in relation to both women and children, although the commitments to Māori contained in the treaty were largely ignored for 145 years (Walker, 2004).

White colonialists often positioned children as unknowing and innocent beings who should be distanced from community practices, as exemplified in the 'lost child in the bush' trope of Australia (Taylor, 2014). In New Zealand the child was more often portrayed as unruly, as in the 'wild colonial child' (Belich, 1996), and the 'larrikin' or 'larrikiness' trope (Morris Mathews, 2002; Brickell, 2014). Larrikins are also celebrated in Australia through for example, Ginger Meggs.[2] In New Zealand, childhood was constructed differently for the Indigenous Māori child and the colonial Pākehā (of European ancestry) child (May, 2001). Katherine Mansfield, the celebrated New Zealand short story writer of the early 20th century, portrayed her Pākehā child characters 'as everything from victims of an insensitive adult world to visionary critics of its blindnesses and hypocrisies' (Prentice, 1997, p. 71). During the 20th century, Māori children 'became a focus of commercial interest' as seen in postcards depicting 'Maori children bathing in hot pools, jumping for pennies, and performing haka (a war dance) for tourists' (May, 2001, p. 12). Renowned Māori authors such as Witi Ihimaera and Patricia Grace have been described as positioning the Māori child as a redeemer, 'as the inheritor of a "cultural" mission or destiny in relation to the ravages of colonial history itself' (Prentice, 1997, p. 66).

From the brutal colonising beginnings in Australia, the trope of 'the lost child' continues to haunt white settler anxieties of being displaced from familiar European landscapes to a remote inhospitable land of strange creatures. The Australian film *Picnic at Hanging Rock* (McElroy et al., 1975), a tale of schoolgirls going missing on a school picnic to Hanging Rock in Victoria, exemplifies this fear. And the fear is kept alive with regular news reports of children lost in the bush. The vulnerability encapsulated in 'the lost child' reflects 'the nation's underbelly of repressed guilt and anxiety related to colonial dispossession and destruction' (Veracini 2010, 175) and continues to perpetuate as a dominant discourse of childhood vulnerability in Australia, through education and social policy and practices that emphasise child safety over child participation.

Molly, Daisy and Gracie's story shared earlier also sits in the metanarrative of the treacherousness of the Australian landscape. The white authorities assumed that the girls would not make it home, seeing the children as vulnerable in the harsh desert. The girls' tenacious self-sufficiency and attunement to country is unfathomable to coloniser ontologies of protecting children in tamed environments. Aboriginal and Torres Strait Islander children were forcibly removed from their kin and country since the first days of European colonisation (Human Rights and Equal Opportunity Commission 1997). The removal of children from their families and communities to be institutionalised in homes, missions or appointed as domestic servants to white families was 'legalised' under varyingly named Aborigines Protection Acts in each colony (and later states) of Australia up to 1970 (Senate Standing Committees on Legal and Constitutional Affairs, 2006; Human Rights and Equal Opportunity Commission, 1997). Children were removed from infancy to 16 years of age resulting in unresolved grief and trauma from sudden unexplained disconnection from family, language, culture and indigeneity with ongoing implications on self-worth, intellectual and social development, relationships, societal participation and future parenting (Human Rights and Equal Opportunity Commission, 1997). Though Aborigines Protection Acts have been abolished, the removal of Indigenous Australian children from their families continues under the guise of welfare and has devastatingly increased by 80% in the last decade without due care to follow the recommendations of the Bringing Them Home Inquiry report (Human Rights and Equal Opportunity Commission, 1997) such as the Aboriginal child placement principle of kin fostering (Wahlquist, 2018).

Colonial discourses result in Indigenous children being denied equal recognition and treatment. Their citizenship is denied on two grounds, that of being both Indigenous and children. Many Indigenous children in Australian and New Zealand were forced to attend missionary schooling for 'protection', conversion from 'barbarism' to 'civilisation' (Walker, 2016, p. 20), with religious instruction and education in English denouncing their mother tongue (Australian Institute of Aboriginal and Torres Strait Islander Studies [AIATSIS], 2014b). The Australian site in this study is an Aboriginal Australian community that was established as a Salvation Army mission, then a government settlement, in which all aspects of Aboriginal peoples' lives were controlled by government administration. Most boys and girls were removed from families and housed in dormitories. Aboriginal people who disobeyed whitefella law were sent to prison or remote reserves. In some missions, Aboriginal people used their schooled English literacy to petition for humanitarian and political objectives in redressing rights abuses (Van Toorn, 2006; Rademaker, 2016). Māori families found the brutality of missionary schools disturbing, and many removed their children (Smith, 1995). Through the imposition of colonial schooling, Māori children faced the constraints of being forced to relinquish their identity and language, in short to become brown-skinned Pākehā, demonstrating obedience to Pākehā authority and subdued by physical punishment enforcing the dominance of the English language and the Victorian etiquette that children should be seen and not heard. Education policies prohibited the speaking of te reo Māori, the Māori language, resulting in generations of Māori children being physically punished, with the consequence that families stopped speaking Māori to their children at home, in order to prevent these beatings. This resulted in multiple generations of Māori being unable to speak their own language (Walker, 2004). Government and missionary actions denied (often through physical brutality) Aboriginal Australians the right to speak and learn in their language (Troy, 2015). In 1977, Grassby declared that of the estimated 600 languages spoken at the point of British colonisation, only 202 remain following 'the heavy hand of colonial conformity' (p. 2), with Aboriginal language genocide spread across the area from 'Adelaide, (to) Broken Hill, Mount Isa, Townsville, Brisbane, Sydney and Melbourne, as well as the whole of Tasmania and the South West of Western Australia' (p. 1).

The legacy of colonialism has had dire ongoing implications for Indigenous children following generations of white government policy enforcing removal from families, harsh discipline and home language denial. Settler and Indigenous children were constructed as needing to be both protected and controlled. In contrast to their inclusion in traditional Indigenous social structures, under the colonisers children were very much subjugated and inequality legitimised. The wild unfamiliar landscapes of Australia and New Zealand, added fear of nature to newly arrived colonisers, as control of it was insurmountable. This fear was magnified in Australia due to its population of deadly fauna, feeding heightened motivation to protect children and childhood.

Progressivism

Progressive thinking of egalitarianism was present, as noted previously, in the British settlement of New Zealand with the Treaty of Waitangi. For children, progressivism forged a notion of child-centredness and experiential learning. In early childhood, these concepts were embedded in Froebel's German kindergartens, spread around the turn of the 19th century with the commencement of kindergartens and nursery schools in Australia (Brennan, 1998) and New Zealand (May, 1997). These philanthropic establishments focussed on education and socialisation for young children (Press & Hayes, 2001) foregrounding discourses of freedom of choice, enabling working-class children to experience the freedom that had historically been denied to those who had been required to work in mines, factories or as farm-hands (Somerset, 1976) or roam the streets (Press & Hayes, 2001). The 'child as an independent and autonomous learner is largely posited on a philosophy of Western individualism' (Ang, 2016, p. 146), and so has served white middle-class children well.

New Zealand's prevailing egalitarian ethos is seen in the 1877 Education Act which determined that all children should have at least an elementary education and again in the 1930s when the progressive ideas of the New Education Foundation were infused into the education system, offering a view of children as competent and capable of democratic collaboration (Campbell, 1938). In New Zealand, a strongly progressive education philosophy was widely disseminated when in 1937 the nation's 6,000 teachers were brought to Wellington to attend a conference organised in association with the New Education Fellowship (NEF) (Brehony, 2004). The NEF was an international organisation dedicated to fostering progressive educational ideas, such as those of Piaget, Dewey, Rousseau, Pestalozzi, Froebel, Tolstoy, Montessori and Freud. Ideals such as the 'principles of democratic government where all had a voice, elimination of class barriers and the full development of the individual' were highlighted by NEF speakers (Abiss, 1998, p. 83).

Yet despite the ostensibly good intention of progressive discourses, they can be critiqued in that their impacts served predominantly the children of the dominant society, that is, white middle-class children. After the 1961 Hunn Report had emphasised that early childhood education was an important focus for addressing the situation of inequitable educational outcomes for Māori, a number of play-centres were established in Māori communities (McDonald, 1973). However, this was just one of many instances whereby racism prevented Māori from accessing the benefits of progressive educational ideas and opportunities.

With the ratification of the United Nations Convention on the Rights of the Child in 1989, children's rights to quality education and care also informed the growth of early childhood education and care provision. According to Prest and Wildblood (2005), two important legal shifts created a climate for the wide acceptance of UNCRC. The first shift was that the state acquired the legal status of obligations towards children, providing additional support to existing parental obligations. The second shift was that international law no longer viewed children as objects needing protection but as subjects entitled to their own rights – a progressive move towards greater equality.

Children's rights have become increasingly influential in Australia and New Zealand, with social and education policy and systems slowly honouring children as rights holders. In Australia, however, the rights mostly recognised for children are those tied to safety and mechanisms of accountability (Van Krieken, 2010), so that discourses of child vulnerability continue to dominate public debate, with, for example the rise of a risk averse culture in recent decades significantly limiting children's independence and physical movement (e.g., see Rudner & Malone, 2011). Both New Zealand (established in 1989) and Australia (established in 2013) now have Children's Commissioners, who play significant roles in the promotion of children's rights, however their role often yields little political power, as they are appointed as public servants who advise and provide information to their respective governments.

A children's rights frame, combined with studies in the sociology of childhood and the worldwide attention on philosophy of early childhood centres in Reggio Emilia, Italy, has witnessed a significant move to acknowledge young children as competent and capable learners and agents in Australia (Bowes, 2007) and New Zealand (New Zealand Ministry of Education, 1996). There has also been increased recognition of children as competent decision-makers in judicial and administrative proceedings in Australia and New Zealand. Examples of children's participation in administrative proceedings in Australia include consultation with children to create government plans that recognise children as active citizens, such The Australian Capital Territory (ACT) Children's Plan 2004–2014 (Australian Capital Territory Government, 2004), The ACT Children and young people's commitment 2015–2025, and The City of Port Phillip Municipal Early Years Plans 2005–2009, 2012–2015 (City of Port Phillip, 2004, 2011, 2013) and now their broader Family, Youth and Children Strategy 2014–2019 provide opportunity for children to be consulted and participate in decision making about their communities.

Such examples were recognised as international best practice in Lundy, Kilkelly, Byrne and Kang's (2012) UNICEF report on legal implementation of UNCRC in 12 countries. More city councils across Australia have actively sought to consult with children and youth on local matters (e.g., Maribyrnong, Logan, Moreland), many motivated by the child friendly city movement (UNICEF, 2018). The establishment of Commissions for Children and Young People in each state and territory of Australia and a National Children's Commissioner has also created avenues for children and young people's participation as citizens. However, the UN Committee on the Rights of the Child (2012) repeatedly noted in their concluding observations on Australia's progress on the implementation of the UNCRC that there were inadequate mechanisms and platforms for Aboriginal and Torres Strait Islander persons under the age of 15 to express their views and contribute to decision-making.

In Aotearoa New Zealand there has been uneven progress in the recognition of the need to establish mechanisms for enabling young children's rights and citizenship enactment. In 2003, under a Labour-led government, the Ministry of Social Development produced guidelines for government and community organisations on involving children in decision-making. The introduction begins with this statement:

> Participation is more than just asking children for their ideas and views. It's about listening to them, taking them seriously and turning their ideas and suggestions into reality. Involving children in decision-making means they can influence some of the things that affect them, and offer a different perspective from adults … It also helps children and young people to gain new skills and knowledge and build their confidence in other processes, including democracy.
>
> *(New Zealand Ministry of Social Development, 2003, p. 3)*

However, obligations under the UNCRC were not prioritised by the subsequent National-led government of 2008–2017. The current UNCRC Work Programme of the New Zealand government includes the goal of 'improving the input of children and young people's views in the formulation of legislation and policies associated with rights under the Convention' (Office of the Children's Commissioner, 2016, p. 2).

Many New Zealand local councils have prominent policies regarding children and young people. For example, the introduction to Porirua City Council's (2018) document 'At the heart of our city – strategic framework for children and young people 2018–2021' recognises that the UNCRC 'means children have a right to say what they think should happen and have their opinions taken into account' (p. 4).

The current Auckland Council Plan's first priority is to 'Put children and young people first' (Auckland Council, 2013, p. 8), and thus 'to involve children and young people in decision-making on policies, plans and projects that affect them' and give them leadership roles (p. 16). The Wellington City Council is a member of the UNICEF Child and Youth Friendly City initiative, supports the Enviroschools programme which includes a strong focus on te ao Māori values such as kaitiakitanga (environmental stewardship) and has a te reo Māori language policy in partnership with local iwi (tribes) (Wellington City Council, 2018).

Though progressivism has largely worked to serve the middle class, it has opened doors for increased acknowledgement of rights for all groups of peoples and asserted collective responsibility for all people's needs. For example, Indigenous and non-Indigenous students' awareness of progressive movements whilst studying at Sydney University led to the formation of the Student Action For Aborigines organisation in 1964 led by Arrernte man Charles Perkins. The group organised a Freedom Ride (inspired by the US Freedom Rides in 1961) for two weeks in February 1965 to bring national and international attention to the widespread racism and poor living conditions of Aboriginal people across rural New South Wales (NITV, 2017; Perkins, 1965).

> The Ride included a survey of Aboriginal living conditions, a direct challenge to a ban against Aboriginal ex-servicemen at the Walgett Returned Services League, and a demonstration against local laws barring Aboriginal children from the Moree and Kempsey swimming pools.
>
> *(AIATSIS, 2014a)*

See Figure 2.3 for media interpretation of the action for Aboriginal children's access to local pools. Another example with significant legacy is the Aboriginal Tent Embassy that was established in front of Parliament House, Canberra in January 1972 and has continued in various forms and locations as a physical site asserting Aboriginal and Torres Strait Islander rights and sovereignty and led to the establishment of the first Aboriginal child care centre, first Aboriginal medical centre and first Aboriginal legal centre (Behrendt, 2014; National Museum Australia, 2018). Services were opened up to Aboriginal people that were previously denied and Aboriginal people had control of them.

Further sovereign acts related to children included the establishment of the Secretariat of National Aboriginal and Islander Child Care (SNAICC) (National Voice for Children) in 1981 to guide the development of government and non-government sector policies and positive developments for Aboriginal and Torres Strait Islander programmes for children and families. Early childhood services specifically for Aboriginal and Islander children and their families for sovereignty and cultural preservation were established in Aboriginal communities across Australia (Department of Education, Employment and Workplace Relations, 2010). And in 1988, National Aboriginal and Islander Children's Day (NAICD) was inaugurated on 4 August to celebrate Aboriginal and Islander children, to give them confidence and pride, and to provide a communal birthday for those not knowing their birthday due to being institutionalised in out of home care.

Māori collective responsibility is embedded in the Māori worldview, evident in ethical values such as mana (power, authority and common good), kotahitanga (unity and solidarity), whanaungatanga (belonging and respect for others), manaakitanga (ethic of care and support) and hau (ethic of spiritual power of obligatory

FIGURE 2.3 Getting in the Swim – artist John First (Melbourne Herald, 1965, 20 February)

reciprocity in relationships with nature) (Henare, 2001). These preceded western constructs of progressivism. Māori, along with Australian and other Indigenous peoples, influenced and were influenced by civil rights movements (Walker, 1990). Māori discontent with the failure of even progressive New Zealand educational initiatives, such as the 'taha Māori' token inclusion of Māori language and customs and in reaction to research that raised serious concerns regarding the imminent demise of their language, led to the Māori early childhood and community development initiative, Te Kōhanga Reo (Ritchie & Skerrett, 2014).

Counter-colonialism

The highly respected Māori legal scholar Dr Moana Jackson recently wrote that:

> colonization was and is a very simple process of brutal dispossession in which States from Europe assumed the right to take over the lands, lives, and power of Indigenous Peoples who had done them no harm. In most indigenous lives it is neither just a past or a memory but a present which links the shock and awe of contemporary international relations to the musings of long dead

European philosophers contemplating how to describe human difference and then how to destroy or control those they saw as inferior because they were different. Decolonization is the process of breaking free from that dispossession and all of the ideas and practices which shaped and were derived from it. It is to interrogate and dismantle all that it has meant and still means to the way we think and live our lives.

(Jackson, 2018, p. 2)

We acknowledge that to consider possibilities for 'post-colonial' thinking is challenging. As if all the atrocities and damage could be somehow undone. This imaginary, according to Linda Smith, 'is best articulated by Aborigine activist Bobbi Sykes, who asked at an academic conference on post-colonialism, "What? Post-colonialism? Have they left?"' (as cited in Smith, 1999/2012, p. 24). It is nonetheless imperative that educators commit to both uncovering and countering the damaging discourses of colonialism that continue to infiltrate the policy-making and spaces in which we work. We acknowledge the challenges, not only faced by Indigenous peoples on a daily basis, but also for those accustomed to their privilege, in committing to resisting the hegemony of colonialist discourses. Counter-colonial theorising attempts to expose this hegemony, as a first step to con-scientising pathways beyond colonisation. Paulo Freire's seminal work, *Pedagogy of the Oppressed* (1972), theorised a counter-colonial vision that has influenced Aboriginal and Torres Strait Islander Scholars such as Pearl Duncan and Martin Nakata, and Māori scholars such as Ranginui Walker, Graham Smith and Linda Smith. Freire himself had been influenced in the final stages of writing his book, by the work of Franz Fanon (Horton & Freire, 1990). In his 1968 book *Black Skins, White Masks*, Fanon writes that 'The *eye* is not merely a mirror, but a correcting mirror. The *eye* should make it possible for us to correct cultural errors' (p. 202). Fanon questioned the white western drive to assume superiority over the 'Other', writing: 'Superiority? Inferiority? Why not the quite simple attempt to touch the other, to feel the other, to explain the other to myself?' (p. 231).

Linda Smith has pointed out that:

Decolonization must offer a language of possibility, a way out of colonialism. The writing of Maori, of other indigenous peoples and of anti-/post-colonial writers would suggest, quite clearly, that that language of possibility exists within our own alternative, oppositional ways of knowing.

(Smith, 1999/2012, p. 324)

Māori resistance to colonisation has been ongoing, since the settlers first betrayed the commitments they had made in Te Tiriti o Waitangi, as have Aboriginal and Torres Strait Islander peoples resisted since British occupation. Resistance has operated in many arenas, including education, through Aboriginal and Torres Strait Islander governed schools and child care centres, and with the Kōhanga Reo language revitalisation early childhood movement the forerunner of Māori medium education which is now available right through to and including tertiary courses. Yet the insidiousness of racism and colonialist impacts still persist, particularly within education and educational research, buried within discourses that privilege western knowledge and paradigms.

Research and scholarship by both Indigenous and non-Indigenous scholars can and should serve as a primary site of counter-colonial re-narrativisation. According to Linda Smith:

> Research begins as a social, intellectual and imaginative activity. It has become disciplined and institutionalized with certain approaches empowered over others and accorded a legitimacy, but it begins with human curiosity and a desire to solve problems. It is at its core an activity of hope.
>
> *(Smith, 1999/2012, p. 322)*

Other sites for counter-colonial re-narrativisation than research and scholarship include television and other media. National Indigenous television channels in both Australia (NITV) and New Zealand (Māori TV) provide an avenue to share culture, histories, storytelling and re-story colonised perceptions of Indigenous peoples. In Australia, contemporary Aboriginal and Torres Strait Islander shows on public broadcasting stations are re-storying hegemonic discourses of Aboriginality, such as *Cleverman* (ABC) which combines Aboriginal mythology, science fiction and political/cultural dystopia, and *Little Cuz and Big J* (SBS) shares Aboriginal worldviews and knowledges through stories of contemporary children's lives in community through animation for children. In New Zealand, Māori TV has contributed to a sea-change whereby being Māori and speaking te reo Māori is now being portrayed as 'cool', as have movies based on the work of Māori writers, such as Witi Ihimaera's 'Whale Rider', as well as the Disney movie 'Moana' which drew on ideas from Polynesian cultures, and was later dubbed into the Māori language, both of which feature strong Māori girl characters.

Counter-colonial re-storying for Indigenous children in Australia and New Zealand offers hope through language revitalisation in schooling and media, indigenised curricula and resources, and resistance of child removal. Kōhanga Reo have been inspirational internationally in providing a model for revitalisation of Indigenous languages and cultures through programmes which bring Elders and the young together (Prochner, 2004). The uptake of Māori communities in kōhanga reo has blossomed into kura kaupapa (primary schools based in te ao and te reo Māori – a Māori world view and the Māori language) and a lesser number of whare kura (secondary schools also with a Māori kaupapa, Māori philosophy and language), as well as Māori medium units within regular primary and secondary schools. Te Whāriki, the New Zealand early childhood curriculum (New Zealand Ministry of Education, 2017), stipulates that 'All children should be able to access te reo Māori [Māori language] in their ECE setting, as kaiako [teachers] weave te reo Māori and tikanga Māori [Māori customs] into the everyday curriculum' (2017, p. 11). There remains, however, a controversy about making te reo a core part of the primary education curriculum, even though official government policy is to make it 'universally available' but not compulsory (Neville, 2018). The 1986 Waitangi Tribunal Report on the Māori language found that the New Zealand government had failed Māori not only with regard to the maintenance of their language, but also by consigning Māori to educational failure. This led in 1987 to the Māori Language Act, which affirmed the status of Māori language status, and obliges government agencies to make sure that they preserve and perpetuate the Māori language in their policies and practices.

In 2018, Craig Ritchie, CEO of the Australian Institute of Aboriginal and Torres Strait Islander Studies, called for similar legislation in Australia. Of the '250 Aboriginal and Torres Strait Islander languages, about 120 are still spoken, but most are severely or critically endangered' (Archibald-Binge, 2018). Aboriginal languages need to be sustained as 'vital carriers of cultural knowledge with relevance for geography, history, the environment, health, literature and philosophy' (Pascoe, 2016). In 2015, the Australian Curriculum introduced a Framework for Aboriginal Languages and Torres Strait Islander Languages, and First Languages Australia was established in 2013 to advocate for and resource Indigenous Australian language communities. The indigenisation of curricula is now evident in Australia in the Australian Curriculum cross-curricular priority of Aboriginal and Torres Strait Islander Histories and Cultures, and the Queensland Department of Education's Foundations for Success. To stop the ongoing colonising practice of child removal, a grassroots movement named Grandmothers Against Removal campaign Australia wide for kinship care.

Despite the advances of counter-colonial re-storying, the sustainability of this re-narrativisation can be impeded by influences of the global neoliberal context in which the market and competition are foregrounded.

Neoliberalism

The globalised neoliberal agenda has widely infiltrated early childhood education. Through domination of private sector early childhood services (two-thirds in Australia) (Munro, 2016) and a similar proportion in New Zealand, state regulations and compliance monitoring, neoliberalism emphasises standardisation and accountability (Baltodano, 2012). 'Neoliberals regard inequality of economic resources and political rights' as 'a necessary functional characteristic of their ideal market system' (Mirowski, 2013). Individual choice is prime and we see that played out in the freeing of the market in early childhood education and care in metropolitan areas in most western democratic nations (Moss, 2014). The individual child is fenced. Neoliberalism revises what it means to be a human – the perpetual market trader, trading in goods, services and self. Early childhood education and care is positioned as a commodity (Moss, 2014).

Curriculum, broadly, 'is now viewed in terms of human capital formations, rather than as a way of developing an informed national citizenry' (Rizvi & Lingard, 2011, p. 12) with a lack of autonomy for educators, described as de-professionalisation (Sims, Forrest, Semann & Slattery, 2014). Following this neoliberal framing of curriculum, many nations have developed early childhood curricula (Sims, 2017). Previously, curriculum content was the professional judgement of early childhood teachers. Though Australian and New Zealand curriculum writers did not intend to produce prescriptive recipes, the curricula are often used in this way, as compliance behaviour of educators increases due to accountability measures enacted through surveillance of practice by external bodies (e.g., see Sims & Waniganayake, 2015; Sims, 2017). 'Freedom of speech, once considered the bastion of education, is now positioned as one of the greatest threats to the state, resulting in increasing compliance enforcement throughout the education sector' (Sims, 2017, p. 3). Further, more academic subjects are increasingly being introduced and assessed in the early childhood sector (Sims, 2014). For example, the New Zealand early childhood framework, *Te Whāriki*, was critiqued for not providing sufficient guidance to address children's literacy and numeracy learning (e.g., McLachlan & Arrow, 2011). *Te Whāriki* (1996), originally crafted with a deeply embedded Māori worldview, could now be seen as 'operating in a context of tension between post-colonialism and neoliberalism' (Sims, 2017, p. 5).

Through neoliberalist thinking, children's learning is understood as an investment in the labour market of the future (e.g., see Lightfoot-Rueda and Peach 2015; Moss et al. 2016), as evidenced in Australia with the conservative government's child care funding package introduced in 2018 entitled 'Jobs for Families', with access and provision of early child education and care based on parental participation in the workforce, not on children's rights to quality early childhood education and care. This funding model is designed for metropolitan middle-class working families, not remote Aboriginal communities where paid work and income is limited. The package has a built-in safety net that Aboriginal and Torres Strait Islander families can apply for, though this means negotiating a complex, humiliating and intrusive bureaucratic system, creating insurmountable obstacles so that children's access to quality early childhood education is reduced (Beutler & Fenech, 2018; Brennan & Adamson, 2015). This funding policy initiative positions children as a burden in the way of workforce participation to fuel the Australian economy, negating children's right to quality care and education. In neoliberalism, children are often referred to by what they will be able to provide to the nation as adult-citizens (illustrated through economic investment arguments, and the measurement of performative outcomes), rather than for the contributions they can make to society as children. The positioning of children as investments increases their 'preciousness' and in turn their surveillance (Stover, 2013).

Three decades of previous New Zealand governments' willingness to embrace neoliberal social and economic policies has contributed to a widening of socio-economic disparity, whereby Māori, having been earlier dispossessed of their lands, fisheries and other resources, are now grossly over-represented in the marginalised sectors of society. These disparities between Māori and non-Māori can be seen in key measures of 'educational achievement, health and economic status' (Smith, 1999/2012, p. 337). According to Linda Smith, the subtext of the neoliberal reforms:

is that Maori are responsible for their own predicament as a colonized people and citizenship for Maori is a 'privilege' for which we must be eternally grateful. Marginalization is a consequence of colonization and the price for social inclusion is still expected to be the abandonment of being 'Maori'.

(Smith, 1999/2012, p. 337)

In tension with counter-colonial initiatives described above, the inequitable negative impact of neoliberal economic and social policies on Māori is evident in the New Zealand government frequently being called to task for failures to attend to issues with regard to the United Nations Convention on the Rights of the Child. These include the ongoing adherence to discriminatory youth pay-rates, large numbers of children living in poverty in which Māori are grossly over-represented, the poor quality of care and outcomes for children in the care of the State, the majority of whom are Māori, and the systemic inequities and poor outcomes for Māori children generally (Office of the Children's Commissioner, 2015). A neo-liberal social agenda was apparent in the previous national government's 'Better Public Services' targeted welfare reforms that required parents on benefits to enrol their children into an early childhood care and education (ECCE) service from the age of three (or themselves to attend an approved parenting programme) or face sanctions including losing half their benefit. With regard to early childhood education, under that government's target of 98% participation, home-based early childhood services burgeoned alongside corporate provision, neither of which ensured high quality programmes since the government permitted home-based carers to be merely supervised via monthly visits from a qualified teacher, and in the other early childhood services a minimum of 50% of teachers needed to be qualified (Ritchie, Harvey, Kayes & Smith, 2014).

'Neoliberalism aggressively privatises public and collective spaces, relationships and institutions' (De Lissovoy, 2015, p. 49), which has worked to feed both overt and covert racism. The liberal focus on the individual for 'the reproduction of social pathologies obscures the persistence of racism and White privilege in material, political, and symbolic terms' (De Lissovoy, 2015, p. 54). The exacerbation of racism in neoliberalism lies in 'neoliberalism's individualization of responsibility in the context of social crisis and longstanding structures of racial affordance and marginalization' so that by 'insisting on race neutrality at the level of law and policy, neoliberalism in effect privatizes racism, allowing systematic discrimination in employment, housing, and other sectors to persist' (De Lissovoy, 2015, p. 54), as illustrated above in the Australian Government's 'Jobs for Families' child care funding package and the New Zealand national government policies mentioned above, along with the disproportionately high incarceration of Aboriginal and Torres Strait Islanders and Māori peoples. Privatisation of prisons is growing in Australia (currently 18.5%) (Andrew, Baker & Roberts, 2016) and 10% in New Zealand (Kuang Keng Kuek Ser, 2016). The trend of increased incarceration and privatisation is, as Gilmore (2007) identified in her analysis of the rapid growth of the prison system in California, a sinister plot by the elite who invest in prisons to control increased unemployed agricultural and manufacturing workers as the value and status of manufacturing and agricultural industries declined. Racialised dehumanisation is produced through the neoliberal project of the growing prison system. Incarcerated family members is a lived reality of Indigenous children in Australia and New Zealand.

Racism

Racism is a powerful overarching discourse that serves to operationalise colonialism. It is based in the assumption of white superiority, as depicted in the Great Chain of Being, outlined in 1579 by Diego Valades, which positioned God at the top, followed by supposedly divine beings such as kings, then successive rankings of humans, '"from civilised to savage"', followed by animals, plants and minerals and the earth in descending order' (Salmond, 2017, p. 35). This hierarchy was repeated in Darwin's portrayal of evolution, and has been used to justify the mistreatment of 'lesser' humans, of animals, and the plundering of the earth. This can be seen reflected in the arrogance of western early childhood models with the implicit assumption of white cultures' superiority, normalising expectations through theories such as Kohlberg's theory of moral development, Piaget's stages of cognitive development and the NAEYC's models of 'developmentally appropriate practice' (O'Loughlin, 1992). It is also evident in the racist imagery that has infused literature for children, as seen in the books for children by Enid Blyton, and *Little Black Sambo*.

The original New Zealand early childhood curriculum, Te Whāriki (New Zealand Ministry of Education, 1996), expected teachers to actively counter racism. It made the statement that: 'the early childhood curriculum actively contributes towards countering racism and other forms of prejudice' (p. 18). It also expected that children would 'see prejudice and negative attitudes being challenged by adults' (p. 67) and that before moving on to primary school, children should 'have some understanding of equity and some ability to identify and challenge bias, prejudice, and negative stereotyping' (p. 65). However, the recently revised Te Whāriki 2017 doesn't mention racism at all and mentions challenging prejudice just once. The Early Years Learning Framework for Australia also offers no mention of racism, but instead offers a subsumed principle of Respect for Diversity and practice of Cultural Competence. Both are constructed under discourses of multiculturalism in which educators paternalistically and often touristically engage with the practices of other cultures (Sims, 2014). Cultural competency is recognised as racist. For example, as Pon (2009) contends, the concept cultural competency positions all except white culture as 'other' and constructs cultural awareness in a way that does not challenge the 'sense of innocence and benevolence' (p. 66) of those who seek to enact it towards their clients of differing cultural backgrounds. In essence, he argues it is an ontology built on forgetting colonialism and racism. The recent revision of the Queensland Kindergarten Learning Guideline removed the declaration in the guideline's purpose for:

all children's appreciation and understanding of Australia's first peoples and promotes learning about Indigenous ways of knowing, being and learning, contexts in which Aboriginal and Torres Strait Islander people live and Aboriginal and Torres Strait Islander peoples' contributions to Australian society and culture.

(Queensland Studies Authority, 2010, p. 3)

despite extensive consultative feedback of the political significance of maintaining the acknowledgement. These are examples of the liberal focus on the individual denying 'the persistence of racism and White privilege in material, political, and symbolic terms ' (De Lissovoy, 2015, p. 54).

The New Zealand Ministry of Education's previous strategy document for Māori education, *Ka Hikitia: Managing for success, Māori education strategy 2008–2012*, aimed to shift educational discourse away from the entrenched deficit thinking in which Māori children and families were positioned as 'the problem', towards instead appreciating culture(s) as an asset, and as being at the heart of learning (New Zealand Ministry of Education, 2008). The expectation was that educators (and the education system) should accept responsibility for supporting Māori children to be successful, rather than perpetuating the historically embedded discourse of blaming Māori children and families for the lack of achievement. Instead, being Māori was to be viewed as an inherent cultural capability, and the foundation for success as Māori. 'Success' was to be defined by students, whānau (families), hapū (subtribes) and iwi (tribes), in negotiation with education professionals and providers, so that Māori learners would excel in the realisation of the cultural identities, and enjoy full participation within and contribute to the multiple sites of their Māori communities, Aotearoa/New Zealand and the wider world. However, the implementation of *Ka Hikitia* was severely underfunded, thus undermining its potential to make any significant challenge to entrenched teacher racism. According to Lyn Provost, the 'Controller and Auditor-General', the implementation of this policy was slow and unsteady, and in addition:

Confused communication about who was intended to deliver Ka Hikitia, unclear roles and responsibilities in the Ministry, poor planning, poor programme and project management, and ineffective communication with schools have meant that action to put Ka Hikitia into effect was not given the intended priority. As a result, the Ministry's introduction of Ka Hikitia has not been as effective as it could have been. There were hopes that Ka Hikitia would lead to the sort of transformational change that education experts, and particularly Māori education experts, have been awaiting for decades. Although there has been progress, this transformation has not yet happened.

(Provost, 2013)

National Indigenous education policy in Australia is focussed on targets of 'closing the gap', and 'is mostly silent on the difficult issue of racism and discrimination'

(Biddle & Priest, 2015). The inclusion of Aboriginal and Torres Strait Islanders Histories and Cultures as one of three Cross Curriculum Priorities in the first Australian Curriculum[3] began implementation in 2010, following feedback from public consultation on the National Curriculum Shape Paper. The National Curriculum Board (NCB) pledged to include 'further reference to the importance of valuing and recognising Australia's Indigenous past, present and future in the Shape Paper. Indigenous perspectives will be considered in all stages of curriculum development process' (NCB, 2009, p. 11). Steps were made to include Aboriginal and Torres Strait Islander knowledges and experience of colonisation. Then in 2014 the Australian coalition government commissioned a review of the Australian Curriculum by two white male conservative education commentators, which in turn orchestrated deletions of any specific inclusion of the contributions of Aboriginal and Torres Strait Islander peoples to the development of Australian society, acknowledgement of National Reconciliation Week, National Aboriginal and Islander Day Observance Committee (NAIDOC) week (Australian Curriculum, Assessment and Reporting Authority, 2015, p. 108), how laws affect Aboriginal and Torres Strait Islander peoples (p. 111) and how Aboriginal and Torres Strait Islander peoples express their identities (p. 112, 142). These deletions were a response to 'fears' that emphasising 'Asia and Indigenous cultural and knowledge' has neglected 'Western traditions and knowledge' (Donnelly & Wiltshire, 2014, p. 138). And despite Aboriginal and Torres Strait Islander Histories and Cultures being a Cross-Curricular Priority (CCP), 'the chair of ACARA chose to defend the curriculum by reinforcing the fact that teachers are under absolutely no obligation to include the CCPs in their classrooms' (Salter & Maxwell, 2016, p. 309).

Recently the term 'unconscious bias' has become more evident in education discourse in Aotearoa New Zealand. 'Unconscious bias' appears to be a euphemism for the less palatable term 'racism'. The Ministry of Education states in its 2018 Annual Report that it has been requiring its staff to attend a programme 'designed to help us build a culturally responsive organisation better able to provide advice that is unbiased. The programme promotes cultural awareness, helps people understand their own unconscious bias and find ways to overcome barriers they may face' (New Zealand Ministry of Education, 2018, p. 41). Whilst the Ministry is currently attempting to get its own personnel to confront their 'unconscious bias', teachers and education scholars also need to address this 'elephant in the room'. Critical theorising is one strategy for this purpose:

> Critical theory must both help to counter the continuing violence of racism and open its ears to the voices of cultural traditions long silenced by Eurocentric approaches to world history. These two objectives constitute the core of radical multicultural forms of critical theory.
>
> *(Pfohl, 1994, pp. 453–454)*

The Early Years Learning Framework for Australia (Australian Government Department of Education Employment and Workplace Relations, 2009) lists critical theories as one of the theories that early childhood educators may draw from to inform their practice: 'critical theories that invite early childhood educators to challenge assumptions about curriculum, and consider how their decisions may affect children differently' (p. 12). This is the only mention and is not expanded on further. The revised New Zealand early childhood curriculum *Te Whāriki 2017* contains a section which is additional to the 1996 version, entitled 'Underpinning theories and approaches'. Towards the end of this short and superficial section, there is a single, very brief paragraph headed 'Critical Theories', which states that:

> Te Whāriki reflects research that adopts critical theoretical lenses to examine the influence of social conditions, global influences and equity of opportunity on children's learning and development. Critical theory perspectives challenge disparities, injustices, inequalities and perceived norms. The use of critical theory perspectives is reflected in the principles of Te Whāriki and in guidance on how to promote equitable practices with children, parents and whānau.
>
> *(New Zealand Ministry of Education, 2017, p. 62)*

It is unclear as to what 'guidance on how to promote equitable practices' is being referred to here, as the 2017 curriculum document is rather short on this. It has not retained the reflective question from the 1996 version: 'In what ways do the environment and programme reflect the values embodied in Te Tiriti o Waitangi, and what impact does this have on adults and children?' (New Zealand Ministry of Education, 1996, p. 56). Nor has it retained the expectation that: 'The early childhood curriculum actively contributes towards countering racism and other forms of prejudice' (p. 18). In fact, *Te Whāriki 2017* doesn't mention racism at all and mentions challenging prejudice just once.

Perpetuating such silences reflects 'a politics of amnesia at both the philosophical level and the official public policy level' (Mills, 2015, p. 22). Critiquing these shifting discourses, including such (newly generated) silences, is important in order to understand the ways in which they shape the views of young children's positionings in society along with influencing the affordances for young children's participation in communities. 'Policy-makers and program developers need to be aware of the inherent racism in targeted programs' (Sims, 2014, p. 92).

Closing thoughts

These contrasting discourses of children and childhood continue in circulation and have influenced the shaping of constructions of children, and their inclusion as citizens and opportunities for civic participation. In particular, the above discussion maps how colonialism, progressivism, counter-colonialism, neoliberalism and racism have and continue to construct Aboriginal and Torres Strait Islander children in Australia and Māori children in Aotearoa New Zealand, and the abuses, and discrimination they and their families continually negotiate to safely express their identities, to have their rights and their contributions to society heard and honoured.

For Aboriginal Australians and Māori, the trauma of colonisation is ongoing, reinforced on a daily basis by racist micro-aggressions (Pihama et al., 2014). Whether 'unconscious' or blatantly deliberate, the impacts of colonisation continue to impact on the capacity of Indigenous children's emotional, physical and spiritual wellbeing, to express their identities and aspirations and to contribute to a wider society that invisibilises their histories and genealogical connections, thus marginalising their citizenship enactment. It is within this context that we sought to frame a study that aimed to re-visibilise Indigenous children and their families' ways of being, belonging, knowing and relating. In the next chapter we outline our methodological positionings for the project.

Notes

1 Transportation continued to Van Dieman's Land up to 1853 and to Western Australia to 1868 (Ballyn 2011).
2 Ginger Meggs is a much-loved Australian comic strip of a red-haired mischievous working-class boy that was first created by Jimmy Bancks in the 1920s and has been sustained by a string of other cartoonists following Jimmy Bancks' passing. It is the most widely syndicated Australian comic strip, published in over 120 newspapers in 34 countries.
3 Previously, school curricula and syllabi have been state developed.

References

Abiss, J. (1998). The 'New Education Fellowship' in New Zealand: its activity and influence in the 1930s and 1940s. *New Zealand Journal of Educational Studies*, 33(1), 81–93.

Alexander Turnbull Library (1856). Artist unknown: Missionary Ref: PUBL-0151-2-014. Wellington, New Zealand./records/23010860.

Andrew, J., Baker, M. & Roberts, P. (2016). *Prison Privatisation in Australia: The State of the Nation Accountability, Costs, Performance and Efficiency*. Retrieved from https://sydney.edu.au/business/__data/assets/pdf_file/0008/269972/Prison_Privatisation_in_Australia-_The_State_of_the_Nation_June_2016.pdf

Ang, L. (2016). Rethinking child-centred education. In *The SAGE Handbook of Curriculum, Pedagogy and Assessment: Two Volume Set* (pp. 141–152). Thousand Oaks, CA: Sage Publications Ltd.

Archibald-Binge, E. (2018, 23 February). Calls for national legislation to protect Indigenous languages in Australia. *NITV*. Retrieved from https://www.sbs.com.au/nitv/article/2018/02/23/calls-national-legislation-protect-indigenous-languages-australia

Auckland City Council (2013). I am Auckland – the children and young people's strategic action plan. Retrieved from https://www.aucklandcouncil.govt.nz/plans-projects-policies-reports-bylaws/our-plans-strategies/topic-based-plans-strategies/community-social-development-plans/Pages/children-young-peoples-strategic-action-plan.aspx

Australian Capital Territory Government (2004). *The ACT Children's Plan 2004–2014*. Canberra: Australian Capital Territory Government Retrieved from www.children.act.gov.au/pdf/childrensplan.pdf.

Australian Curriculum, Assessment and Reporting Authority (2015). September 2015 tracked changes to F-10 Australian Curriculum. Retrieved from https://acaraweb.blob.core.windows.net/resources/Changes_to_the_F-10_Australian_Curriculum.pdf

Australian Government Department of Education Employment and Workplace Relations (2009). *Belonging, Being and Becoming: The Early Years Learning Framework for Australia.* Canberra: Australian Government Department of Education, Employment and Workplace Relations for the Council of Australian Governments. Retrieved from https://docs.education.gov.au/documents/belonging-being-becoming-early-years-learning-framework-australia

Australian Institute of Aboriginal and Torres Strait Islander Studies (AIATSIS) (2014a). *1965 Freedom Ride* Retrieved from https://aiatsis.gov.au/explore/articles/1965-freedom-ride

Australian Institute of Aboriginal and Torres Strait Islander Studies (AIATSIS) (2014b). *Remembering the Mission Days: Stories from the Aborigines' Inland Missions.* Retrieved from https://aiatsis.gov.au/exhibitions/remembering-mission-days

Ballyn, S. (2011). *The British Invasion of Australia. Convicts: Exile and Dislocation.* Retrieved from http://www.ub.edu/dpfilsa/2ballyn.pdf

Baltodano, M. (2012). Neoliberalism and the demise of public education: the corporatization of schools of education. *International Journal of Qualitative Studies in Education, 25*(4), 487–507.

Behrendt, L. (2014). Foreword. In G. Foley, A. Schapp & E. Howell (Eds) *The Aboriginal Tent Embassy: Sovereignty, Black Power Land Rights and the State.* Abingdon, UK: Routledge.

Belich, J. (1996). *Making Peoples. A History of the New Zealanders from Polynesian Settlement to the End of the Nineteenth Century.* Auckland: Penguin.

Beutler, D. & Fenech, M. (2018). An analysis of the Australian government's 'jobs for families child care package: The utility of Bacchi's WPR methodology to identify potential influences on parents' childcare choice. *Australasian Journal of Early Childhood, 43*(1), 16–24.

Biddle, N. & Priest, N. (2015, 29 September). Racism hits Indigenous students' attendance and grades. *The Conversation.* Retrieved from https://theconversation.com/racism-hits-indigenous-students-attendance-and-grades-48233

Bowes, J. (2007). Australia: Pedagogies in early childhood educationIn R. New & C. Mocrieff (Eds), *Early Childhood Education International Encyclopedia* (Vol. 4, pp. 883–887). Westport, CT: Greenwood Publishing.

Brehony, K. J. (2004). A new education for a new era: the contribution of the conferences of the New Education Fellowship to the disciplinary field of education 1921–1938. *Paedagogica Historica, 40*(5 & 6), 733–755.

Brennan, D. (1998). *The Politics of Australian Child Care: Philanthropy to Feminism and Beyond* (Rev. edn). Cambridge: Cambridge University Press.

Brennan, D., & Adamson, E. (2015). *Baby Steps or Giant Strides?* Retrieved 21 June 2015, from https://mckellinstitute.org.au/app/uploads/The-McKell-Institute-Baby-Steps-or-Giant-Strides-June-2015.pdf

Brickell, C. (2014). Sensation and the making of New Zealand adolescence. *Journal of Social History, 47*(4), 994–1020.

Campbell, A. E. (Ed.) (1938). *Modern Trends in Education: the Proceedings of the New Education Fellowship Conference held in July, 1937.* Wellington: Whitcombe and Tombs.

City of Port Phillip (2004). *Creating a Child-Friendly Port Phillip: Framework for Action 2005–2009.* Retrieved from http://www.portphillip.vic.gov.au/eyp-framework-for-action-2005-2009.pdf

City of Port Phillip (2011). *Creating a Child-friendly Port Phillip: 2012–2015.* Retrieved from http://www.portphillip.vic.gov.au/Report_5_-_Attachment_1_-_Early_Years_Plan_2012_-__2015.pdf

City of Port Phillip (2013). Family, youth and children strategy 2014–2019. Retrieved from http://www.portphillip.vic.gov.au/Endorsed_Family_Youth_and_Children_Strategy_2014_to_2019.pdf

Cultural Atlas of Australia (2012). Rabbit proof fence. Retrieved from http://australian-cul tural-atlas.info/CAA/listing.php?id=133

De LissovoyN. (2015). *Education and Emancipation in the Neoliberal Era*. New York: Palgrave Macmillan.

Department of Education, Employment and Workplace Relations (2010). *Multifunctional Aboriginal Children's Services (MACS) and Creches*. Retrieved from https://www.anao.gov.au/ work/performance-audit/multifunctional-aboriginal-childrens-services-macs-and-creches

Donnelly, K., & Wiltshire, K. (2014). Review of the national curriculum: Final report. Retrieved from https://docs.education.gov.au/system/files/doc/other/review_of_the_na tional_curriculum_final_report.pdf

Fanon, F. (1968). *Black Skin White Masks* (C. L. Markmann, Trans.). London: MacGibbon & Kee.

First, J. (1965, 20 February). Getting in the swim! [image] *Melbourne Herald*. Retrieved from http://indigenousrights.net.au/resources/documents/getting_in_the_swim!

Freire, P. (1972). *Pedagogy of the Oppressed*. London: Penguin.

Gilmore, R.W., (2007). *Golden Gulag: Prisons, Surplus, Crisis, and Opposition in Globalizing California*. Berkeley: University of California Press.

Grassby, A.J. (1977). Linguistic genocide. In E. Brumby & E. Vaszolyi (Eds) *Language Problems and Aboriginal Education* (pp. 1–4). Mount Lawley, WA: Mount Lawley College of Advanced Education.

Henare, M. (2001). Tapu, mana, mauri, hau, wairua: A Māori philosophy of vitalism and cosmos. In J. A. Grim (Ed.), *Indigenous Traditions and Ecology. The Interbeing of Cosmology and Community* (pp. 197–221). Cambridge, MA: Harvard University Press.

Horton, M. & Freire, P. (1990). *We Make the Road by Walking. Conversations on Education and Social Change*. Philadephia: Temple University Press.

Human Rights & Equal Opportunity Commission (1997). *Bringing Them Home: Report of the National Inquiry into the Separation of Aboriginal and Torres Strait Islander Children from Their Families*. Sydney: HREOC. Retrieved from http://www.austlii.edu.au/au/journals/ AILR/1997/36.html.

Jackson, M. (2018). In the end 'The hope of decolonisation'. In E. A. McKinley & l. T. Smith (Eds), *Handbook of Indigenous Education* (pp. 1–11). Singapore: Springer Nature.

Jenkins, K. & Harte, H. M. (2011). Traditional Maori parenting. An historical review of literature of traditional Maori child rearing practices in pre-European times. Retrieved from www.ririki.org.nz/wp-content/uploads/2015/04/TradMaoriParenting.pdf

Kuang Keng Kuek Ser (2016). Australia and the UK have a higher proportion of inmates in private prisons than the US. Retrieved from https://www.pri.org/stories/2016-09-01/a ustralia-uk-have-higher-proportion-inmates-private-prisons-us

Lightfoot-Rueda, T. and Peach, R. L. (2015). Introduction and historical perspective. In T. Lightfoot-Rueda and R. L. Peach (Eds), *Global Perspectives on Human Capital in Early Childhood Education: Reconceptualizing Theory, Policy, and Practice*. New York: Palgrave Macmillan.

Loos, N. (2007). *White Christ: Black Cross*. Canberra: Aboriginal Studies Press.

Lundy, L., Kilkelly, U., Byrne, B. & Kang, J. (2012). *The UN Convention on the Rights of the Child: A Study of Legal Implementation in 12 Countries*. Retrieved from http://www.unicef. org.uk/Documents/Publications/UNICEFUK_2012CRCimplementationreport% 20FINAL%20PDF%20version.pdf

McDonald, G. (1973). *Maori Mothers and Pre-school Education*. Wellington: New Zealand Council for Educational Research.

McElroy, H. & McElroy, J. (Producers) & Weir, P. (Director). (1975). Picnic at hanging rock [Motion picture]. Australia: Australian Film Commission.

McGillivray, A. (1997). *Governing Childhood*. Aldershot: Dartmouth Publishing Company.

McLachlan, C., & Arrow, A. (2011). Literacy in the early years in New Zealand: policies, politics and pressing reasons for change. *Literacy*, 45(3), 126–133. doi:10.1111/j.1741-4369.2011.00598.x

May, H. (1997). *The Discovery of Early Childhood*. Auckland: Bridget Williams Books, Auckland University Press.

May, H. (2001). Mapping some landscapes of colonial-global childhood. ece@2000.europe. antipodes. *European Early Childhood Education Research Journal*, 9(2), 5–20. doi:10.1080/13502930185208731.

Mills, C. W. (2015). Decolonizing western political philosophy. *New Political Science*, 37(1), 1–24. doi:10.1080/07393148.07392014.07995491.

Mirowski, P. (2013). The thirteen commandments of neoliberalism. Retrieved from www.the-utopian.org/post/…/the-thirteen-commandments-of-neoliberalism

Morris Mathews, K. (2002). The deviant child and larrikin youth in colonial towns: State intervention and social control through education in New Zealand. *Educational Review*, 54(2), 115–123. doi:10.1080/00131910220133202

Moss, P. (2014). *Transformative Change And Real Utopias In Early Childhood Education*. Abingdon, UK: Routledge.

Moss, P.*et al.* (2016). The organisation for economic co-operation and development's international early learning study: opening for debate and contestation. *Contemporary Issues in Early Childhood, 17*, 343–351. doi:10.1177/1463949116661126

Munro, K. (2016, 13 November). Boom time for corporate childcare in Australia. *The Sydney Morning Herald*. Retrieved from https://www.smh.com.au/education/boom-time-for-corporate-childcare-in-australia-20161109-gslgx2.html

National Curriculum Board (NCB) (2009). Shape paper consultation report. Retrieved from http://docs.acara.edu.au/resources/Shape_Paper_consultation_report.pdf

National Museum of Australia (2018). Aboriginal tent embassy. Retrieved from http://www.nma.gov.au/defining-moments/resources/aboriginal-tent-embassy

National Indigenous Television (NITV) (2017). *Explainer: What was Australia's Freedom Ride.* Retrieved from https://www.sbs.com.au/nitv/nitv-news/article/2015/02/18/explainer-what-was-australias-freedom-ride

Neville, A. (2018). Why making te reo Māori a core subject is not as simple as it seems. *Metro*, Auckland, NZ. Retrieved from https://www.noted.co.nz/currently/education/should-te-reo-maori-be-compulsory/

New South Wales Migration Heritage Centre (2010). *1840 Order Ending Transportation To New South Wales*. Retrieved from http://www.migrationheritage.nsw.gov.au/exhibition/objectsthroughtime/order-ending-transportation-to-nsw/index.html

New Zealand Ministry of Education (1996). Te Whāriki. He whāriki mātauranga mō ngā mokopuna o Aotearoa: Early childhood curriculum. Retrieved from https://education.govt.nz/assets/Documents/Early-Childhood/Te-Whariki-1996.pdf

New Zealand Ministry of Education (2008). *Ka hikitia. Managing for Success. Māori Education Strategy 2008–2012*. Wellington: Ministry of Education.

New Zealand Ministry of Education (2017). Te Whāriki. He whāriki mātauranga mō ngā mokopuna o Aotearoa. Early childhood curriculum. Retrieved from https://www.education.govt.nz/early-childhood/teaching-and-learning/te-whariki/

New Zealand Ministry of Education (2018). Annual report. Retrieved from https://www.education.govt.nz/assets/Documents/Ministry/Publications/Annual-Reports/2018-MOE-Annual-Report-WEB-Final.pdf

New Zealand Ministry of Social Development (2003). *Involving Children. A Guide to Engaging Children in Decision-making*. Wellington, NZ: MSD.

Ngata, A. S. (1951). Introduction to Maori Poetry. *Arachne*, 3, 2–6. Retrieved from http://nzetc.victoria.ac.nz/tm/scholarly/tei-VUW03Arac-t1-body-d2.html

Noyce, P., Olsen, C. (Producers) & Noyce, P. (Director) (2002). Rabbit proof fence [Motion picture]. Australia: Rumbalara Films.

Office of the Children's Commissioner (2015). *Report of the NZ Children's Commissioner to the Committee on the Rights of the Child*. Wellington, NZ. Retrieved from https://tbinternet.ohchr.org/Treaties/CRC/Shared%20Documents/NZL/INT_CRC_NGO_NZL_22410_E.pdf

Office of the Children's Commissioner (2016). *Supplementary report from the Office of the Children's Commissioner to the United Nation's Committee on the Rights of the Child*. Wellington, NZ. Retrieved from http://www.occ.org.nz/childrens-rights-and-advice/uncroc/uncroc-reporting/

O'Loughlin, M. (1992). Appropriate for whom? A critique of the culture and class bias underlying Developmentally Appropriate Practice in early childhood education. Paper presented at the 3rd Reconceptualizing Early Childhood Education: Research, Theory, and Practice Conference: Reclaiming the Progressive Agenda, Chicago, Illinois.

Pascoe, B. (2014). *Dark Emu Black Seeds: Agriculture or Accident*. Broome, Australia: Magabala Books.

Pascoe, B. (2016, 26 May). It's a great time to be teaching about Indigenous Australian languages. *ABC Education*. Retrieved from http://education.abc.net.au/newsandarticles/blog/-/b/2290623/it-s-a-great-time-to-be-teaching-indigenous-australian-languages-

Perkins, C. (1965, 16–18 April). Student Action for Aborigines Report. Eighth Annual Conference on Aboriginal Affairs, Canberra, ACT. Retrieved from http://indigenousrights.net.au/__data/assets/pdf_file/0005/382676/f90.pdf

Pfohl, S. (1994). *Images of Deviance and Social Control: A Sociological History*. New York: McGraw-Hill Publishing Co.

Pihama, L., Reynolds, P., Smith, C., Reid, J., Smith, L. T. & Te Nana, R. (2014). Positioning historical trauma theory within Aotearoa New Zealand. *AlterNative: An International Journal of Indigenous Peoples*, 10(3), 248–262.

Pilkington, D. (1996). *Follow the Rabbit Proof Fence*. Brisbane: University of Queensland Press.

Pon, G. (2009). Cultural competency as new racism: An ontology of forgetting. *Journal of Progressive Human Services*, 20, 59–71.

Porirua City Council (2018). At the heart of our city. Strategic framework for children and young people 2018–2021. Retrieved from https://poriruacity.govt.nz/your-council/city-planning-and-reporting/our-strategic-priorities/children-and-young-people/

Prentice, C. (1997). 'Born in a marvellous year'?: The child in colonial and postcolonial New Zealand literature. *New Literatures Review*, 33, 65–80.

Press, F. & Hayes, A. (2001). *OECD Thematic Review of Early Childhood Education and Care Policy: Australian Background Report*. Sydney, NSW: Institute of Early Childhood, Macquarie University.

Prest, C. & Wildblood, S. (2005). *Children Law: An Interdisciplinary Handbook*. Bristol: Jordan Publishing Ltd.

Prochner, L. (2004). Early childhood education programs for indigenous children in Canada, Australia and New Zealand: an historical review. *Australian Journal of Early Childhood*, 29, 7–16.

Provost, L. (2013). *Education for Māori: Implementing Ka Hikitia – Managing for Success*. Wellington, NZ: Office of Controller and Auditor-General. Retrieved from http://www.oag.govt.nz/2013/education-for-maori

Queensland Studies Authority (2010). *Queensland Kindergarten Learning Guideline*. Brisbane: QSA.

Rademaker, L. (2016). 'We want a good mission not rubbish please': Aboriginal petitions and mission nostalgia. *Aboriginal History*, 40, 119–143.

Ritchie, J., Harvey, N., Kayes, M. & Smith, C. (2014). Our children, our choice: Priorities for policy. Child Poverty Action Group Policy Paper Series. Part Two: Early Childhood Care & Education (ECCE). Retrieved from https://www.cpag.org.nz/resources-2/our-children-our-choice-priorities-for-policy-7/part-2-early-childhood-care-and-education/

Ritchie, J. & Skerrett, M. (2014). *Early Childhood Education in Aotearoa New Zealand: History, Pedagogy, and Liberation*. New York: Palgrave MacMillan.

Rizvi, F. & Lingard, B. (2011). Social equity and the assemblage of values in Australian higher education. *Cambridge Journal of Education*, 41, 5–22.

Roberts, J. (1981). *Massacres to Mining: The Colonisation of Aboriginal Australia*. Melbourne: Dove Communications.

Roche, J. (1999). Children: Rights, participation and citizenship. *Childhood*, 6(4), 475–493.

Rudner, J., & Malone, K. (2011). Childhood in the suburbs and the Australian dream: How has it impacted children's independent mobility? *Global Studies of Childhood*, 1(3), 207–225.

Salmond, A. (2017). *Tears of Rangi. Experiments Across Worlds*. Auckland: Auckland University Press.

Salter, P., & Maxwell, J. (2016). The inherent vulnerability of the Australian Curriculum's cross-curriculum priorities. *Critical Studies in Education*, 57(3), 296–312.

Senate Standing Committees on Legal and Constitutional Affairs (2006). Unfinished business: Indigenous stolen wages. Retrieved from https://www.aph.gov.au/parliamentary_business/committees/senate/legal_and_constitutional_affairs/completed_inquiries/2004-07/stolen_wages/report/c02

Sheldon, R. (2010). *The Rhetoric of Future Harm: Representations and Figurations of Child in Contemporary American Discourses of Catastrophe*. Doctor of Philosophy thesis, The City University of New York.

Sims, M. (2014). Racism. Surely not? *Australasian Journal of Early Childhood*, 39(1), 89–93.

Sims, M. (2017). Neoliberalism and early childhood. *Cogent Education*, 4, 1–10. Retrieved from https://cogentoa.com/article/10.1080/2331186X.2017.1365411.pdf

Sims, M., & Waniganayake, M. (2015). The performance of compliance in early childhood: neoliberalism and nice ladies. *Global Studies of Childhood*, 5, 333–345.

Sims, M., Forrest, R., Semann, A., & Slattery, C. (2014). Conceptions of early childhood leadership: Driving new professionalism? *International Journal of Leadership in Education: Theory and Practice*, 18, 149–166.

Smith, L. T. (1995). The colonisation of Māori children. *Youth Law Review*, August/September/October, 8–11.

Smith, L. T. (1999/2012). *Decolonizing methodologies. Research and Indigenous Peoples*. London and Dunedin: Zed Books Ltd and University of Otago Press.

Somerset, G. (1976). *Vital Play in Early Childhood*. Auckland: New Zealand Playcentre Association.

Stover, S. (2013). Working theories on 'unintended consequences' of early childhood education in Aotearoa, New Zealand. *Australasian Journal of Early Childhood*, 38, 4–8.

Taylor, A. (2014). Settler children, kangaroos and the cultural politics of Australian national belonging. *Global Studies of Childhood*, 4(3), 169–182.

Troy, J. (2015, 1 December). The first time I spoke in my own language I broke down and wept. *The Guardian*. Retrieved from https://www.theguardian.com/commentisfree/2015/dec/01/the-first-time-i-spoke-in-my-own-language-i-broke-down-and-wept

UNICEF (2018). Child friendly cities initiative. Retrieved from https://childfriendlycities.org

UN Committee on the Rights of the Child (2012). Consideration of reports submitted by States parties under article 44 of the Convention: Concluding observations: Australia.

Retrieved from http://www2.ohchr.org/english/bodies/crc/docs/co/CRC_C_AUS_ CO_4.pdf

van Krieken, R. (2010). 'Childhood in Australian sociology and society.' *Current Sociology* 58(2), 232–249.

Van Toorn, P. (2006). *Writing Never Arrives Naked: Early Aboriginal Cultures of Writing in Australia*. Canberra: Aboriginal Studies Press.

Veracini, L. (2010). *Settler Colonialism: A Theoretical Overview*. London: Palgrave MacMillan.

Wahlquist, C. (2018, 25 January). Indigenous children in care doubled since stolen generations apology. Retrieved from https://www.theguardian.com/australia-news/2018/jan/25/indigenous-children-in-care-doubled-since-stolen-generations-apology

Waitangi Tribunal (1986). *Report of the Waitangi Tribunal on the Te Reo Maori Claim (WAI 11)*. Wellington, NZ: Waitangi Tribunal. Retrieved from http://www.justice.govt.nz/tribunals/waitangi-tribunal

Walker, R. (1990). *Ka Whawhai Tonu Matou. Struggle Without End*. Auckland: Penguin.

Walker, R. (2004). *Ka Whawhai Tonu Matou. Struggle Without End* (revised edn). Auckland: Penguin.

Walker, R. (2016). Reclaiming Māori education. In J. Hutchings & J. Lee-Morgan (Eds), *Decolonisation in Aotearoa: Education, Research and Practice* (pp. 19–38). Wellington: NZCER.

Wellington City Council (2018). *Te Tauihu. Te reo Māori Policy*. Wellington, NZ. Retrieved from https://wellington.govt.nz/your-council/plans-policies-and-bylaws/policies/te-tauihu-te-reo-maori

Western Australia Government (1905). *Aborigines Act*. Retrieved from https://aiatsis.gov.au/sites/default/files/catalogue_resources/52790.pdf

Wyness, M. G. (2000). *Contesting Childhood*. London: Falmer Press.

3

DECOLONISING METHODOLOGIES
WITH CHILDREN AND COMMUNITY

Scientific research has a legacy of tyranny for colonised peoples across the globe. Linda Tuhiwai Smith (1999) opens her now legendary book *Decolonizing Methodologies: Research and Indigenous Peoples* with this powerful statement:

> From the vantage point of the colonized, a position from which I write, and choose to privilege, the term 'research' is inextricably linked to European imperialism and colonialism. The word itself, 'research', is probably one of the dirtiest words in the indigenous world's vocabulary.
>
> *(p. 1)*

She points out that Māori, like many other Indigenous peoples, have been over-researched, and that the majority of this research has been done to them, in an exploitative manner, whereby western researchers 'steal' knowledge from Indigenous groups and then use it for their own benefit (Smith, 1999; 2012, p. 114). Aboriginal children have been part of the Aboriginal Australian experience of being over-researched, 'without the permission, consultation, or involvement of Aboriginal people' 'generating mistrust, animosity, and resistance' in communities (Martin, 2003, p. 203).

Education was a key site for colonisation, deliberately undermining Indigenous knowledge systems and values. As Leonie Pihama and Jenny Lee-Morgan have pointed out:

> Colonial processes, underpinned by an unfettered arrogance and self-asserted superiority, have shaped our shared, but different, experiences as Indigenous people. From our natural environment and relational structures that enabled collective wellbeing to our cultural knowledge systems to our languages and

ceremonial practices, colonialism has sought to explicitly and implicitly disrupt and fragment our ways of being.

(2018, p. 2)

Mere Skerrett (in Skerrett and Pence, forthcoming) has recently highlighted the colonial project of domination as involving displacement and replacement of Indigenous peoples by colonisers who misleadingly claim 'discovery' of these Indigenous lands. She points out that colonialism constructs both racism and linguicism. Applying her analysis to the context of early childhood education, she writes that the 'undercurrents of imperialist projects steeped in 200 years of paternalistic colonial mind-sets continue their efforts to silence Māori Indigeneity through policy in text and policy in practice' (Skerrett, 2017, p. 4). Skerrett highlights that Indigenous languages hold one key to decolonisation, as the conceptualisations they bring serve to affirm Indigenous frameworks, such as self-determination, as expressed in the Māori term tino rangatiratanga. Reinstating such concepts into education, according to Skerrett, facilitates 'the power of Indigenous languages to liberate minds through language' (p. 4).

Educational research is fraught with the potentiality to perpetuate, or reinscribe, colonialist oppression. Researching with young children can be, and often is, a colonising practice, through unequal power structures with adults determining what, how and who are researched, often objectifying children and oversimplifying their experiences and understandings for adult knowledge gain (Cannella & Viruru, 2004). Researching with young Indigenous children requires multimodal sensitivity and responsivity to the complex layers of historical, contemporary, coloniser, racist, economic and adultist oppressions that may exist, including in our own histories and realities as teachers and researchers.

Tuck and Yang (2014) have highlighted the tendency for white liberal teachers and researchers to elicit 'pain narratives' from members of Indigenous and other disenfranchised communities. And yet, it is impossible to avoid the realities of pain that emerge during a research process. As researchers, we cannot remain indifferent or impartial when teachers share stories of difficulties they or the families and children are facing. These difficulties are compounded by histories of colonisation having created conditions of socio-economic disenfranchisement.

Research that aims to be decolonising therefore needs to intentionally, and proactively, counter the potential for it to in fact be re-colonising. This means that western trained methodologists need to proactively shift from 'an individualistic, linear, hierarchical, authoritarian, majoritarian, patriarchal, compartmentalized, white-privileged complacency, to an unsettled, contingent, relational, spiritual, and emotional positioning' (Ritchie, 2015, p. 83). Shawn Wilson, an Opaskwayak Cree from northern Manitoba, who has developed his research paradigm via his experiences working with Indigenous scholars in both Australia and Canada, highlights that a core aspect of an Indigenous ontology and epistemology is relationality, and that central to an Indigenous axiology and methodology 'is that research must maintain accountability to all the relationships that it forms' (2008,

p. 137). We consider both relationality and accountability to be central components in any research that has an intention of being decolonising. Margaret Kovach (2010) points out that Indigenous communities 'demand a decolonizing outcome from research' (p. 86), and employs a theoretical positioning that employs some tools of western critical theory to this end.

It is important to interrogate the purposes and processes of any research involving young children and their families, and in particular when working with Indigenous communities. Russell Bishop (2011) emphasises some fundamental critical questions to be asked of any proposed research with/in Indigenous communities: Who benefits? Will the community in which the research takes place find the outcomes meaningful and useful? Who is initiating this study? Whose concerns, interests and perspectives are prioritised in designing and carrying out the study? To whom are the researchers accountable? How are the findings being represented? Who is legitimating this study and its findings and in relation to whose worldviews? (Bishop, 2011, pp. 3–4).

The necessary orientation of ongoing reflexivity and self-scrutiny can be guided by consideration of the following provocations:

- In what ways has the focus of the research taken into account consideration of historical/political/social/cultural contexts?
- What 'homework' does the researcher(s) need to do, in critiquing and deconstructing her/his/their cultural/historical boundedness, interests and motivations?
- What ethical responsibilities emerge from this consideration? How can the research focus be jointly determined so it operates in service of the community that is to be 'researched'?
- How does the research agenda address social, cultural and environmental justice considerations?
- How does the proposed study respond to considerations of self-determination by Indigenous peoples; protect their lands, languages, identities and traditions; and ensure that they are not remarginalised?
- How might participant communities be affirmed and enabled to operate as collectives within the research process?
- How is the research design relevant to diverse cultural groups that may be represented as participants? How will cultural specificities be acknowledged and highlighted?
- How will Elders of relevant communities be informed and involved? What spiritual processes and protections will need to be incorporated?
- How will the findings be analysed and theorised (and in what ways are participants to be included in this process)? What accountability mechanisms can be included to ensure that participants feel that their understandings have been honoured and are represented in ways that feel appropriate to them?
- And 'who benefits'? Will the research contribute to better understandings of ways in which educators can serve to enhance life-worlds of children

and families and the well-being of the more-than-human world? How will the knowledge that is generated be disseminated in ways that will be accessible, transformative and influential?

(Ritchie, 2017, pp. 477–478)

These questions need to be considered in relation to the ethics and values of the particular research community (Canosa et al., 2018). In the case of Aotearoa, Linda Tuhiwai Smith's (1999) list of culturally embedded Māori ethical considerations, often overheard spoken by Kuia (women Elders) on the marae, continue to resonate:

1   Aroha ki te tangata (a respect for people).
2   Kanohi kitea (the seen face, that is present yourself to people face to face).
3   Titiro, whakarongo … korero (look, listen … speak).
4   Manaaki ki te tangata (share and host people, be generous).
5   Kia tupato (be cautious).
6   Kaua e takahia te mana o te tangata (do not trample over the mana of people).
7   Kaua e mahaki (don't flaunt your knowledge).

(p. 120)

These also align with the set of ethics outlined by Manuka Henare (2001), which we described in Chapter One of this book. Such relational ethics, of reverence for life (mauri), for spiritual interconnectedness (wairuatanga), for the spiritual power of obligatory reciprocity (hau), for care and support (manaakitanga) and so on, provide guidance for researchers who are working in an Indigenous context. Having the spiritual guidance of Indigenous Elders is important in this work.

Aboriginal Australians are globally one of the most researched people (Martin, 2003; Rigney, 1999). Aboriginal scholars Narungga, Kaurna and Ngarrindjeri man Lester Irabinna Rigney (1999) and Noonuccal woman Karen Martin (2003) are key contributors of knowledge of Aboriginal worldviews on ethics in research. Rigney advocated for Indigenist research drawing from 'insights and principles of feminist research that involve emancipation and liberation strategies (Lather; Waldby; Ebert; Weiler)', to foreground research that is culturally safe and culturally respectful. He proposed three fundamental and interrelated principles: resistance, political integrity and privileging Indigenous voices. Martin (2003) expanded on Rigney's work on indigenist research to include Aboriginal worldviews drawing from her Quandamooka ontology. Some examples of how Quandamooka values inform ethical research practice include that:

• The prime concern is to protect and preserve 'country and its Entities and the protection and preservation of our Ways of Knowing, Ways of Being and Ways of Doing' (p. 211).
• The research design is based on recognition of 'the way relations are maintained between and amongst Entities' (p. 212).

- Researcher 'conduct is ... driven by our Ways of Knowing and Ways of Being, to know and to observe protocols and respect relations and earn rights to continue the research' (pp. 212–213).
- The 'fieldwork ... immerses the researcher in the contexts of the Entities and to watch, listen, wait, learn and repeat these processes as methods for data collection' (p. 213).
- The 'data interpretation accords respect to the country and Entities in allowing these to tell the patterns within their own stories, in their own ways. It may also require the Indigenist researcher to watch and wait with patience as the interpretations and representations of these patterns emerge' (p. 213).
- The 'reporting is culturally regulated through respect of protocols to others, such as asking permission, using preferred language, terms and expressions, with the ultimate aim of maintaining relations' (p. 213).

Such principles work to foreground Aboriginal ways of being, knowing and doing and foreground Aboriginal sovereignty over research.

> Acknowledging sovereignty changes the conversation from considering whether to engage respectfully with Indigenous peoples to a meaningful exploration of how, and more broadly, of the ways in which we all might live together so as to sustain the land upon which all depend for survival.
>
> *(Kwaymullina, 2016, p. 442)*

Along with this primary respect for Indigenous onto-epistemologies, guidance can also be found in critical qualitative methodologies such as critical ethnography and critical narrative methodologies. Inherent to these approaches is a deep, ongoing critical reflexivity, researcher humility and a commitment to ongoing collaboration. Relationships forged are likely to be lifelong, as exemplified in the work of New Zealand anthropologists Joan Metge and Anne Salmond. Time, trust, honesty, respect, patience, being able to listen and 'really hear' and being open to challenge and critique are important qualities in these relationships.

In addition to ethnographic presence, and the ethical relationality this entailed, we adopted specific data gathering methods of fieldnotes, supported by audio and video recording. Through our physical presence and engagement with the teachers and children and in viewing the video data, we came to realise that the children's embodied ways of being, doing and relating, whilst often non-verbal, were a source of meaning that had great relevance to our study. Donna Haraway, in an explanatory footnote in her book *How Species Meet*, relates how Cary Wolfe, in a piece reflecting on his learning from Temple Grandin, recognised that thinking and understanding can be non-verbal, exploring 'ways out of the premises of liberal humanism and its language-sated versions of epistemology, ontology, and ethics that Grandin offers in her explorations of sensory modalities of knowing' which critique 'the implicit assumption and explicit premise that all that is truly thinking must be linguistic' (Haraway, 2008, p. 371).

An aspect of modernist, positivist science that has been particularly colonising is the denial of ways of knowing that are sensory, intuitive, spiritually sourced and embodied. The Māori word 'rongo' means to sense, and includes intuition along with other senses of hearing, seeing, smelling, tasting, feeling. In a Māori world-view, humans are positioned alongside the plants, insects, birds and other creatures, all descend from the original parents, Papatūānuku, the Earth Mother, and Ranginui, the Sky Father, and thus operate in ongoing intra-activity with the spiritual and physical worlds. From a Māori perspective, verbal language is merely one way of being and relating:

> The Māori language, as a metaphorical means of communication, clears the way for Being to emerge in ways that respect its primordiality. Its metaphorical nature allows for gaps in understanding so that Being can appear from time to time. Silence is therefore highly valued amongst Māori, allowing more to divulge itself than what was possible solely through utterance. Being itself is affected by the interrelationship between the self and the natural world, with the result that speaking, art, silence, and contemplation produced a conduit for Being to hold sway.
>
> *(Mika, 2012, p. 1083)*

A methodology that aims to avoid re-colonising needs therefore to be similarly sensorarily attuned and responsive. Borrowing from Carl Mika (2016, p. 9), it would be problematic to make the claim that our methodology was actually 'decolonizing' since, as he points out, 'most likely, nothing fully decolonizes'; however, we fully intended our approach to be counter-colonial, that is, to contribute to challenging the politics and policies of amnesia (Mills, 2015) with regard to the ongoing impacts of colonisation, which will otherwise perpetuate social, cultural and ecological injustices. 'Respectful research, in relation to Indigenous peoples, requires engaging with and through new modes of interaction that begin with the recognition of that which the colonial project has long denied: the inherent sovereignty and humanity of Indigenous peoples' (Kwaymullina, 2016, p. 447).

Louise, Kerryn and Bena's story of decolonising research

LOUISE: Acutely aware of my whiteness and outsider positioning, I first shared the idea of the project[1] with Kerryn who I knew through the early childhood sector. Kerryn already had a six-year plus relationship with the Gundoo child care community as a mentor.

KERRYN: We talked about relationships being important, and how having a relationship with community comes first. We talked about whether Gundoo community may be interested, so we took those questions to the community, for the community to answer. I don't speak for any community other than the country I belong to, Luritja country. I can't speak on behalf of other people, so I can only share relationships. We took that yarn, with no preconceived notions, to the beautiful custodians of Gundoo's community and the leaders of Gundoo early childhood community (Bena being one of them).

LOUISE: We visited the child care centre a couple of times to get to know each other, talking about the centre, community, early childhood education and the project. Kerryn and I referred to the project in terms of children having voice, rights and being active contributors to community.

BENA: When I heard about the project I was surprised. I saw it as a good opportunity to share our way of living. Our culture is so often looked down upon, so I was proud that our centre was recognised. Not just our centre, the community, our culture. We had that opportunity to represent the Aboriginal people. Share our knowledge with others. To learn from one another – two-way learning.

LOUISE: With support from the Gundoo educators, the director took Kerryn and I to the home of an Elder who was executive officer on the centre's committee, to talk about the project. It was a very humbling experience to be welcomed into an Elder's home. I have never been to the homes of, say, principals of schools in which I have researched. I was struck by the intimacy and generosity of this encounter. The Elder agreed, on behalf of the community, to approve the study taking place. I understood that her decision was guided by the physical presence of the director and Kerryn standing beside me on this project.

Kerryn and I visited a few more times across a year to build relationships with educators and discuss what children's rights and citizenship means to them. I would have visited more if they were closer, though the community is half a day's travel away from my home. It wasn't until 15 months after I had first visited the community that we entered classrooms to spend time with children and seek the children's consent and became involved in their everyday practices. We sought to decolonise conventional research methodologies of distance between researcher and participants and built relationships first (L. T. Smith, 2012).

KERRYN: Time underpinned. We walked alongside. It was the time of the country and the time of the community. Time of the research agenda points of reference – but the priority came to be the time of the children, the community and to build relationships, because there has to be trust for people to come into community. There has been a long history of people coming and taking. Looking through a lens, as Bena said, that views Aboriginal culture as having deficits, but instead to see the strengths and to hear the cultural strengths and ways of being and knowing. The strengths of community and what keeps culture alive. Taking the time to build relationships was pinnacle. And be part of the community. Not to come in and view from a lens, but to come and play and work together. Be seen to be a part of, not as something separate.

LOUISE: We were there. We were responsible for those who we were with.

BENA: Children learn from what they see. Because they saw that we trusted you, then they were able to too. You weren't just coming to take. You also came to give. You shared your knowledge with us. That helps us too. We also need knowledge to live in a changing world. We learn to walk in two worlds. But we develop in our own children to be able to do that. We don't want to take our culture, our beliefs, our values for our children. Having an understanding of our beliefs and values. Acknowledging them and accepting them.

LOUISE: Transitioning into the rhythms of Gundoo and community from the city and academic mechanistic operations was not smooth and easy but rather about episodically letting go.

KERRYN: Looking at our watches feeds deficit thinking. When it is going to happen? Well we don't know but it will. Research has its roots in ideology in western constructs such as time with an individual agenda rather than a collective agenda.

BENA: Learning as a collective not as an individual. Our way of life is built on the collective. We don't just take one person away to teach them something. It wasn't just one teacher. There were many. And children teaching one another.

KERRYN: Having respect that they lead some decisions. That they have autonomy. Negotiating the regulations, such as the fences. Strong community wrap around care.

BENA: To know who they are and where they come from.

KERRYN: Yes and to quickly climb that fence.

BENA: And why we were placed in the remote areas. Forcibly removed not by cars but by foot. All them years ago. They have that sense where they come from originally and they can identify that. When you did the research you just opened my eyes more to what we were already doing and what we already taught. It was always part of our lives. Then they introduce that children should be treated like this and they have rights, but we always given children these rights. You know. It was always a part of our culture for them to learn to be a part of the community.

KERRYN: Giving children autonomy to do what they need to do to survive.

BENA: It's always been our way of being. My awareness only came about when you came, but I've always done this. I'm just doing what my Mum and Dad taught me. And you coming and showing the videos. You saw what we were doing. You didn't ask kids questions and you looked at children's rights and citizenship and you said I see this and I see this. We doing it all the time without thinking or knowing we was doing it. We know what we doing but sometimes it's hard to write on paper. It's our way of life, something we do naturally every day.

LOUISE: As early childhood teachers, Kerryn and I readily joined in the children's activities and co-played building relationships and getting to know the children. We played with the children and took part in all the day's activities – playing inside and out, setting up equipment, comforting children, serving food, cleaning, and settling children to sleep. We did everything the educators did. I understood this as a cultural value – if you are there you are responsible – you contribute. After a few days, we introduced the video camera – showing the children what it did and asking if they wanted to be filmed. With the use of the camera's built-in projector, we played footage back to the children at group time, gleaning their feedback and response. The children could see and comment on what we were doing. To nurture reciprocity, we did what they did – so they did what we did – cameras were shared with the children. Our notebooks were also shared – the children too wanting to make notes. We provided a University ethics committee approved consent form with pictures of craft-making, a camera, video camera, an audio recorder and hand-writing, asking them to tick what they agreed to in data gathering of the project. But it was in their actions that they really communicated their consent and trust in our presence and the project. Such as running to hug us on arrival, and calling us Aunty, inviting us to film their activities, and my most treasured moment, when Ezra (4), who carried his small backpack of toys everywhere, chose me to look after it when he wanted to enter a spontaneous soccer game outside. He had carried this small child's novelty backpack of toys everywhere with him for many weeks. He did everything with the bag on his back, until one day a football game started up in the backyard past the climbing fort. And he walked over to me and placed his bag at my feet, then ran over to join the game. An educator nearby looked at me, surprised: 'that's the first time I've seen him without that bag.' I don't recall him looking back to check. When we caught eyes later on, I smiled, nodded and give him the thumbs up, and pointed to the bag and I together.

I was an outsider to the community, but I had a close bond with Ezra. We were always delighted to see each other. I shared cameras with him and many a piggy-back ride. This is a story about trust. In terms of young children's community building, that for young children to build community, energy and commitment into relationship building is necessary between adults and children with reassurance when they make that decision to trust what is precious, that the trust is honoured, so that a sense of security grows, along with confidence.

BENA: You were a constant, you were accepted. You were called 'Aunty'.

LOUISE: Our research design originally was to observe young children's civic action in practice and to guide these observations we had developed a framework of five civic concepts: Civic identity, Social responsibility, Civic agency, Civic deliberation, Civic participation. After writing up a few observations, I felt like I had drifted back to my early days of early childhood teaching in the 1980s writing developmental anecdotal records. I then began to read Bronwyn Davies (2014) book in this series *Listening to Children* and realised from Bergson (1911/2007) that observing and categorising the children's actions like such were 'lines of descent' that 'unwinds a roll already prepared … it might be accomplished almost instantaneously, like releasing a spring' (Bergson, 1911/ 2007, p. 7). I felt unsettled by this, the automation of the spring unwinding felt almost mindless, but worse it was colonising – we were categorising according to whitefella constructs. There were many questions about what I was observing, experiencing and feeling that required further attention. I read how Bergson refers *to lines of ascent* as corresponding to an inner work of ripening or creating, that '*endures* essentially, and imposes its rhythm on the first, which is inseparable from it' (Bergson, 1911/2007, p. 7). Davies (2014) explained in her application of Bergson's thinking that lines of descent and ascent continually affect and depend on each other.

Lines of descent may foreclose the disclosure the emergence of new thought, but they also create a coherent space in which the new can emerge. Lines of ascent ... are life-giving and powerful, but they are not always good and may sometimes be sad and even dangerous.

(p. 8)

LOUISE: I let go of prior assumptions and categories to be fully present to notice what emerges.

The research plan had proposed that the children would engage in three civic action projects (one class-based, one centre-based, one community-based). For months Kerryn and I endeavoured to support civic action projects taking place with the kindergarten group: through conversations with educators about what we observed and what issues could be explored further, through sharing Aboriginal children's literature as provocations, through community walks, through inviting the children to take pictures of what they don't like – what they feel uncomfortable about – to see if any of these may incite a project. And across four months there was multiple changes to the teaching team, with at least eight different educators. The constant rupture in the teaching team meant they were in survival mode with no space to be pro-active. As Linda Tuhiwai Smith (2012) noted, the lived reality is that 'Indigenous peoples are not in control and are subject to a continuing set of external conditions' (p. 206). We became acutely aware that the research agenda was not aligned with the community's pressing needs and reality, though they so wanted the children to engage in civic action. The constant barrage of crises demanded urgent attention. And what was more important was for us to show support and be there with community.

Kerryn and I talked for hours and hours, and we talked for hours with the director and Bena, the pedagogical leader, and we read Indigenous and non-Indigenous female scholars to locate possibilities for making meaning with ethical and culturally sensitive sensibilities that did not add to the colonising project, but rather, offered what I saw in Barad's (2012) reference to 'justice-to-come':

living compassionately requires recognizing and facing our responsibility to the infinitude of the other, welcoming the stranger whose very existence is the possibility of touching and being touched, who gifts us with both the ability to respond and the longing for justice-to-come.

(p. 10)

LOUISE: With heartfelt sensitivity for the beautiful people of the community, we foregrounded relationship building, over research agendas. To be with the children and community and to fully commit to ethical research, I drew from Barad (2007) and asked, 'what is being made to matter here?' and 'how does that mattering affect what is possible to do and think?'.

And drawing from Linda Tuhiwai Smith's (2012) lived wisdom, we sought to decolonise our research by seeking to understand the colonising experience, valuing Aboriginal knowledges and ways of being, and questioning what do we have to do to reframe knowledge and knowledge making.

I listened intently to children, educators, families and community members to glean multi-directional layers of meaning, somewhat aligned with what Bronwyn Davies (2014) refers to as emergent listening (drawing from Henry Bergson's (1911/2007) theory of creative evolution and Barad's (2007) theory of agential realism and diffractive analysis). I noticed what emerged from what became automated such as our taken for granted practices and assumptions. And, as Barad suggests, asked how what matters affects what is possible to do and think.

I played with Barad's (2007) suggestion of diffractive analysis, so rather than reflecting or representing what is there as research typically seeks to do, through diffraction I worked with the ongoing production of what is there. As Laurel Smith (2012) explains in her ethnographic work on videos by Oaxaca mediamakers 'Diffracted stories contribute to the decolonization of hybrid knowledge production by not only revealing disconnects, but also common – and uneven – grounds' (p. 331). Kerryn and my presence influenced the ongoing production of what citizenship might be for these children in this context. And so we were open and noticed thoughts as they passed in and out – letting go of desire to fixate – noticing how ideas and matter affect each other. Much of the listening was not verbally focussed; rather we read bodies engaged with environments. And we sat with the unsettling and troubling – how the all-pervasive parasitic racism crept into every crevice of life in this community.

We sat and listened to Elders, to educators, to families, to children – hearing their stories of discrimination, of hurt, of illness, of loss, of struggles, of wins, of hilarious misadventures, of love for others and country. Through these stories and witnessing the children's actions, we came to know core values that guide Aboriginal knowledges and ways of being. I came to see that the children were initiating civic action projects on daily basis. To really see what citizenship meant to young children, I noticed how they negotiated co-existence with each other in the shared space of an early childhood centre.

We shared stories and videos of children's actions back with children, educators and families, to hear their readings of what mattered – what was valued. We did this daily so they knew what we were doing. Not to just take their consent and that's the end of contact, but to talk all the way through. Across the ongoing years of this research, we have questioned how the knowledges of this community can reframe what citizenship is, and what it can be for children. From years of listening and letting go of research agenda, and all prior identities and just simply being there with community, I have been gifted with profound wisdom that I carry like a fragile ancient egg, wrapping for protection in transit and carefully consultatively and collectively choosing where and when to place it in public. It takes time and it takes patience, and pushing back against institutional deadlines and timeframes. I (Louise) as a non-Indigenous scholar have sought to, as Kwaymullina (2016) advised, 'to highlight and support Indigenous voices' (p. 440).

Jenny's story of decolonising research

As Linda Tuhiwai Smith (1999, 2012) reminds us, for Indigenous peoples research is seen as a 'dirty' word, associated with being victimised, labelled, categorised and objectified. Wary of my positioning as a Pākehā, of Cornish and Jewish descent, I have deliberately sought to challenge Pākehā hegemony in all my teaching, writing and research. This has always involved working very closely with Māori colleagues and friends, taking guidance from them on research processes and, in particular, on interpretations of te ao Māori constructs.

Despite coming from an academic family, I did not aspire to be an academic, avoiding university study for several years before eventually training as a kindergarten teacher. During the 1980s I was privileged to study te reo Māori and Māori studies courses at the University of Waikato taught by Tīmoti Karetu, Wharehuia Milroy, the late Hīrini Melbourne and the late Murumara John Moorfield. My experiences as a kindergarten teacher in Rotorua and Huntly during the 1980s alerted me to the incongruities of many middle-class Pākehā women teacher colleagues' failure to respect and respond to Māori communities. As a single parent I returned to university and completed a social sciences degree in Māori studies and education, and then, desperate not to return to the boredom of stay-at-home solo parenting, a Master's in counselling. During the final years of this university study, leading up to the 1990 New Zealand commemoration of 150 years since the signing of Te Tiriti o Waitangi, I began facilitating anti-racism workshops that had a strong focus on the treaty. I have continued to facilitate Te Tiriti o Waitangi workshops for a wide range of groups ever since. For my Master's dissertation I outlined the pedagogy we utilised in our workshops, which was heavily influenced by my Master's study of the work of Paulo Freire, in a year-long course taught by Peter Roberts. My PhD research focussed on the implications of implementing a commitment to Te Tiriti o Waitangi within early childhood education and teacher education. My interview participants, half of whom were Māori, were colleagues and former students. I followed the kaupapa Māori research process emphasised by Russell Bishop, one of my supervisors, regarding issues of initiation, benefits, accountability, representation and legitimation. The final hui with the Māori participants to co-theorise the project findings proved to be a particularly worthwhile aspect of the study.

In the 1990s I was most fortunate to have as a student Cheryl Rau, who completed her Master's dissertation (2002) on the retention of Māori identity, despite the impact of colonisation, by four generations of her whānau. Cheryl and I graduated together and almost immediately afterwards were successful in obtaining a grant from the New Zealand Teaching and Learning Research Initiative (TLRI) to study bicultural implementation within early childhood education, professional development and teacher education (Ritchie & Rau, 2006). Our participants, who we viewed as co-researchers, came from our wide networks within the early childhood sector. We again followed a process of co-theorising, identifying our methodology as a convergence of collaborative and narrative processes, informed by kaupapa Māori methodologies. We felt anxious after completing this study that we hadn't been particularly successful in obtaining 'child and parent voice' and this became the focus of a second study, which also included as a research question a focus on narrative methodologies (Ritchie & Rau, 2008). Cheryl and I worked closely together on these projects and then with colleagues Iris Duhn and Janita Craw on a third TLRI study (Ritchie, Duhn, Rau & Craw, 2010) which focussed on 'caring for ourselves, others and our environment' in early childhood settings.

Over this period of time we learnt from working closely with our co-researcher teachers and in particular from Māori teachers and parents. We described our collaborative, narrative research process as a form of counter-colonial renarrativisation (Rau & Ritchie, 2014; Ritchie, 2015, 2017; Ritchie, Craw, Rau & Duhn, 2013; Ritchie & Rau, 2010, 2012, 2013). Cheryl and I maintain a close friendship, and have shared many research experiences over the years, our dialogues and reciprocal challenging, respect and honesty having generated a depth of shared understanding that we have applied in our joint research and writing. Key to our research process has been our close relationships with the wonderful, generous, insightful and committed teachers with whom we have worked on the research, and who have been clearly focussed on our shared obligation with regard to implementing Te Tiriti o Waitangi within early childhood care and education. These teachers have done the 'hard yards' in our collaborative research projects, and we greatly appreciated how they drew upon their deeply respectful knowledge of tamariki and whānau.

Returning to my birthplace of Wellington in 2014 after many years in the Waikato, I was keen to find an early childhood centre with whom to progress the 'Young Children's Civic Action' project. Through the Whānau Manaaki Wellington Kindergarten Association I was invited to make an approach to Katoa Kindergarten in Porirua, who agreed to join me in this study. The teachers from Katoa – Trinity, Katrina, Sonya, Garth, Scott, Madeline, Jessica, Jesse, Cinnamon and Jared as well as a number of student teachers who came and went during the project – were all wonderful contributors to the study, and I thank them all – ngā mihi nūnui rawa atu ki a koutou katoa – along with Amanda Coulston the Chief Executive and the Senior Teachers of the Association. Walking into an unknown kindergarten to conduct a study was a new experience for me, as previous studies had involved teachers with whom we already had long-standing relationships. The Katoa team were warm and welcoming and interested in the kaupapa of the study. They also embraced the two research assistants who contributed their not inconsiderable efforts to the project, Elisabeth Jacob, a doctoral intern from Quebec, and anthropology student Rolene Watson, both of whom made invaluable contributions.

I am very grateful to them both, Elisabeth for her efforts in overseeing firstly the ethical consent process, and then her sterling job on gathering video data, coding this data, and producing the 'day in the life' video, and Rolene for her work producing in-depth fieldnotes. These sources of data were particularly valuable, since as a kindergarten teacher at heart, on my regular visits I was invariable commandeered immediately by tamariki to participate in their activities. I provided two digital cameras and a set of notebooks with matching pens, so that the children could utilise these (and in an unsuccessful attempt to divert them so that I would be freed from requests for the use of my notebook to enable me to actually *be* a 'researcher' and record my observations). The cameras were a great favourite, and no sooner had I walked in the gate, I would immediately be asked for them. Elisabeth and Rolene's excellent data gathering fortunately more than compensated for my inability to escape being commandeered.

The teachers were generous in sharing their insights on a regular basis. I made it a point to make time during each weekly visit to talk with each of the teachers. I was fascinated in that they quite often would all individually share with me during these informal conversations a version of the same observations of interesting examples of young children's empathy and community building. They also demonstrated a respectful and wide-ranging knowledge of the parents, whānau and community in which they worked, and the challenges faced by many of these families. This sense of a shared, respectful understanding indicated to me that the teachers worked closely together and were seemingly 'on the same page' when it came to their reading of children's contexts, challenges and contributions. Kindergartens are busy places, with so many relationships and interactions to monitor and support, let alone participating in a research project. The Katoa teachers faced all these challenges with warm-hearted, good-spirited orientations, laced with a shared sense of joy, respect and humour.

Working alongside Louise in this study, I was privileged to be able to observe her gentle, respectful and inclusive work with teachers and children. I remember during a visit to Gundoo the day before we were going to present some material on the project at a seminar at her university, Louise was careful to sit with the children and talk with them about what she was planning to do, and to show them the video of their play that she was planning to use, checking in with them carefully about her intentions, and whether they were clear and comfortable about these. This seemed to me to be a most genuine demonstration of an ongoing commitment to informed consent and an ethic of care in research processes.

An important ethical principle was the sharing of videos with children, whānau and community and seeking their permission for sharing with others.

Jared's research story

What did it feel like to be a researcher? It was an amazing feeling, I remember when I first started at Katoa Kindergarten I was so excited to have a fresh beginning. I was already learning a lot from the teaching team and head teacher within that first term. Then one day Jenny showed up to Kindergarten and talked to me about this research project. I felt honoured, and excited to get to take part in it.

As Jenny and I have discussed, all committed and passionate teachers are researchers, they notice, recognise, respond, record and revisit their practice regularly. It is just a natural part of the role. However, participating in this particular piece of work with such prestigious mentors and guidance felt like a dream come true.

I enjoyed working with Jenny to identify learning emerging through the data she had collected, specifically through individual learning stories, group planning and videos. We unpacked the learning together and discussed which strategies had been intentional from the teaching team, as well as the learning that was child initiated and led. Jenny has the skills to take such a complex and meaningful piece of research and ground it in realism. Making it achievable and fun, I absolutely loved playing my role in the end part of the research at Katoa Kindergarten.

As for the reading and writing for publishing a folio article and this book, it was incredibly nerve racking. It took me back to studying at Whitireia Polytechnic where I was reading and gathering information and data, then using this to reinforce my own view and conceptualise the idea of civic action. It was full on at times, but thoroughly enjoyable, and once again a high honour to take part in.

Jenny and I met regularly to discuss content and specific topics to cover in our publications, we talked about the emerging learning we identified as stated above and wrapped it in theoretical discourse. Once again, it speaks to Jenny's ability to bring high academia to a grounded level that teachers can relate to while working with and alongside children, in everyday teaching and learning.

Collaborative methodology: sharing between sites

Mindful of our (Louise and Jenny) roles as university-based researchers and of the issues raised earlier in this chapter our methodological processes aimed to foreground the ways of being, knowing, doing and relating of the early childhood communities in which we were engaged. Spending regular extended periods of time in the two centres built trust, enabling deep sharing. Fieldnotes were recorded of incidents noticed or shared by children and teachers. The use of video recordings enabled recognition of unvoiced expression. Analysis was produced collectively through multiple layers of discussion. To engender dialogue between Gundoo and Katoa, we shared videos between the sites. Firstly, we shared a three-minute video from each site of children engaging in what we recognised as civic action. Each site (which also included the US site – though not discussed in this book) viewed the other sites' videos then educators at each site gathered online through google hangout to dialogue responses and queries about what was witnessed in the videos. The idea for this approach drew from Joe Tobin and colleagues' video-cued multivocal ethnography, in which videoed scenarios are shared to provoke transnational/intercultural dialogues about pedagogical ideas (Tobin, Hsueh, & Karasawa, 2009; Tobin & Hsueh, 2007; Tobin, Wu, & Davidson, 1989; Tobin, 1988). The provocations for this dialogue are edited videos with components chosen to portray 'rich interactions' and 'tiny dramas' that are likely to provoke interest and discussion, via the 'telling and retelling of the same event from different perspectives; an ongoing dialogue between insiders and outsiders, between practitioners and researchers, and between people of different cultures' (Tobin, 1988, pp. 176–179). In our project, the focus of these video-cued discussions was on young children's civic action which we came to view as community building.

The first phase of the sharing was a three-way viewing of two–three minute video clips followed by a real-time dialogue between the US, Australian and New Zealand sites. We then created 'day in the life' videos which were 10–20 minutes long. At Gundoo we produced a collation of vignettes of children's civic actions in collaboration with children and educators with playful titles and subtitles and popular Aboriginal music as soundtrack for a family evening. We also produced a 10-minute video that followed the daily routine at Gundoo illustrated through clips of children illustrating civic action at these routine times. To prepare the 'day in the life' video of Katoa Kindergarten, we initially shared with the teachers some examples of video clips that Elisabeth Jacob, the research assistant who had been responsible for videoing, had selected as demonstrating young children's civic action. We discussed with them what elements of their philosophy they would like to share in a 'day in the life' video, and which of the video clips they thought would be valuable to share with the teachers from Gundoo and the USA site. Here is some of the dialogue that was recorded at this meeting with teachers Maddie, Scott, Sonya, Garth, Katrina, Jesse, Lisa (student teacher), Trinity (Head Teacher) plus Elisabeth and Jenny.

JENNY: Question One is: 'What elements of the Katoa philosophy would you like to see represented in the edited video of a "day in the life" of Katoa kindergarten'?

KATRINA: Okay, so firstly, children being independent and advocating for others. You know, just doing things for themselves.

GARTH: As a teacher, I think I'm supporting children to have their own conversations with others. I am giving them extra words and modelling to them and hopefully adding to their learning through various teaching techniques.

SONYA: I think problem solving too, where children can negotiate and work out their differences or not. By giving them the tools.

GARTH: And love and cuddles. I'm doing that too.

MADDIE: Teachers using consistent language.

KATRINA: And also I'll just add onto that with getting them to actually see and feel that actually they've hurt someone rather than just go up and say: 'Oh, I'm sorry' and they didn't actually mean it. Getting them to get an icepack for their friend, you know, getting them to empathise and understand how that person is feeling and hurting. It's huge.

TRINITY: Take responsibility for their actions. Be accountable. That's huge.

SCOTT: Also building language so that they already have that language so giving them words to use.

SONYA: Because I think it comes down to, I've heard a few kids coming over to me and saying: 'So and so has hurt my feelings.' So, it's building on that empathy.

TRINITY: And I noticed that today, like, when we went to the Ngāti Toa concert, the principal came over and talked to our children. And they were really responsive. And they answered her. And they smiled. They weren't shy.

GARTH: And another example is our older children including the newcomers, the younger children.

KATRINA: And including them immediately, yeah, I have been just so impressed with that, actually. It's like everybody's different but they are just so accepting of anyone that comes. You know? It's uncanny. It's like there's no judgements. They don't make judgements.

GARTH: And I've got a really good example in that Rex,[2] just how people are just really tolerant with him. Even though sometimes he's a bit full-on in his reactions but that's an acceptance. They're not judging him, they're not banishing him.

KATRINA: Children being accepting of anyone.

GARTH: Rex, in terms of empathy, he came from a deficit model, not much empathy, amazing to see how he is growing. The peer influence is strong.

SCOTT: Children learning life skills that are really applicable.

JENNY: Question two is: What activities would you like us to include in the 20 minute edit?

TRINITY: Kai [food], the rolling aspect, really good space for social learning.

KATRINA: It is a huge one. Children are very independent with breakfast, then take the scraps down to the worms, put their plates in the dishwasher themselves. Taking responsibility.

GARTH: And noticing when glasses have run out.

TRINITY: And using the scissors by themselves to cut open their chip packets.

GARTH: How space is used for running, freedom to run freely, negotiate the bumps.

KATRINA: And we had such great play with the mud the other day.

GARTH: The puddle down in the corner, active exploration, let them explore it, throw the trucks in. Opportunity to explore freely. Although safety is a consideration of course.

KATRINA: Can be a challenge.

GARTH: I want the video to show that freedom.

TRINITY: Te reo Māori, kaupapa Māori, so things around obviously our group times, te wā kotahitanga, the emphasis that we put on those concepts would be cool. Our relationships with whānau.

GARTH: Tuakana teina [older children taking care of younger siblings].

TRINITY: The integrated nature of the kindergarten and the playgroup.

We then shared a sheet explaining aspects of civic action (civic identity, collective responsibility, civic agency, civic deliberation and civic participation). We asked the teachers to bear these in mind whilst we watched a series of video clips from the kindergarten. For reasons of brevity, just the teachers' responses to the first clip are recorded below. The clip featured two boys playing at the water trough, when one, Tane, is alerted to the situation that the other boy has a bleeding nose, and then goes to tell teacher Jesse.

TRINITY: Definitely: voicing concern

GARTH: Tane was exploring what was happening, he knew what he needed to do. Independence, going for help. Both non-verbal and verbal communication. It was interesting he was also, Tane was exploring what was happening with the nose quite ... Yeah, quite literally hey?

GARTH: Like, this is happening. Okay and working through what he needed to do next. Wasn't it? He was really thinking about it. You could tell, couldn't you? He knew something's wrong here. I need to plan what to do next and I'll get help. Wasn't it?

JENNY: Yeah, he had a strategy and he followed through.

SCOTT: But, it was also, the '*again*' – it's happened before, and he kept saying: 'Again. It's bleeding again.'

GARTH: So that's him trying to think why's this still happening?

KATRINA: A working theory.

GARTH: Yeah, totally. So the independence, and then the going for help and then the clear communication, the non-verbal pointing, as well. Although his verbals were strong. But, you know Tane really followed through on it.

KATRINA: Yep, he did.

JENNY: He picked up that concern.

KATRINA: Took that responsibility hey? To advocate.

GARTH: Yeah. Yeah. Papa [Tane's grandfather] will love to see that hey?

KATRINA: Yeah, he would.

TRINITY: Yeah.

The above excerpts of teachers' discussions demonstrate the thoughtful ways in which the teachers engaged with the project, in collectively prioritising what they wanted to see included in the 'day in the life' video, and in analysing the community building actions and dispositions of the children. The 'day in the life' videos of each site were also shared with the educators at the other sites. Responses to these videos are shared in Chapter Six, as they produced fruitful dialogue on environments and pedagogies for children's community building.

Children's photography

In enactment of a commitment to reciprocity and full participation as a key ethical value and principle in research with Indigenous communities (e.g., Australian Institute of Aboriginal and Torres Strait Islander Studies, 2012; National Health and Medical Research Council, 2018) and with children and young people (e.g., Alderson, 2008), data recording with cameras was also done by children. This shared access to the technologies for digitally recording meant that filming became an everyday practice that everyone did – a community practice rather than a scientific mode of distancing between researcher and observed. At Gundoo, a new set of ten children's cameras were purchased to enable greater access amidst the children. We also involved the children in usage of our camera by playing back to the children daily what we had videoed through the camera's inbuilt data projector. Children were very interested in all the cameras. When we went for our first community walk in week one of data collection the children who carried the cameras took great care, being very attentive to securely holding them as they walked. Ezra[3] filmed whilst we were in the hospital waiting room. He filmed his peers and showed them what he had filmed (see Figure 3.1).

Much of the children's usage of the cameras was focused on exploring what they could do. To focus their attention on the research topic of children's civic action, Louise asked the children to take photos of what they don't like or want changed at Gundoo. Ezra, whose verbal language was challenged by speech difficulties, immediately took this provocation up, took photos and then showed us his photos. They were of the children's toilets (see Figure 3.2) – three in a row with no walls for privacy. Later when we looked at them on the computer he pointed at the toilet photo – 'that one' affirmed with his serious nod. Talia also took photos and selected a photo of a closed door (see Figure 3.3) and declared 'can't get in'. The cameras gave the children another language to express their interests and concerns.

At Katoa Kindergarten, the two user-friendly children's video cameras were very popular, and involved a great deal of cooperation, patience and negotiation around turn-taking. The children also enjoyed using the three sets of 'research notebooks' with matching pencils. Their images captured aspects of the children's interest in the study (see Figures 3.4 and 3.5).

When the images the children had captured were shared back to the children on the large kindergarten screen there was great excitement and enjoyment as children recognised their friends, teachers and different favourite aspects of the kindergarten environment such as the climbing area, swings, sandpit, outdoor climbing equipment, the vegetable gardens and the kindergarten cat, 'Ngeru'. Jared recalls:

FIGURE 3.1. Ezra sharing photos with group.

FIGURE 3.2 Photo of children's toilet by Ezra

The children absolutely loved seeing themselves on the video. Heaps of children were empowered to share their learning with their peers because of it. Another thing the children loved seeing was Ngeru the local cat who often came into Kindergarten and the tamariki [children] would come into the kitchen with one of the kaiako [teachers] to feed the cat with us – they loved being kaitiaki [carers/guardians] for Ngeru.

Further thoughts regarding our research processes

> *It matters what thoughts think thoughts.*
> *It matters what knowledges know knowledges.*
> *It matters what relations relate relations.*
> *It matters what worlds world worlds.*
> *It matters what stories tell stories*
> *(Haraway, 2016, pp. 38–39)*

As neither Louise nor Jenny are Indigenous, we were constantly mindful of the ethical relationality of our role in facilitating this study, in negotiating our pathways amongst the entangled layers of tensions and dilemmas embedded in the historicity and contemporaneity of the communities in which we were working. Linda Smith highlights that engaging in social justice oriented research can be perilous for researchers:

> In these conservative times the role of an indigenous researcher and indeed of other researchers committed to producing research knowledge that documents social injustice, that recovers subjugated knowledges, that helps create spaces for the voices of the silenced to be expressed and 'listened to', and that challenges racism, colonialism and oppression is a risky business.
>
> *(L.T. Smith, 2012, p. 316)*

FIGURE 3.3 Closed door photo by Talia

She cautions researchers and scholars to be mindful of the responsibility that comes with the privileged positions we hold, in that:

> academic writing is a form of selecting, arranging and presenting knowledge. It privileges sets of texts, views about the history of an idea, what issues count as significant; and, by engaging in the same process uncritically, we too can render indigenous writers invisible or unimportant while reinforcing the validity of other writers. If we write without thinking critically about our writing, it can be dangerous. Writing can also be dangerous because we reinforce and maintain a style of discourse which is never innocent.
>
> *(1999, p. 36)*

Engaging in research across vastly different international contexts can be problematic in all these respects. Mathias Urban writes that:

> Like in other areas, globalisation in early childhood has become a powerful force for the spread of a supposedly universalised, western (minority world) set of values (e.g. capitalism, free enterprise, competition, and individualism) resulting in an all-encompassing economic, social, cultural, and political hegemony.
>
> *(2018, pp. 6–7)*

Urban and many other early childhood scholars have critiqued the International Early Learning and Child Wellbeing Study (IELS) currently being conducted under the auspices of the OECD in only three countries: England, Estonia and the USA (Carr, Mitchell & Rameka, 2016; Mackey, Hill & De Vocht, 2016; Moss et al., 2016; Moss & Urban, 2018; Pence 2016; Urban, 2018). Urban characterises this form of universalising international study as resembling a neocolonial benevolent dictatorship, providing only a 'narrow, utilitarian, and largely decontextualised understanding of educational practices on children, practitioners and communities, and [which] dismisses the diversity of ways of being, knowing and

FIGURE 3.4. Child's photo of another child writing in research notebook, Katoa Kindergarten

doing in this world' (2018, p. 3). He further highlights the study's 'disregard for diversity, children's rights, and the rights of Indigenous peoples to self-determination and "education in a manner appropriate to their cultural methods of teaching and learning" (United Nations Declaration on the Rights of Indigenous Peoples, 2007: Article 14)' (Urban, 2018, p. 4).

Our study serves as an alternative model to such decontextualised international research, whereby in working closely, ethically and relationally in community with teachers, children and families we seek nuanced collectively shared understandings. We therefore advocate for the inclusion of Indigenous co-researchers and community members in all early childhood research endeavours, from the outset in terms of research design and ethical undertakings as well as throughout the research enactment and data analysis. As opposed to large universalising meta-studies, we see value of in-depth localised research, bringing forth the particularities of place, and the specificities of cultural histories and knowledges of children, families, Elders and communities.

We see time, place and relationality as our core principles. As Kerryn explains:

> In my view, it is the concepts of time and place, reflecting the community and cultural context of family and way of being, rather than set timeframes and tight scheduled events that reflect a Western concept of time. The research project took the time, and the time taken is what was required to ensure we were walking with the stories of place and people and connecting to country.

It is about fully being in the here and now, as Deborah Bird Rose (2004) notes: 'the ethical challenge of decolonisation illuminates a ground for powerful presence' (p. 213).

Relationality, mutuality and connectivity are asserted to engage in responsiveness in the present. Time and relationality continued as prime throughout the writing of the book with our preferred modus operandi being physically present with each

FIGURE 3.5. Child's photo of research assistant Elisabeth, videoing

other yarning around the kitchen table with a phone audio recorder on. We revisited stories of children's community building from fieldnotes and videos and shared our readings of what we saw, what they made us think about and what we read as mattering. In Chapters Four and Five, we share these stories from Gundoo and Katoa followed by readings from different authors with association with that site, creating diffractive, hybrid knowledge production revealing disconnects, alignments and surprises. We all embody different worldviews some more closely aligned than others. We did not all share the same yearnings to know the same things; as L.C. Smith (2012) explains that's the whole point of diffraction. The varied ontological readings we believe produce more insightful and more valuable reconstructions of knowledge 'than expert deconstructions delivered from nowhere' (p. 343). We walked and talked beside each other in place.

Notes

1 This project 'Civic Action and Learning with Young Children: Comparing Approaches in New Zealand, Australia and the United States' was funded by the Spencer Foundation of Chicago, USA. There were three sites in the project, one in the USA. This book reports on the Australian and New Zealand sites.
2 Katoa Kindergarten children's names have been changed to pseudonyms.
3 Pseudonyms have been used for each child mentioned form Gundoo.

References

Alderson, P. (2008). Children as researchers: Participation rights and research. In P. Christensen & A. James (Eds), *Research with Children: Perspectives and Practices* (2nd ed., pp. 276–290). Abingdon, UK: Routledge.

Australian Institute of Aboriginal and Torres Strait Islander Studies. (2012). *Guidelines for Ethical Research in Australian Indigenous Studies*. Retrieved from https://aiatsis.gov.au/sites/default/files/docs/research-and-guides/ethics/gerais.pdf

Barad, K. (2007). *Meeting the Universe Halfway: Quantum Physics and the Entanglement of Matter and Meaning*. Durham: Duke University Press.

Barad, K. (2012). On touching – the inhuman that therefore I am. *Differences: A Journal of Feminist Cultural Studies*, 23(3), 206–223.

Bergson, H. (1911/2007). *Creative Evolution* (A. Mitchell, Trans.). London: MacMillan.

Bishop, R. (2011). *Freeing Ourselves*. Rotterdam: Sense.

Cannella, G. S. & Viruru, R. (2004). *Childhood and Postcolonization. Power, Education and Contemporary Practice*. New York: RoutledgeFalmer.

Canosa, A., Graham, A. & Wilson, E. (2018). Reflexivity and ethical mindfulness in participatory research with children: What does it really look like? *Childhood*, 25(3), 400–415. doi:10.1177/0907568218769342

Carr, M., Mitchell, L. & Rameka, L. (2016). Some thoughts about the value of an OECD international assessment framework for early childhood services in Aotearoa New Zealand. *Contemporary Issues in Early Childhood, 17*(4), 450–454. doi:10.1177/1463949116680705

Davies, B. (2014). *Listening to Children: Being and Becoming*. Abingdon, UK: Routledge.

Haraway, D. J. (2008). *When Species Meet*. Minneapolis, MN: University of Minnesota Press.

Haraway, D. J. (2016). Staying with the Trouble. Anthropocene, Capitalocene, Chthulucene. In J. W. Moore (Ed.), *Anthropocene or Capitalocene? Nature, History, and the Crisis of Capitalism* (pp. 34–76). Oakland, CA: PM Press.

Henare, M. (2001). Tapu, mana, mauri, hau, wairua: a Māori philosophy of vitalism and cosmos. In J. A. Grim (Ed.), *Indigenous Traditions and Ecology. The Interbeing of Cosmology and Community* (pp. 197–221). Cambridge, MA: Harvard University Press.

Kovach, M. (2010). *Indigenous Methodologies. Characteristics, Conversations, and Contexts*. Toronto: University of Toronto Press.

Kwaymullina, A. (2016). Research, ethics and Indigenous peoples: an Australian Indigenous perspective on three threshold considerations for respectful engagement. *AlterNative: An International Journal of Indigenous Peoples*, 12(4), 437–449.

Mackey, G., Hill, D., & De Vocht, L. (2016). Response to the colloquium 'The Organisation for Economic Co-operation and Development's International Early Learning Study: Opening for debate and contestation', by Peter Moss, Gunilla Dahlberg, Susan Grieshaber, Susanna Mantovani, Helen May, Alan Pence, Sylvie Rayna, Beth Blue Swadener and Michel Vandenbroeck, Contemporary Issues in Early Childhood 17(3). *Contemporary Issues in Early Childhood, 17*(4), 447–449. doi:10.1177/1463949116680699

Martin, K. (2003). Ways of knowing, being and doing: a theoretical framework and methods for indigenous and indigenist research. *Journal of Australian Studies*, 27(76), 203–214.

Mika, C. T. H. (2012). Overcoming 'Being' in favour of knowledge: The fixing effect of 'mātauranga'. *Educational Philosophy and Theory*, 44(10), 1080–1092.

Mika, C. (2016). A counter-colonial speculation on Elizabeth Rata's –ism. *Journal of World Philosophies*, 1, 1–12.

Mills, C. W. (2015). Decolonizing western political philosophy. *New Political Science*, 37(1), 1–24. doi:10.1080/07393148.07392014.07995491

Moss, P., Dahlberg, G., Grieshaber, S., Mantovani, S., May, H., Pence, A., … Vandenbroeck, M. (2016). The Organisation for Economic Co-operation and Development's International Early Learning Study: opening for debate and contestation. *Contemporary Issues in Early Childhood, 17*(3), 343–351. doi:10.1177/1463949116661126

Moss, P., & Urban, M. (2018). The Organisation for Economic Co-operation and Development's International Early Learning Study: what's going on. *Contemporary Issues in Early Childhood.* doi:10.1177/1463949118803269

National Health and Medical Research Council (2018). Ethical conduct in research with Aboriginal and Torres Strait Islander Peoples and communities: guidelines for researchers and stakeholders. Retrieved from https://nhmrc.gov.au/about-us/publications/ethical-conduct-research-aboriginal-and-torres-strait-islander-peoples-and-communities

Pence, A. (2016). *Baby PISA: dangers that can arise when foundations shift. Canadian Children,* 41(3), 54–58.

Pihama, L. & Lee-Morgan, J. (2018). Colonization, education, and Indigenous peoples. In E. A. McKinley & L. T. Smith (Eds), *Handbook of Indigenous Education* (pp. 1–9). Singapore: Springer Nature.

Rau, C. (2002). *Te Ahutanga Atu o Toku Whanau.* (Masters Dissertation). Hamilton: University of Waikato.

Rau, C. & Ritchie, J. (2014). Ki te whai ao, ki te ao marama: early childhood understandings in pursuit of social, cultural, and ecological justice. In M. N. Bloch, B. B. Swadener & G. S. Cannella (Eds), *Reconceptualizing Early Childhood Care and Education. Critical Questions, New Imaginaries and Social Activism: A Reader* (pp. 109–130). New York: Peter Lang.

Rigney, L.I. (1999). Internationalization of an Indigenous anticolonial cultural critique of research methodologies: a guide to Indigenist research methodology and its principles. *Wicazo Sa Review,* 14(2), 109–121.

Ritchie, J. (2015). Counter-colonial research methodologies drawing upon postcolonial critique and Indigenous onto-epistemologies. In G. S. Cannella, M. S. Perez, & P. A. Pasque (Eds), *Critical Qualitative Inquiry. Foundations and Futures* (pp. 77–90). Walnut Creek, CA: Left Coast Press.

Ritchie, J. (2017). Diverse complexities, complex diversities. Critical qualitative educational research in Aotearoa (New Zealand). *International Review of Qualitative Research,* 10(4), 468–481.

Ritchie, J., Craw, J., Rau, C. & Duhn, I. (2013). Ko koe ki tēnā, ko ahau ki tēnei kīwai o te kete: Exploring collaboration across a range of recent early childhood studies. In J. Duncan & L. Connor (Eds), *Research Partnerships in Early Childhood Education. Teachers and Researchers in Collaboration* (pp. 93–113). New York: Palgrave Macmillan.

Ritchie, J., Duhn, I., Rau, C., & Craw, J. (2010). *Titiro Whakamuri, Hoki Whakamua. We Are the Future, the Present and the Past: Caring for Self, Others and the Environment in Early Years' Teaching and Learning. Final Report for the Teaching and Learning Research Initiative.* Wellington, NZ: TLRI. Retrieved from http://www.tlri.org.nz/tlri-research/research-completed/ece-sector/titiro-whakamuri-hoki-whakamua-we-are-future-present-and

Ritchie, J. & Rau, C. (2006). *Whakawhanaungatanga. Partnerships in Bicultural Development in Early Childhood Education. Final Report to the Teaching & Learning Research Initiative Project.* Wellington, NZ: TLRI. Retrieved from http://www.tlri.org.nz/tlri-research/research-completed/ece-sector/whakawhanaungatanga%E2%80%94-partnerships-bicultural-development

Ritchie, J. & Rau, C. (2008). *Te Puawaitanga – Partnerships with Tamariki and Whānau in Bicultural Early Childhood Care and Education. Final Report to the Teaching Learning Research Initiative.* Wellington, NZ: TLRI. Retrieved from http://www.tlri.org.nz/tlri-research/research-completed/ece-sector/te-puawaitanga-partnerships-tamariki-an

Ritchie, J. & Rau, C. (2010). Kia mau ki te wairuatanga: Counter-colonial narratives of early childhood education in Aotearoa. In G. S. Cannella & L. D. Soto (Eds), *Childhoods: A Handbook* (pp. 355–373). New York: Peter Lang.

Ritchie, J. & Rau, C. (2012). Exploring possibilities for critical relational de/colonising methodologies in early childhood education contexts in Aotearoa. In G. S. Cannella & S. R. Steinberg (Eds), *Critical Qualitative Research (CQR) Reader* (pp. 536–547). New York: Peter Lang.

Ritchie, J. & Rau, C. (2013). Renarrativizing Indigenous rights-based provision within 'mainstream' early childhood services. In B. B. Swadener, L. Lundy, J. Habashi & N. Blanchet-Cohen (Eds), *Children's Rights and Education. International Perspectives* (pp. 133–149). New York: Peter Lang.

Rose, D. B. (2004). *Reports From a Wild Country: Ethics for Decolonisation*. Sydney: University of New South Wales Press.

Skerrett, M. (2017). Colonialism, Māori early childhood language, and the curriculum. In E. A. McKinley & L. T. Smith (Eds), *Handbook of Indigenous Education* (pp. 1–22). Singapore: Springer Nature.

Skerrett, M. & Pence, A. (forthcoming). Untitled. In *Springer Encyclopedia of Teacher Education*. Singapore: Springer.

Smith, L.C., (2012). Decolonizing hybridity: Indigenous video, knowledge, and diffraction. *Cultural Geographies*, 19(3), 329–348.

Smith, L. T. (1999). *Decolonizing Methodologies. Research and Indigenous Peoples*. London and Dunedin: Zed Books Ltd and University of Otago Press.

Smith, L. T. (2006). Researching in the margins. Issues for Māori researchers: a discussion paper. *AlterNative: An International Journal of Indigenous Peoples*, 2(1), 4–27. doi:10.1177/117718010600200101

Smith, L. T. (2012). *Decolonizing Methodologies: Research and Indigenous peoples* (2nd edn). London: Zed Books.

Tobin, J. J. (1988). Visual anthropology and multivocal ethnography: A dialogical approach to Japanese preschool class size. *Dialectical Anthropology*, 13(2), 173–187.

Tobin, J. & Hsueh, Y. (2007). The poetics and pleasures of video ethnography of education. In R. Goldman (Ed.), *Video Research in the Learning Sciences* (pp. 77–92). NY: Lawrence Erlbaum Associates.

Tobin, J., Hsueh, Y. & Karasawa, M. (2009). *Preschool in Three Cultures Revisited. China, Japan and the United States*. Chicago: University of Chicago Press.

Tobin, J., Wu, D. Y. & Davidson, D. H. (1989). *Preschool in Three Cultures: Japan, China, USA*. New Haven, CT: Yale University Press.

Tuck, E. & Yang, K. W. (2014). R-Words: refusing research. In D. Paris & M. T. Winn (Eds), *Humanizing Research: Decolonizing Qualitative Inquiry with Youth and Communities* (pp. 223–247). Los Angeles, CA: Sage.

Urban, M. (2018). The shape of things to come and what to do about Tom and Mia: interrogating the OECD's International Early Learning and Child Wellbeing Study from an anti-colonialist perspective. *Policy Futures in Education*. doi:10.1177/1478210318819177

Wilson, S. (2008). *Research is Ceremony. Indigenous Research Methods*. Black Point, Nova Scotia: Fernwood Publishing.

4

GUNDOO COMMUNITY AND HOW GUNDOO CHILDREN SHOW COMMUNITY BUILDING

In this chapter, we introduce you to the Aboriginal Australian governed Gundoo early learning centre for Aboriginal and Torres Strait Islander children in a regional Queensland Aboriginal community. This is where Kerryn and Louise spent about nine months regularly visiting to be with the children to understand civic action demonstrated by three- to five-year-olds. Bena was the pedagogical leader at Gundoo at the time of the study. We first set the scene of how the community came to be: its history, and ways of being and knowing. We then provide some background context to help you imagine the centre. Then we share stories of children's community building in action with our diffractive, conversational readings of what was happening and mattering. We acknowledge the collective wisdom of the ancestors, and of all who have welcomed and supported children's community building on the place that we meet. We graciously thank the children for welcoming us into their lives and community and sharing their joy, tenacity and wisdom. This chapter is a small gesture to keep the wisdom and memories alive.

Community

The community in which Gundoo is located was established by 'herding' Aboriginal peoples from 35 tribes across Queensland and Northern New South Wales to a fenced policed government settlement. All the people were wards of the state under *The Aboriginals Protection and the Restriction of the Sale of Opium Act*[1] (1897) and the subsequent amending Acts of 1901, 1927, 1928 and 1934. The Queensland legislation gave the 'government complete authority and control over the lives of Aboriginal people' (The State of Queensland (Queensland Museum), 2019) authorised through the Chief Protector of Aboriginals, as well as the individual regional Protectors. Aboriginal peoples had to seek permission from their local Protector to go anywhere and to do anything. For example, permission from the

Protector needed to be sought to marry, or to leave the town to visit family. Children were separated from families and placed in dormitories and anyone of working age was allocated to white settlers as unpaid (or minimally paid) domestic servants or labourers. 'Part 5, section 31 of the 1897 Act provided the Chief Protector with the power to control the wages of Aboriginal people living on a reserve and to apportion the net produce of their labour amongst all the Aboriginals on the reserve' (Frankland, 1994). Food was allocated through weekly rations of flour, sugar, tea, dried peas and boney meat. As a Community Elder who lived under the Act explained 'we were slaves on our own land' (Strong and Smart, 2004).

Children were treated harshly under the Act, as many have come to know through the *Rabbit Proof Fence* story and film that we have proposed as illustrative of the Aboriginal child citizen as a resistant, resilient survivor. Aunty Ruth Hegarty (1999) described her dormitory life experiences in the 1930s and 1940s under the Act:

> Punishment meted out for misbehaviour or disobedience was accepted almost as if we thought we deserved it. Having our heads shaved was one form of punishment that was cruelly used in the Home (p. 41) … Another way they punished us was locking us in gaol. It was a small building in the backyard of the dormitory … many times we were locked up in the gaol for misbehaviour, little things like being late for meals, or playing somewhere out of bounds. We would scream and yell from fear; at the same time we'd hope someone might get sorry for us and let us out (p. 42) … The very thought of being put away on your own in a locked cell, with high barred windows, no lights and very little ventilation, no bed and a drum in the corner – this was enough to terrorise any child … (p. 43)

The lived trauma of the daily violations and liberty denial are embodied by the grandparents of the community.

In 1965, the passing of the Queensland Aborigines and Torres Strait Islanders Affairs Act (Queensland, Department of Aboriginal & Island Affairs, 1965) began the slow removal of some of the government restrictions on Aboriginal people living on reserves and allowed the community to form their first Aboriginal governed council (Queensland, Department of Aboriginal & Island Affairs, 1966, 1) with limited local government powers (Frankland, 1994). Under this reformed Act, Frankland records that Aboriginal peoples were no longer defined as wards of the state, but now assisted persons and the Director of Aboriginal and Torres Strait Islander Affairs now had control of Aboriginal peoples' personal property and movement. The location formed through a government settlement was 'given back' (with conditions) to the Aboriginal peoples of the community through deed of grant in trust legislation in 1984. Such legislation placed the local Aboriginal council as trustees of the land for the Aboriginal residents of the settlement (Brennan, 1992).

From this history, the population of the community is predominantly Aboriginal and continues to be heavily government managed under government infrastructure and policy designed for what is referred to in government speak as a *discrete*

Indigenous community defined by being a location, that is bounded by physical or legal boundaries, inhabited predominantly by Indigenous people, with housing or infrastructure that is managed on a community basis (Australian Institute of Health and Welfare, nd). The community has a community managed radio station, medical centre, museum and child care centre. There's no petrol station, no public transport, and only one small shop.

The community town is not on the way to anywhere, so there is no through traffic. All vehicles are community members or visitors. Children play in the street. This is accepted community practice. Central cultural value is everyone looks out for each other. From about three years of age children independently wander the community of less than 2,000. Most everyone knows each other – they go to visit cousins, Aunties, Uncles, Grans, Pops daily – in and out of each others' houses. Boundaries of personal property are much more softened than in Australian metropolitan neighbourhoods. In a study by Kreutz (2015), she found that 9–12-year-olds have a home range of independent mobility of 7.8 square kilometres (whereas rural children in England have a 1.8 kilometre home range).

FIGURE 4.1 Sunset by Samuel Murray (Bena's Dad)

Children are treasured and the fear of child removal continues to be very real. Many grandmothers care for many children to ensure they stay with community – active in the Grandmothers Against Removal campaign for kinship care mentioned in Chapter Two. Community values are strong. Resilience and sticking together are strong threads for a community that was formed through such adverse liberty abuse.

> When someone is sad, when someone loses a family member, the sadness and the other kids crying. How they'll like go and pat each other's backs. They learn that at such a young age.
>
> *(Sylvia, community leader)*

It is a community that cares for each other, informed by kinship lore but also by bonding in supporting cultural identity and rights in the face of ongoing colonialism. Knowing where you from and who belong to is core.

> You can't go forward without knowing where you're coming from. And we were taken away from country in the first place ... bringing those kids up understanding who they are, who their mob is, who they belong to, and branching out to respect those other's clans and mobs and how they're connected somewhere along the line.
>
> *(Sylvia, community leader)*

There is strong community pride, with regular community events that are well attended and a community museum was established in 2004 that retains and builds on the memories. Many community and cultural stories have been co-created into books and videos by local artists and children.

Respect is a strong community value, that is talked and enacted through kinship roles and responsibilities that children are taught from infancy. Such as knowing who you refer to as Aunty, Uncle, Mum, Dad, Nan, Pop, Sis, Brotha, and Cus, not based on biological relations but more so on generational. Respect is reciprocal. Older children and adults take care and time with younger children.

> They see someone giving them time and patience and they look up to that fellow or that person as an uncle or aunty or brother. And when they see someone giving them the time, showing them what they need to do, or how to do it, you know, and then they feel respect.
>
> *(Gino, Dad)*

As Community leader Sylvia further explains:

> We grew up with values that was all based on, that respecting first. And to go with respect. If you want respect, you earn it. And you know we were taught to earn it when we were growing up. And where the boundaries were for us growing up. And the importance of the old people they said, 'you respect the

white man like you respect your own mob'. Respect. That's your weapon there. That tongue is mightier than the sword, or any other weapon. So talk first.

A place and practice of respect nurtures community.

The community constantly works together on many projects, such as the museum and community events, but also by collectively governing the community town through the Aboriginal council. When the town is say affected by natural disasters, crime, or resource access, community gather to all 'chip in'.

> You go with your people, your family. You go together and you'll win or you'll finish it that day and sort it out. Cos you're not being a proper black fella unless you're going together. That togetherness and getting your strength from each other and support.
>
> *(Sylvia)*

The community is a strong proud community that has survived slavery and incarceration on their own land. What keeps everyone going is each other, as Sylvia asserts it's about keeping that strength and that community spirit going in everybody.

Gundoo early learning centre structure, philosophy and pedagogy

Gundoo early learning centre is governed by a committee of Aboriginal community members. At the time of the study, the centre was funded under the federal government budget-based funding programme, which provided 'access to childcare in communities where mainstream or conventional childcare services are not available or viable, and where there is a need for culturally competent services, in particular Indigenous focused childcare' (Department of Education, Employment and Workplace Relations, 2010). Most of the staff (bar one or two at any given time) identified as Aboriginal or Torres Strait Islander. The centre has five playrooms, four for different age groups established to follow child care licensing regulations with different ratios for different age groups. In more recent years, when licensing became more open to mixed age grouping ratios, a mixed age group room was added. The centre is licensed for 81 and is open Monday to Friday from 8am to 4pm. The stories that we share are mostly from the kindergarten room with three- to five-year-olds and some primary school aged children in school holiday times.

Gundoo provides a culturally supportive programme for young children and families, so that they feel culturally safe and cultural pride is nurtured. Aboriginal and Torres Strait Islander people often do not feel safe or welcomed to enter and be in many mainstream institutions and services, from the long legacy of deficit positioning.

> Cultural safety … encompasses the whole person, the whole family, the whole community. It is related to economic and social safety, as well as land, a

recognition of prior ownership and all that entails. To ensure a culturally safe environment *you need someone [Aboriginal] there so that they are comfortable and can see something familiar, have people around them that can speak the same language, have someone that you know can give support when you need it.*

(italics in original, Eckermann, Dowd, Martin, Nixon,
Gray & Chong, 1992, p. 167)

Aboriginal community members govern and staff the centre, so that the centre is known as a community space, known as a space where lingo is spoken and community values and practices enacted. Cultural safety is felt through being amidst your own kind and community ways of being.

The pedagogy of the centre flows from the community child raising practices, of providing children with freedom to explore and learn through trial and error. Child initiated play provides the main platform for learning. Children know adults are there if needed. Educators provide a watchful presence and environments rich with Aboriginal and Torres Strait knowledges that affirm cultural pride.

Children's learning is framed by the Early Years Learning Framework for Australia (Australian Government Department of Education Employment and Workplace Relations, 2009) which is based on the view of children's lives 'characterised by belonging, being and becoming' (p. 7). Gundoo philosophy defines these states of being as:

Belonging – recognises the interdependence the child has with others; family, community members, friends – significant others who form his/her identity.

Being – the here and the now – how s/he sees themselves now in relation to others and what he/she knows.

Becoming – supports this child through this rapid stage of development from birth to school age.

Collectively, the Gundoo educators seek for the young children:

- To gain a strong sense of identity
- To gain a strong sense of wellbeing
- To be confident effective learners
- To be connected with and contribute to their world (key outcomes of the Early Years Learning Framework).

Gundoo provides a space for young children to build community.

Stories of Gundoo children's community building in action

To be with the children and community and to fully commit to ethical research we asked, as Barad (2007) suggests, what is being made to matter here and question how that mattering affects what is possible to do and think. And by doing this we collated stories on what was mattering to the children and the community: community membership, looking out for mob, collective spirit, caring for country, non-judgement and resistance. These concepts are discussed and illustrated with stories of the children in action followed by Bena, Kerryn and Louise's differing readings, and summation of what is being made to matter.

Community membership stories

Community membership for Aboriginal Australian peoples is more than belonging to a political community as in western constructions of citizenship (Bellamy, 2008). As foregrounded in Chapter One, it is about connection to country – to all living entities (Martin, 2003; Pascoe, 2014). Early childhood settings provide a community space (polis) in which young children negotiate co-existence with unknown others (MacNaughton, 2007) and thus provide a space to experiment with and develop community membership, rights and participation. We share two stories that illustrate how young Aboriginal children in community demonstrate community membership through resonant connection to country.

Knowing country

> One day we were talking to the children about culture and country and where we belong. And we brought out the Australian Institute of Aboriginal and Torres Strait Islander Studies map of Aboriginal Australia with all nations. We pointed out Wakka Wakka country that we were on. Then Jack (4) was looking at it and he was really getting close to the map and he said he was going to go to his Poppa in his country in Yarrabah and he went straight up along the coast line with his fingers up along the Queensland coast right up to where he could have just put his finger on Yarrabah country near Cairns. He knew where Yarrabah country was. He knew he had to go up along the coast and he was looking forward to seeing his Poppa. And he talked about how he was going crabbing up there in that country. He brought others children in. Then Talia (4) she said she was going to the beach and her country was right up in islands. And she pointed up to the top of Australia – to the Torres Strait. And everything in her conversation was around salt water. She knew she was from salt water country. I (Kerryn) shared where my country was and educators in the room and we talked about where we belonged.

KERRYN: There was a strong sense of children knowing about their country and what country they belong to. Even though they hadn't seen this map, but not fully understanding what it was, they had a concept of knowing straight where their country was. And in my view demonstrated interest in looking at the map and analysing it. It was very powerful. A lot of pride shown in the children in talking about their country and where they belong. It's important to have those explicit conversations in the context of learning at kindy. The next day I shared it with Jack's Mum and she was really proud and confirmed they were going up to Yarrabah to see Poppa and her eyes lit up and you could see she was looking forward to that country too. Knowing we are one mob but different and respect for each other.

LOUISE: A map is an abstract concept, so to intuitively know was striking to witness. To accurately orient and navigate locate places that are thousands of kilometres away indicates something much stronger than a cognitive process, but rather an embodied spiritual connection to country. Membership of place/country/community known with pride.

BENA: I was not there to witness the experience but I did see it on the video and was surprised about what they were talking about where they come from and you could see that pride when they talking about it. Later Jack in the nursery was talking about fishing with the boat that was set up in the sandpit and they started talking about what they was fishing for and Jack was saying 'when I go to Yarrabah we catch stingrays there'. And Archy said 'when I go to Hopevale we catch turtles'. Another boy said 'Well we catch jewfish in our creek'. Then we was talking about it that they have identification of their culture and country. They knew the names for the animals from their country. When their parents came in, and then they shared their knowledge of their country too. And connection to language of country. They know their country. Great to see their pride. The children showed us the ways to catch stingray and turtles. Learning from one another that each community is different and has their own values and views. Learning from one another about those as well. This was important to them.

KERRYN: These are stories from their culture that supports knowing their identity. The survival of identity that continue through all those battles.

Walking on country

We asked them where would you take us in the community. The children voiced their ideas about where they would like to show us. We shared a printed map of the community. Quincey and Jack looked at the map with real intrigue and we asked them where will we go for a walk tomorrow. Quincey pointed down Murray St to trees. Jack pointed to the sewage plant on way into town. They both insisted their position. 'I want go there' 'No there' 'No There'. Then Quincey pointed over where the football field is – Louise read the map 'that's the football field. Do you want to go there?' 'Yeah' they both replied with sheer delight. And there were ideas to go to the Ration Shed and someone else said 'no, let's go to the shop'. There were a couple of ideas and we tallied up who wanted to go where. For the football field, we talked about how it was hot and that it was quite a distance to walk to the football field. They realised that. Then we thought we'd go to the Ration Shed and that there is the hospital on the way. When we walked down the road, cars slowed down to see what we were doing in community and the children waved and said hello. They were showing respect for each other. There were children coming along, so cars went slow. And the children waved at passing family.

When we got to the hospital we were told to wait in the waiting area, and Ezra had a camera and he took a photo of the group and then immediately shared the image on viewfinder to the rest of the group. He knew to share back. He also reminded everyone to sit and wait as a natural leader.

And at the Ration Shed they knew to wait for Uncle to come and talk to us and put the film on. They knew to sit and wait and show respect. They knew the place held importance for the community. The important messages in that whole place.

They pointed out where the helicopter lands. And people's houses. Talking as we walked about who lives where.

KERRYN: The children had a real strong sense of place. They knew their community well and they knew how to get there. They knew where the hospital was, they knew where the Ration Shed was.

BENA: They knew what it was for too.

KERRYN: It was more than an excursion from a child care centre. It was a walk on country.

LOUISE: They were showing us. They were the leaders.

KERRYN: The children knew that the Ration Shed is important to community to suggest it as a place to visit and to show respect when we were there. Demonstrated important part of community's history.

BENA: They know too that you only go there on special occasions, so they have to be on their best behaviour. Showing their respect to the place also feeling that this is time to act proper. Everybody knows it. And community celebrations are always there. Celebrations with significant meanings – like NAIDOC celebrations.

LOUISE: It's the hub of the community.

BENA: And they know that when helicopter lands there that someone very sick. They know that. It's more than just knowing places in the community. It's knowing what they for. They know the places like the radio station, they know what it's for, not that it's just there.

KERRYN: Non-indigenous children have an understanding of their own yard and own house. Community children know more than that. Responsibility is broader than that yard and that house and that square block.

BENA: It may not be the number and the name of the street. But they have that identity of knowing where they staying and who stays in that area. There was a concern at the school that children did not know the name and number of their address. They know where they live.

KERRYN: If we were to walk with them to say take me to your house they would know.

BENA: It's more important to know their surroundings than to know the number and street name.

Community membership is known, felt and enacted as connection to country. It's about knowing your ancestral homelands, and knowing all the features of your community and their role. It's highly visual and embodied. Intergenerational bodily memories hold the ancestral connection to country. As Aunty Margaret Kemarre Turner (2010) explains:

> The only way we can translate into English how we see our relationship with the Land is with the words 'hold' and 'connect'. The roots of the country and its people are twined together. We are part of the land. The land *is* us, and we are the Land. That's how we hold our Land.

(p. 15).

Looking out for mob stories

A collective ontology runs deep in Aboriginal Australian ways of knowing, being and relating. Kinship systems define relationships to others (Yeo, 2003). As noted in Chapter One, children learn kinship relations and responsibilities from a very young age (Daylight & Johnstone, 1986). The following three stories illustrate how young Aboriginal children enact kinship relations and responsibilities, referred to in community as 'looking out for mob'.

Magpie warning

> It was magpie season and they were swooping around. Jakirra and Ezra had an eye out for their movement. And every so often they would quickly yelp: 'magpie!' to let everyone know. Not just caring about their own safety but having a responsibility for everyone's safety who was there. Children would check and stop where they were playing and look around and remind each other. They were keeping an eye out for everyone.

KERRYN: This is about children showing leadership. Jakirra and Ezra were natural leaders. No one told them. They assumed that role and responsibility.

BENA: They had role of chasing it away.

KERRYN: Children have a responsibility to each other – as community family members. It's not just to yourself or your siblings. They see themselves as a collective, as a family.

BENA: Day care is another family.

Packing beds away

> Saul started lifting his bed, then Aiden joined in to lift the other end of the bed. Without any instruction from adults, Jack, Cedric, Tammy and Jakirra also joined in carrying one bed each over their heads. They knew how to order it so they packed away neatly. They knew one needed to hold the storage room door open so that they could come in and out. Working as one entity to get the job done. Jakirra turned the lights on. Jack, Cedric and Jakirra worked as a team to carry one bed together. Nothing was spoken. No directions given.

KERRYN: They read each other's cues. There was no one saying there that is not your job, that's someone else's job. Or it's the teacher's job.

BENA: Like some teachers do, they give out cards or have charts on the wall that says this is your responsibility now. The children here had the freedom to help if they wanted to.

KERRYN: They could make the choice.

LOUISE: And self-initiate. There was not a need to speak they knew how to read the situation and what help to offer.

KERRYN: My Pop used to say there is too much of this (hand mimicking chatter) all the time. And that is part of survival and being able to listen to the land. And listen to everything around you so you can be attuned to it, so you can be responsive to it. That's for survival.

BENA: You don't need to speak – there's a lot that can be communicated non-verbally.

Getting rope ladder down

> A rope ladder was wound up on timber frame to put it out of reach because children had been fighting over it. A group of 5 girls aged 2–5 gathered under it collectively trying to reach it. Older taller girls tried to jump up to reach it, then one kneeled on all fours and another climbed on her back, but she struggled to balance. Then older girls took turns picking up a younger girl to get her to pull but still they couldn't reach it. Then they saw me (Louise) filming and they called to me – 'hey aunty' and gestured to me come over and help.

LOUISE: They worked together on it and it was an intergenerational effort. You don't see that often in mainstream education, as we have a system that insists on learning in age group batches. There was no resistance like I don't want to be picked up, I don't want to be stood on.

KERRYN: They were working as one. They worked as one entity to get this done. That's how you play, that's how you work. You work as one.

Aboriginal Australian worldview is rooted in collectivist principles of working as one. From the grand scale of the whole nation that Bruce Pascoe (2014) explained as the 'epic integrity of the land' (p. 138) in which each clan and tribe have different but aligned responsibilities to care for country, to the micro where it is about everyone around pitching in to get a job done, as happens in the community. The collectivist ontology of Aboriginality informs knowing, being, doing and relating, so that people think of themselves in terms of their relationship to others and their community (Yeo, 2003). This shared way of thinking informs how Aboriginal people work together (Lohoar, Butera & Kennedy, 2014). As community leader, Sylvia declared: 'you're not being a proper black fella unless you're doing together'. Doing together keeps the community spirit going.

Respecting Elders

The relatedness to others is specified through kinship systems. Children are provided opportunities and knowledge required for them to be Wakka Wakka, to be Gubbi Gubbi, to be Barunggam, to understand their cultural ways of being, knowing and doing (Arbon, 2008). And through modelling, children come to know to respect Elders. As Margaret Kemarre Turner (2010) explains:

> Aboriginal people's way is to respect elders ... Our way is to understand elders, to be with them, to see and recognise all the old people from around *apmereyanhe*. Never to speak in any improper way to them, and always live right within your kinship. To understand clearly who you are to them, to sit and listen and learn. But above all to relate, to follow *anpernirrentye*. All that is respect.
>
> (p. 211)

There is no one story to share to illustrate respect for Elders, because it is embedded in the everyday. It is core practice at Gundoo. Everyone knows kinship roles and who has authority to give permission.

KERRYN: Educators are referred to as aunty and uncle or nan, because they are seen as community leaders. Someone we respect and listen to. They are more than educators to them. They are kin. This is the way people have been for thousands of years. You respect Elders. They hold the knowledge, and you need to seek their permission for what you do, so they know.

LOUISE: Like we went and sought permission from Elders to come into community and research with educators and children about how children's citizenship plays out at Gundoo.

BENA: And the children would have come to call you two, Aunty.

LOUISE: Yes, I felt so accepted when I was called Aunty.

Next door to Gundoo is the community's aged care facility. Providing a very special opportunity, for young and old to connect. Bar be it through a six-foot high steel fence. Whitefella law scarring and dividing precious young and elder relations. The children call it the Nanna and Poppy's home.

BENA: One of the Elders does the washing there. And the children go to the fence and they sing out 'Nan'. They bring some of the Elders in wheelchairs to the fence. The children sing out to them. They know to care for each other. Respect grows from a young age.

KERRYN: One time we took the babies into visit the old people. The joy on the old people's faces when we put a baby on their lap. They wanted to know who was who. And one granny said when holding her great grandson 'he needs a haircut'.

BENA: And we told his Mum. And the next day he had a haircut. They knew to listen to Elders.

Respect for Elders has largely diminished in broader society. Especially in the neoliberal agenda, where people are seen in economic terms, as human capital, and so older people who are no longer working are no longer seen as valuable. Further, rapid technological advancements position those who are up to speed with the latest innovations as holding greater knowledge status. A society that respects their Elders brings greater reverence in social exchanges, and honours accumulated knowledge and experience. Respect for Elders recognises the mentorship Elders provide. This is not only traditional and community Elders but anyone older. Children know it is their responsibility to look after and mentor anyone younger than them (Arbon, 2008), which was widespread in the practices of the children at Gundoo. For example, we saw Jarrah (just learning to walk) pat baby Latayla's head as she lay in a rocker crying. We often saw older children bring younger children into Gundoo, and when a younger child was upset or struggling with something, older children would comfort them or help out.

Caring for country stories

Aboriginal peoples' connection to country runs deep (Pascoe, 2014). Responsibility to country is profound (Rose, 1987). Animals, plants, land and water are all respected as kin, as sacred.

Connecting with stick insects

Ezra had a stick insect in a container when he came into the classroom and was eager to show everyone who he has with him today. He proudly held up the container and pointed to the large moving antennas of the stick insect. The children all looked on at this and Jack moved closer to Ezra and the stick insect and placed his hands on the lid of the container and put his fingers under the lid and then looked at Ezra seeking his okay to continue and open the lid of the container. Ezra frowned at Jack and a shook his head and puts his hands firmly over the lid. Jack smiled and moved his hands away and continued observing the insect.

Ezra carried the insect around for the morning putting it on the edge of tables to get a good look at it from low while squatting down on the floor to look up at it and in the block area where he covered it with blocks. When I (Kerryn) approached, Ezra he put his finger to his mouth and shushed me to be quiet, I nodded and whispered 'Is the stick insect sleeping?' Ezra nods yes and smiled while looking down at the covered insect.

In the afternoon, when we entered the outside space Ezra took the stick insect down the back near the large gum tree and opened the container and put it against the tree. It was staying in the container and as I approached I said, 'Can I help you Ezra?' Ezra said 'up there' and several children had noticed what was going on and come over to the tree to watch. I picked up a stick and said to Ezra 'we can help the insect onto the tree'. I moved the stick over for Ezra to hold also and we held the stick together and nudged the stick insect onto the tree. The stick insect took a few steps on the bark and then Ezra pointed at the insect and said looking around to all proudly 'Look, look!'

KERRYN: Ezra shows respect for insects as living beings and displays responsibilities for living beings that inhabit Gundoo, from catching bees that are swarming a flowering tree on the fence line (see Adair, Phillips, Ritchie & Sachdeva, 2017), to chasing and catching small moths in his hands that have just hatched in the grass from overnight rains and now to a catch and release stick insect. During these experiences Ezra displays interest in the details of these beings and makes close observations and is then happy for them to be on their way. He is connecting and caring for country; knowing the beings on the country we walk. He showed a real sense of responsibility and empowerment in the knowing and doing.

BENA: In our community, because we are a small community and we have a lot of Aboriginal artists who do Aboriginal artwork and most of the animals children see, they see in the paintings, and the story that goes behind the paintings. Sharing the stories, so children respect nature because they know that the animals have their part to do with looking after the country as well. Most of the stories are about animals and their part in looking after community and providing in our way of culture. The stories are in the storybooks we share and when the Elders come they tell the stories and most of the Elders are the local artists. Ezra knows this through these stories.

Connecting with rocks

In the yard, Talia has formed a mound of dirt where it is loose near the fence. She carefully lays some small rocks in a circle on top of the mound. Talia gathers more rocks. She holds up a small rock, calling it a baby rock. And continues collecting more rocks. Talia often collects rocks and has collections in her pockets, bag and room. One day when Kerryn shares ochre rocks and crushing them to make paint, she watches eager to learn. The next day her Nan shares that Talia was enthusiastically telling her cousin about painting rocks.

KERRYN: I know that on that particular day there was some fresh soil from the new gate that had been put in, and a lot of new soil turned around in that area and Talia was there going through the soil and looking for rocks. And I'd seen her putting these rocks together – a small collection throughout the day and taking particular care with them and arranging them and looking at them. That resonated for me as my grandfather would often say not to pick up rocks or living things and move them from their place. Everything has its home and who am I to take a rock from its home that comes back to that tracking and survival and old people's way of reading the land. Also, that we are all connected to country. In Arrente/Luritja country growing up there you are surrounded by rocks and rocks are your kin. Rocks of the great caterpillar that we call the MacDonnell Ranges which keep the wind from the people and keep everyone safe. Talia's care resonated with me and I asked about the rocks and she showed me her rock collection that she was gathering. They appeared to be very special to her. Rocks are very special to me. They are living entities and we do need to think of them as that. And everything has its place. We overlook the little things. I then brought in some of my rocks for Talia later that we could make in to paint. It was a sense of joy and connection for me as I think we all should have time to play but connection to country also and that caring for country even this steel fence had been placed into the ground, it's artificial, but from that new dirt stirred Talia's bonding with rocks. It's like she's trying to heal the wound, playing around in the dirt, finding the treasure. I think that's something Aboriginal communities are so resistant and get on with it and in these high fences, find some fun and positive in that, with Talia finding some beautiful gems in this bare yard with a steel fence. That shows her own connection to country and respect for country. Even amongst this she could still find pride and connection to country. Resistance.

And the time taken. If we were to look at footage with Talia and those rocks – it was the intention. She took herself away from group play to do something with intent. To carefully place them and mound the dirt up and show off these rocks. And looking at them and taking them back. She had a little container and put them in her bag. She wrapped one up in some tissue. A conversation we had afterward and she had taken them home and they were in her bedroom. She knew where they were and they had place in her life now.

BENA: I think that each rock represented someone significant to her and they were special and she took them home and how she lined them up in a circle. It might have been those special people in her life. Her Mum had just had baby. Her sense of identity and her rights of belonging to a family.

LOUISE: It's about recognising the different languages the children communicate with, in that placing rocks and forming patterns communicates as well.

Embodied knowledge becomes known through keen interest of entities of country, as we see above in Ezra's close observations and connection with insects and Talia's with rocks. The project of co-existence with others is with all entities in Aboriginals' ways of knowing, being, doing and relating.

Acceptance and non-judgement of others' stories

By seeing others as they are a part of you, as Margaret Kemarre Turner (2010) explained, builds foundations for greater empathy and inclusivity and seeing that we are all in this together – we are a family – we are a community. It is disrespectful to ask direct questions.

Nurturing acceptance

> Bena sits in the middle of the room with Tallara and Dheran leaning and climbing on her, whilst Teddy and Jarrah walked around the room and Latayla lay in a cot drinking her bottle. Jarrah (1) sat in chair next to the cot and patted her. Latayla reached out to him through the bars of cot. Then Jarrah stood up on the chair. Bena calmly said 'sit down Jarrah' and he followed. Teddy stands on the edge of a foam mattress bouncing. Bena offers: 'jump Teddy jump' he steps off with a big smile. He enthusiastically repeated this a few times. Bardo (Bena's 9-year-old son) is visiting and lying on another mattress. He calls to Teddy who toddles over arms wide open falling warmly into an embrace. Coco (an educator from neighbouring room) visits to cuddle her daughter, earlier her brother visited.

LOUISE: Bena projects comfort, acceptance and encouragement to nurture a strong sense of security and belonging for all in the space (young and old), so that they peacefully negotiate with each other and confidently take risks. Bena is the mothership providing security and encouragement for these very young children (all under 2) to take risks, eased with gentle cautionary reminders.

BENA: It's about love and doing everything out of love and with love and that children get a sense of what it feels like through a sense of encouragement, hugs and cuddles, and speaking with respect and care. Learning to share with others. Older children then share with younger children. Showing how – and the children learn it's a cycle. Love is there to share and is entwined with others. The babies always looked out for Bardo when he came to visit. They had such big smiles on their face when they see him.

Across the duration of our visits to Gundoo for the project in 2015 and 2016, the children were very accepting of each other's different ways of being and doing. For example, Ezra had a small backpack bag of his treasures that he carried with him everywhere for a couple of months (as mentioned in Chapter 3) and no other child showed interest in it.

LOUISE: There seemed to be a general acceptance that this was Ezra's way. I don't recall children asking why someone doing something. I sense children learn from their community from a young age to interpret what is going on – to read the landscape, rather than ask explicit directed questions.

BENA: I can't say how they feel or how they know but they know if someone has something special and that they need time and space. Needing to belong. They knew to respect him and not to torment him. And that he'd share with them when he was ready to share. They knew to be patient and just wait. I think that is some of the values that we try and teach the children: being patient, learning to share with others and show love. Teaching them what respect looks like, feels like – show them.

LOUISE: There's something about time here as well. It will happen in good time. It's not like western white way in which we are very strict and time scheduled.

BENA: Mmm. Allowing time. You need time.

It's the knowing, and feeling that another is a 'part of us' (p.7) that Margaret Kemarre Turner (2010) described that nurtures acceptance and non-judgement. This notion of relating to others as they are a part of us seems to offer profound potential for community building – an ontology to be central to all education.

Stories of resistance

Australian early childhood education and care legislation, policy and practice are built on whitefella laws: invisible and visible fences. Gundoo is surrounded by 6 foot high steel fences, and the outdoor area is divided into six separate outdoor spaces and framed by multiple 1.2 metre high fences for different age groupings.

> (1) The approved provider of an education and care service must ensure that any outdoor space used by children at the education and care service premises is enclosed by a fence or barrier that is of a height and design that children preschool age or under cannot go through, over or under it.
>   Penalty $2000
>
> *(State of Queensland, 2018, Regulation 104)*

The Building Code of Australia (BCA) requires that fencing surrounding education and care services meets the following

> (c) Each group has access between the group's indoor play area and an outdoor play area without passing through another group's indoor play area or a functional area.

(d) Fencing not less than 1200mm high complying with AS 1926.1–2007, is provided around those parts of a centre where children are cared for, including all buildings and grounds accessible to children.

(Department of Housing and Public Works, 2012, p. 14)

All traffic in the community is local. Children play in the street. This is accepted community practice.

BENA: We didn't want fences but the Department ordered installation of fences.

Here are three stories of children at Gundoo resisting the fences; resisting the demarcation of property zoning per age group; resisting the colonising of country and collective spirit; resisting fences 'as a powerful signifier for Aboriginal people of the regulation of their and their children's lives in the making of the Australian nation' (Power & Somerville, 2015, p. 67).

Under and over fences – to include all beings

A small dog came in under the back boundary fence. A sign at the front entrance states 'no dogs allowed' placed by an education department representative. Nowhere in the Queensland Education and Care Services National Regulations is there a stipulation about animals in child care centres. In the local community there are town dogs – dogs that wander the community living off scraps, and families have pet dogs and hunting dogs. Jakirra (4) noticed the dog immediately in the Emu playground, she was in the neighbouring kangaroo playground and leapt over the 1.2 metre welded mesh fence, grabbed the dog in her arms then climbed back over the kangaroo playground fence all before I (Louise) really registered any of this. An educator soon ushered the dog back under the boundary fence.

LOUISE: Jakirra desired to be with dog – she desired a more-than-human community. Like Uncle Bob Anderson (1998) noted 'All living things, be they mammals, birds, reptiles, insects or trees are our sisters and brothers and therefore we must protect them' (p. 8).

The imposed regulating force of the fence did not obstruct her desire. Her dexterity enabled rapid negotiation over fence. Children can be with dogs in community but not in this regulated institution. I see that an altered controlled community is enforced and often struggled with to reconcile community ways of being.

BENA: Dogs have always been an important part of family. That's why they have the dogs painted on the wall walking with people on the front of the Ration Shed. They provide protection and meals and making sure there were nutrients in the food.

KERRYN: A lot of poisonous things to sniff out.

BENA: Everyone knows the dogs. Dogs protect us. Important part of family.

KERRYN: Dogs look out for his mob. Dogs hunt with you. If dog doesn't eat the meat – it not good. In this story of Jakirra we see risky play: allowing to learn through trial and error. Learning by doing. Scaling fences like lightning, navigating through different lays of the land. Using toes to wrap around thin vertical strips of steel. She was not escaping. Like in mainstream child care if you saw a child scaling a fence the assumption would be that they are escaping to go into unknown territory. Jakirra had purpose and intent – to be with the dog.

Climbing over fences for community resources

Jack had a small toy car that he momentarily left on the ground then Ezra picked it up. Jack asked: 'give it back' reaching for it and chasing Ezra who quickly threw it over the fence. Jack then quickly scaled the 1.2 metre welded mesh fence grabbed his car then scooted all the way to the adjacent corner of the fenced unused yard and picked up all the other toys and threw them back over the Echidna class's fence and then came back and threw over a ball and ninja turtle toy that had been tossed over by the Kangaroo class earlier then he scaled the fence with his car in hand to return to his playground.

LOUISE: Ezra knew the fence demarcated where they could partake, and where they couldn't. Jack's desire to partake with his small car, made the fence penetrable. The yard where the small car had landed was a zone in which no child was permitted according to the regulated fencing regime, yet many play items had landed there, to work with the policing regime of fenced areas and his peers desire for all of the out-of-reach play items, Jack took responsibility to relocate each item to its respective zoned area. As Jack's grandmother said: 'You are not being a proper blackfella if you don't think of others in your mob.'

Giving through fences

Frequently each day we saw children giving to siblings and kin through the bars of the fences. Siblings know to always get one for your brother or sister. When lolly snakes were given out Ezra took two. An educator was about to reprimand him though a visiting gran said 'wait let's see what he does'. And he took the other snake over to the age group dividing fence to pass to his younger brother. On another day, when soft fine beach sand was delivered to the kindergarten sandpit. Jakirra carried two handfuls of sand to her sister through the fence.

KERRYN: You can't fence them off from family, their country. From a very young age these children know to look after anyone younger and your kin. By learning from a very young age that you care for each other and you work together as a large extended family.

LOUISE: Kinship duty prevails through fences. The fences were not felt so much by the children as a physical barrier. They were just a thing to get over or the thing in between us playing. You just climb it or put your hands through it. And I wonder what point you start to feel that the fence locks you in.

KERRYN: I think for any Aboriginal person in Australia, your identity is so linked with politics; it is out there at the front. There is always something to fence you everyday. Identity is always questioned. We still have cultural capability frameworks that people are supposed to be working with to ensure there is no racism, but we don't even name racism. We don't name institutional racism in education systems. We pander around it. It's too harsh a word to use.

LOUISE: In terms of children feeling those barriers. Remember when I asked a couple of them to take photos of what don't you like here. And Talia took a picture of a closed door and said 'can't get in'.

KERRYN: What I was brought up with was you don't have a door shut on a baby or any one child. Need to keep doors open. And that whole idea of putting babies in a cot is unthinkable. When I go home I'll be sleeping in a bed with aunties, cousins and nieces. Because we don't buy single beds we buy double beds for more people.

BENA: When we have a new baby at Gundoo, we lay them on a mattress on the floor. And when the Department comes they ask why the baby was there. And I explain that at home they don't sleep in a cot they sleep with their Mum and Dad.

LOUISE: The cot is another fence.

KERRYN AND BENA: Yes.

BENA: Parents don't like them. Due to past incidents that happened to their grandparents or parents. About being shoved in a cot. And stolen generation experiences.

Segregation and separation wounds run deep in a kinship entwined ontology. Child care fences divide children by age, separating and excluding family members and defining participation – what can be done by whom, and when and where. The fences act as what Jacques Ranciere (2010) defines as policing, and partition of the sensible – in defining whom, when and where can partake in society. In the name of protection, fences define children's citizenship – as only with those of same age and only within the confines of the fence. The outside world is dangerous and so are those older – even in many cases only days older. We question the fences, their imposition, their colonising force and how they act as regimes of regulation and control. We see and feel the violence of the fences' cuts and divisions. The children actively mediated the fences and community building through cultural values of care for kin and country and a tenacious spirit to work through, under and over fences. The children desire to move in, with, over and under – their bodies are entangled with the matter of structures. They diverge from colonising conventions of usage. These children were not disembodied as is required in western education. They are very much embodied – as they readily ask themselves what can my body do in this space, as opposed to what am I meant to do. As Veronica Arbon (2008) explains, Aboriginal ways of doing is 'a signifier of embodied knowledge' and 'concerns all senses' (p. 49).

Sharing with community – family video night

> After six months of 25 whole days of being with community, we wanted to share back with community so everyone could see what we had been doing at Gundoo with their little ones. From talking with Jacqui (Gundoo Director) and Bena, they shared how they have a family night the week before Christmas as an end of year celebration and graduation for those going on to school the following year. It seemed a perfect occasion to share a video composition of how we had seen the children building community. When Jenny was visiting from New Zealand and Jenn Adair from the USA in November, Bena arranged for us to be interviewed on the local radio Aboriginal station so we could share with community about the study, we also talked up the family night that was planned for December. Bena made posters for the family night that were put on the walls of the local cafe, and shop and medical centre. The family night was set to be a key community event. When Kerryn and I (Louise) started to make the video we looked at iMovie templates and saw a blockbuster theme and agreed to go with that to add spark and humour. In all honesty, it was actually the first film we had edited with titles and music and credits, so edits and rendering happened right up unto last minute before family night opening. Kerryn and I brought our families too. My Mum and in-laws were treated so respectfully as Elders, being given the best chairs and first serve of food. My partner rigged up a projector and speakers in one of the playrooms. The film was titled 'Our Children, Our Community' as the educators had come to name the project and shared a series of clips of children illustrating knowing who they are in community; knowing what they can do for community; caring for others and environment; and including and acting with and for others. And familiar Aboriginal music was overlaid, such as the children's lullaby 'Inanay' and 'Sing about Life' by Tiddas (Bennett, 1993). When each child saw themselves on the screen they sat taller with beaming smiles. About a hundred people came to the gathering and there was real hush and focus when the film played. Family were so proud of their children. Community members told us that it was so good to see the positives of our young ones. And the resounding comment from most was 'that was deadly eh' and 'Should be on NITV [National Indigenous Television] Bub'.

KERRYN: I think it's a very important part of the whole project to give back to community so that Elders know. That's how I was raised to be transparent in every move we make. This is the story that will be told, so they can know and know what we were doing at Gundoo in community. And giving back. Give back the story. So that they can hear. I remember one of the older boys making signs 'movie night this week' and no one asked them to do that. The ownership of that. It became more a community event more than a research project, because that was a celebration to see all the beautiful work that happens in this community.

BENA: Yes, the ownership – everyone playing their part and everyone knows. You not just gaining trust in the centre but also in the community. That was good. The feedback was good. Seeing the children proud with their chests puffed out. It brings community together.

KERRYN: To know what's going well. There are a lot of people continually coming to Gundoo, but to fix things. A problem to be fixed. But rather we looked at what they have and honoured that.

LOUISE: I so wanted to share back with community in a way that was accessible, welcomed and appreciated by the community. I had the great privilege of being with their little ones. In return, I wanted to gift back what reflected deep appreciation of this honour. I spent days and days working on the video. I wanted it to be perfect. It was a creation and a sharing I will never forget. For the community to continue to share with family and community who couldn't make it that night, I created a Gundoo YouTube channel and multiple copies for families on DVDs.

What we came to know about young children's community building

The above collection of stories is offered to share Aboriginal children's knowledge of community building – attuned with Aboriginal ways of knowing through story. National and cultural conceptualisations of young children mediate young children's community building. But these children also define it themselves. They know, feel and enact their cultural and community identity and claim it with pride through embodied connection to kin and country. They know to look out for each other and for the collective good – from that deep rooted knowing that they are all a part of each other. They know it is their responsibility to look after and mentor anyone younger than them and to respect Elders. Their knowing is embodied and entangled with all entities. And workarounds to barriers are readily accessed in pursuit of collective interests.

Our research design originally was for the children to initiate and engage in three civic action projects (one class-based, one centre-based, one community-based). For months, we endeavoured to support civic action projects taking place with the kindergarten group at Gundoo. Through conversations with educators about what we observed and what issues could be explored further, through sharing Aboriginal children's literature as provocations, through community walks, through inviting the children to take pictures of what they don't like – what they feel uncomfortable about – to see if any of these may incite a project. And across four months there was multiple changes to the teaching team, with at least eight different educators. They were in survival mode with no space to be pro-active. As Linda Tuhui Smith (2012) noted, the lived reality is that 'Indigenous peoples are not in control and are subject to a continuing set of external conditions' (p. 206). We became acutely aware that the research agenda was not aligned with the community's pressing needs and reality. Though they so wanted the children to engage in civic action. The constant barrage of crises demanded urgent attention.

Kerryn and I talked for hours and hours and we talked for hours with the director Jacqui and Bena and we read widely to locate possibilities for making meaning with ethical and culturally sensitive sensibilities – that did not add to the colonising project but rather offered hope for justice to come. With heartfelt sensitivity for the beautiful Gundoo community, we foregrounded relationship building, over research agendas.

We let go of prior assumptions and categories, to be fully present to see what emerges and in this state of being – we came to realise that the children were initiating community projects constantly right under our noses:

The be with dog project
The return of property to respective mobs project
The giving to kin project.

Note

1 The explicit reference to the sale of opium reflects the perception at the time that Chinese people in Queensland were the principal suppliers of opium, and so were understood as the source of the problems experienced by Aboriginal people. 'Eleven of the Act's 32 sections deal stringently with control of the supply of opium to Aboriginal people' (Commonwealth of Australia (Museum of Australian Democracy), 2011).

References

Adair, J. K., Phillips, L., Ritchie, J. & Sachdeva, S. (2017). Civic action and play: examples from Maori, Aboriginal Australian and Latino communities. *Early Child Development and Care*, 187(5–6), 798–811.

Anderson, B. (1998). No application forms. In *Arts Nexus*. Brisbane: Queensland Community Arts Networks.

Arbon, V. (2008). *Arlathirnda Ngurkarnda Ityirnda: Being-knowing-doing*. Teneriffe: Post Pressed.

Australian Government Department of Education Employment and Workplace Relations (2009). *Belonging, Being and Becoming: The Early Years Learning Framework for Australia*. Canberra: Australian Government Department of Education, Employment and Workplace Relations for the Council of Australian Governments. Retrieved from https://docs.education.gov.au/documents/belonging-being-becoming-early-years-learning-framework-australia

Australian Institute of Health and Welfare (n.d.). *Discrete Indigenous Community – Indigenous Community Identifier*. Retrieved from https://meteor.aihw.gov.au/content/index.phtml/itemId/269732

Barad, K. (2007). *Meeting the Universe Halfway: Quantum Physics and the Entanglement of Matter and Meaning*. Durham: Duke University Press.

Bellamy, R. (2008). *Citizenship: A Very Short Introduction*. Oxford, UK: Oxford University Press.

Bennett, L. (1993). Inanay [Recorded by Tiddas] on *Sing about Life*. Australia: Phonogram.

Brennan, F. (1992). *Land Rights Queensland Style: The Struggle for Aboriginal Self-determination*. St Lucia: University of Queensland Press.

Commonwealth of Australia (Museum of Australian Democracy) (2011). *Aboriginals Protection and Restriction of the Sale of Opium Act 1897 (Qld)*. Retrieved from https://www.foun dingdocs.gov.au/item-sdid-54.html

Daylight, P. & Johnstone, M. (1986). *Women's Business, The Aboriginal Women's Task Force Report*. Canberra: AGPS.

Department of Education, Employment and Workplace Relations (2010). *Multifunctional Aboriginal Children's Services (MACS) and Crèches*. Retrieved from https://www.anao.gov. au/sites/default/files/ANAO_Report_2010-2011_8.pdf

Department of Housing and Public Works (2012). *Queensland Development Code – MP 5.4 Child Care Centres*. Retrieved from http://www.hpw.qld.gov.au/SiteCollectionDocum ents/MP5.4ChildCareCentres18July2012.pdf

Eckermann, A., Dowd, T., Martin, M., Nixon, L., Gray, R. & Chong, E. (1992). *Binan Goonj: Bridging Cultures in Aboriginal Health*. Armidale (NSW): University of New England Press.

Frankland, K. (1994). *A Brief History of Government Administration of Aboriginal and Torres Strait Islander Peoples in Queensland*. Retrieved from http://www.slq.qld.gov.au/__data/assets/p df_file/0008/93734/Admin_History_Aboriginal_and_Torres_Strait_Islanders.pdf

Hegarty, R. (1999). *Is That You Ruthie?* St Lucia, Qld: University of Queensland Press.

Kreutz, A. (2015). *Children and the Environment in an Australian Indigenous Community: A Psychological Approach*. Abingdon, UK: Routledge.

Lohoar, S., Butera, N. & Kennedy, E. (2014). Strengths of Australian Aboriginal cultural practices in family life and child rearing. *Child Family Community Australia Information Exchange*. Melbourne: Australian Institute of Family Studies. Retrieved from https://aifs. gov.au/cfca/sites/default/files/publication-documents/cfca25.pdf

MacNaughton, G. (2007). *Trials and transitions to citizenship: What really matters in early childhood education?* Paper presented at the Dean's Lecture Series, Faculty of Education, University of Melbourne.

Martin, K. (2003). Ways of knowing being and doing: a theoretical framework and methods for Indigenous and Indigenist re-search. *Journal of Australian Studies*, 27(76), 203–214

Pascoe, B. (2014). *Dark Emu Black Seeds: Agriculture or Accident*. Broome, WA: Magabala Books.

Power, K., & Somerville, M. (2015). The fence as technology of (post-) colonial childhood in contemporary Australia.' In V. Pacini-Ketchabaw and A. Taylor (Eds), *Unsettling the Colonial Places and Spaces of Early Childhood Education* (pp. 63–77). New York: Routledge.

Queensland, Department of Aboriginal and Island Affairs (1965). *Annual Report of the Director of Aboriginal and Island Affairs*. Brisbane: Department of Aboriginal and Island Affairs.

Queensland, Department of Aboriginal and Island Affairs (1966). *Annual Report of the Director of Aboriginal and Island Affairs*. Brisbane: Department of Aboriginal and Island Affairs.

Ranciere, J. (2010). *Dissensus* (S. Corcoran Ed.). London: Continuum.

Rose, D. B. (1987). Consciousness and responsibility in Aboriginal religion. In W. H. Edwards (Ed.), *Traditional Aboriginal Society: A Reader* (pp. 257–269). South Melbourne: MacMillan.

Smith, L. T. (2012). *Decolonizing Methodologies: Research and Indigenous peoples* (2nd edn). London: Zed Books.

State of Queensland (2018). *Education and Care Services National Regulations*. https://www.legislation.qld.gov.au/view/pdf/inforce/current/sl-2011-ecsnr

State of Queensland (Queensland Museum) (2019). *Government Settlements*. Retrieved from http://www.qm.qld.gov.au/Events+and+Exhibitions/Exhibitions/2015/01/Dandiiri+Maiwar/Living+under+the+Act/Government+settlements#.XEfrvs8zZuU

Strong and Smart (2004). *The Early Days* [video file]. Duration 16 mins. Ration Shed Museum.

Turner, M. K., with McDonald, B. & Dobson, V.P. (Trans.) (2010). *Iwenhe Tyerrtye: What It Means to Be an Aboriginal Person*. Alice Springs: IAD Press.

Yeo, S. S. (2003). Bonding and attachment of Australian Aboriginal children. *Child Abuse Review*, 12(3), 292–304.

5

KATOA COMMUNITY AND CHILDREN'S COMMUNITY BUILDING AT KATOA KINDERGARTEN

This chapter begins by contextualising the Katoa Kindergarten site for this study. It briefly overviews the context provided by the Aotearoa New Zealand (NZ) early childhood curriculum, *Te Whāriki*, and other key documents. It then highlights the situation of benefits of having fully qualified teachers, being well staffed, and a supportive Kindergarten Association which supports staff through regular relevant professional learning conferences. These documents and the support in implementing them form part of the scaffolding required to enable teachers to grasp the significance of these documents and thus utilise them effectively. We then move to outline some of the key Māori values that featured in the work of Katoa Kindergarten, before describing how they underpinned the teachers' pedagogical approaches and offering some stories of young children's community building at Katoa.

Te Whāriki – 'bicultural' early childhood curriculum

Whilst the phrase 'civic action' has not been visible in early childhood discourse in Aotearoa NZ, the notion of children and their whānau/families experiencing a sense of 'empowerment' through their engagement with an early childhood service is integral to the early childhood curriculum document *Te Whāriki* (NZ Ministry of Education (MoE), 1996, 2017). During the period of the data collection for the study, the kindergarten was using the original 1996 version of the curriculum. Towards the end of the study, Te Whāriki was 'refreshed' by the Ministry of Education, resulting in the promulgation in 2017 of a revised version of the curriculum.

The introduction to the original Te Whāriki made a strongly stated commitment to Te Tiriti o Waitangi, the Māori version of the treaty that legitimised British settlement of Aotearoa:

This is a curriculum for early childhood care and education in New Zealand. In early childhood education settings, all children should be given the opportunity to develop knowledge and understanding of the cultural heritages of both partners to te Tiriti o Waitangi. The curriculum reflects this partnership in text and structure.

(NZ MoE, 1996, p. 9)

Interestingly, this same statement is relegated to the final page of the 2017 version (NZ MoE, 2017, p. 69).

Both versions of the curriculum have the same key overarching principles:

Empowerment | Whakamana
Holistic Development | Kotahitanga
Family and Community | Whānau Tangata
Relationships | Ngā Hononga

It should be noted that the Māori principles above are not direct translations of the English words. They are two parallel sets of constructs, representing two different world views, hence the 'bicultural' description of the document.

The original *Te Whāriki 1996* had been visionary in honouring commitments to Te Tiriti o Waitangi and to Māori, the Indigenous people of Aotearoa, seeking expression of the treaty commitment to Māori of tino rangatiratanga (absolute authority, self-determination), as seen in the following quotes from *Te Whāriki 1996*:

Particular care should be given to bicultural issues in relation to empowerment. Adults working with children should understand and be willing to discuss bicultural issues, actively seek Māori contributions to decision making, and ensure that Māori children develop a strong sense of self-worth.

(p. 40)

Decisions about the ways in which bicultural goals and practices are developed within each early childhood education setting should be made in consultation with the appropriate tangata whenua [Indigenous people].

(p. 11)

Neither of these statements were retained in the revised *Te Whāriki 2017*. (Nor were other key commitments, such as to countering racism and reflecting on the commitments contained within Te Tiriti o Waitangi as previously mentioned in Chapter Two.)

The philosophical framework for *Te Whāriki 1996* was underpinned by a te ao Māori conceptual framework provided the two Māori writers, Tamati and Tilly Reedy (Te One, 2003, p. 19). The other key writers of *Te Whāriki 1996*, Helen May and Margaret Carr, acknowledged a depth and range of theoretical inspiration that underpinned their work on the document:

If we look for a philosophical framework to encompass the work that has gone before, it may be a useful metaphor to think of the enormous quantity of writing on early childhood curriculum as a forest of kauri, rimu, and rata ... [and this] forest is also strewn with ideological disputes and conflicting beliefs (Katz, 1975; Roopnarine and Johnson, 1987). We can do no more here than find a tentative path through the forest ... Four tall kauri provide important guides: Piaget (Piaget and Inhelder, 1969), Erikson (1950), Vygotsky (1968), and Bruner (Bruner and Haste, 1987). They help us to describe an early childhood path, in particular they provide two main principles of learning: we are concerned with the whole child and a developmental framework (Piaget and Erikson), and with learning in a social and cultural context (Bruner and Vygotsky).

(Carr & May, 1991, pp. 223–224)

Helen and Margaret drew upon a wide range of research and theory beyond these four tall 'kauri', and worked closely alongside Tilly and Tamati Reedy, who provided the Māori conceptual framework, in developing *Te Whāriki 1996*. Their process also involved wide-ranging, in-depth consultation throughout the early childhood care and education sector in Aotearoa NZ.

Tiriti o Waitangi commitments in policy and assessment documents

The promulgation of *Te Whāriki 1996* was followed by a series of other key education documents also grounded in recognition of Te Tiriti o Waitangi. These include the series of 20 booklets, *Kei Tua o te Pae/Assessment for Learning: Early Childhood Exemplars* (NZ MoE, 2004–2009) illustrating exemplars of assessment using the 'learning stories' model developed by Margaret Carr. Booklet three focuses on Bicultural Assessment (NZ MoE, 2004).. A further document *Te Whatu Pōkeka* covers assessment in early childhood care and education from a Māori worldview (NZ MoE, 2009b).

Tātaiako; Cultural Competencies for Teachers of Māori Learners (2011) is a document jointly produced by the Ministry of Education and the Teachers Council, that outlines key competencies which, as has been previously suggested, are appropriate for *all* teachers in Aotearoa NZ contexts (Ritchie, 2012). *Tātaiako* links strongly to the Ministry's Māori education strategy documents, *Ka Hikitia.Managing for Success. Māori Education Strategy 2008–2012* and *Ka Hikitia: Accelerating Success (2013–2017)* (NZ MoE, 2009a, 2013). The Māori education strategy emphasised important discursive shifts with regard to conceptualising 'being Māori' as an educational asset, based on the 'Māori potential approach' of Te Puni Kōkiri, the Ministry for Māori Development. This approach emphasised 'Māori self-development and self-determination, and represents a move away from a focus on deficit, problems, failure and risks, to a focus on making the most of opportunities for success' (NZ MoE, 2009a, p. 11).

All of these documents, in alignment with honouring a commitment to Te Tiriti o Waitangi, reflect a deep respect for core te ao Māori values, such as whanaungatanga (relationships), manaakitanga (caring, generosity, hospitality), as well as recognition of the importance of te reo Māori (the Māori language) and of those who are the local peoples of each tribal area, that is, those who hold mana whenua.

Some examples drawn from the above documents will now be provided in order to illustrate the Tiriti o Waitangi based alignments that guide early childhood pedagogy in Aotearoa. To firstly briefly recap: Article Two of the treaty affirmed Māori self-determination, via their chiefly authority over their lands, resources and everything that Māori valued. Article Three undertakes that Māori will have equal citizenship rights to the settlers. *Te Whāriki 2017* makes the following statement:

Te Tiriti | the Treaty has implications for our education system, particularly in terms of achieving equitable outcomes for Māori and ensuring that te reo Māori [the Māori language] not only survives but thrives. Early childhood education has a crucial role to play here, by providing mokopuna [grand-children/children] with culturally responsive environments that support their learning and by ensuring that they are provided with equitable opportunities to learn.

(2017, p. 3)

Te Whāriki 2017 elaborates further in the strand 'Mana Whenua | Belonging', which requires that: Teachers/kaiako are to acknowledge the particular status of Māori as tangata whenua, the original people of the land and to support children to be kaitiaki, guardians of the earth and more-than-human co-habitants:

Kaiako are cognisant of the concept of tangata whenua and the relationship that Māori have to each other and to the land. This guides kaiako relationships with whānau, hapū and iwi. Kaiako share appropriate histories, kōrero and waiata with mokopuna to enhance their identity and sense of belonging.

(p. 33)

Kaiako support mokopuna to engage respectfully with and to have aroha for Papatūānuku. They encourage an understanding of kaitiakitanga and the responsibilities of being a kaitiaki by, for example, caring for rivers, native forest and birds.

(p. 33)

In order to fulfill these expectations, the curriculum requires that 'Appropriate connections with iwi [tribes] and hapū [sub-tribes] are established' (2017, p. 35). It poses the reflective question: 'In what ways can kaiako support children to take care of or become kaitiaki of this place?' (p. 35).

Like Te Whāriki, *Te Whatu Pōkeka* (NZ MoE, 2009b) recognises the intrinsic mana (esteem) of the child, and thus seeks to privilege the child's voice:

We want to ensure that the culture and the voices of the children are heard throughout, rather than those of the adults or the organisations. We also want to ensure that the identity of the Māori child is not marginalised during the course of their experiences from birth to adulthood.

(p. 47)

Children are to be recognised as being embedded in the histories of their communities:

Te Whatu Pōkeka requires that we recognise what the children bring to the context. This includes not only their inherent strengths but also their traditions and history, their whānau, and their whakapapa [genealogical inter-relationships].

(p. 49)

Te Whatu Pōkeka highlights the importance of engagement with the child's extended family/whānau, privileging their perspectives, and thus shifting the power dynamics away from a western hierarchical view of teachers as experts:

Whānau are intrinsically involved in the child's learning and therefore must be intimately involved in the assessment process of Te Whatu Pōkeka. Embedded within the notion of whānau are concepts of rights and responsibilities, obligations and commitments, and a sense of identity and belonging. The role of kaiako as the expert, with the power to judge and classify children, must be redefined as that of a contributing whānau member. Teaching and assessment must be perceived and recognised as a collaborative activity where whānau and kaiako both have a valued contribution.

(p. 54)

Tātaiako: Cultural Competencies for Teachers of Māori Learners (NZ MoE & Teaching Council, 2011) provides pedagogical elaboration in support of the Ministry's Māori education strategy. It comprises five overarching competencies:

- Wānanga: participating with learners and communities in robust dialogue for the benefit of Māori learners' achievement.
- Whanaungatanga: actively engaging in respectful working relationships with Māori learners, parents and whānau, hapū, iwi and the Māori community.
- Manaakitanga: showing integrity, sincerity and respect towards Māori beliefs, language and culture.
- Tangata Whenuatanga: affirming Māori learners as Māori. Providing contexts for learning where the language, identity and culture of Māori learners and their whānau is affirmed.
- Ako: taking responsibility for their own learning and that of Māori learners.

(NZ MoE & Teachers Council, 2011, p. 4)

Applying the value of 'manaakitanga' is defined in this document as 'Caring for Māori learners as culturally-located beings' and 'Treating Māori students, whānau, and iwi equitably with sincerity and integrity' (p. 16). Key indicators of this competency to be displayed by registered teachers are:

- Displays respect, integrity and sincerity when engaging with Māori learners, whānau, hapū, iwi and communities.
- Demonstrably cares about Māori learners, what they think and why.
- Displays respect for the local Māori culture (ngā tikanga- ā-iwi) in engaging with Māori learners, their parents whānau, hapū, iwi and communities.
- Incorporates Māori culture (including tikanga-ā-iwi) in curriculum delivery and design processes.
- Can describe how the Treaty of Waitangi influences their practice as a teacher in the New Zealand educational setting (p. 10).

In 2017 the Education Council, now Teaching Council, produced a further document that will be integral to initial teacher education and to the registration and ongoing appraisal of all teachers in Aotearoa NZ, *Our Code, our Standards: Code of Professional Responsibility and Standards for the Teaching Profession*. Whilst it was yet to be published at the time of our study, it will provide strong impetus to Tiriti o Waitangi based commitments. It has four overarching values:

- WHAKAMANA: empowering all learners to reach their highest potential by providing high-quality teaching and leadership.
- MANAAKITANGA: creating a welcoming, caring and creative learning environment that treats everyone with respect and dignity.
- PONO: showing integrity by acting in ways that are fair, honest, ethical and just.
- WHANAUNGATANGA: engaging in positive and collaborative relationships with our learners, their families and whānau, our colleagues and the wider community (p. 2).

The *Code and Standards* document includes the following statement that reinforces the centrality of a commitment to Te Tiriti o Waitangi for all teaching practice in our country: 'As teachers, we are committed to honouring Te Tiriti o Waitangi and we understand this has implications in all of our practice' (Education Council, 2017, p. 4). Furthermore, teachers are to demonstrate their commitment to society by 'promoting and protecting the principles of human rights, sustainability and social justice' and by 'demonstrating a commitment to a Tiriti o Waitangi based Aotearoa New Zealand' (p. 12).

Whilst the discursive context signalled in the brief overview above ostensibly provides the scaffolding for early childhood teachers in Aotearoa, it should not be assumed that all early childhood services draw as deeply as did the teachers at Katoa Kindergarten on the available documents. Practice in our diverse range of early childhood services and settings is extremely variable, particularly with regard to the implementation of Māori language and content (Education Review Office (ERO), 2013, 2018). A national evaluation by the Education Review Office (ERO) in 2013 found that many early childhood settings fail to deliver on Te Tiriti o Wait-angi obligations as outlined in the above documents:

> Many services made reference to Te Tiriti o Waitangi and to New Zealand's dual cultural heritage and bicultural practice in their philosophy statements. However, only a few services were fully realising such intent in practice by working in partnership with whānau Māori and through the provision of a curriculum that was responsive to the language, culture and identity of Māori children.
>
> *(ERO, 2013, p. 13)*

ERO reported that very few centres had strong partnerships with parents and whānau Māori whereby they responded to their aspirations for their children. The report listed its concern that few centres included a focus on bicultural practice or used *Ka Hikitia* and *Tātaiako* (ERO, 2013, p. 13). The report concluded that 'ERO's findings suggest that Te Whāriki is not well understood and implemented as a bicultural curriculum' (p. 13). The report posed the following questions for early childhood services to consider:

- What informs and guides our bicultural curriculum?
- How do Te Whāriki, Ka Hikitia and Tātaiako inform our bicultural practice?
- What do we know about the impact of our bicultural curriculum for Māori children? For all children in our service?

(ERO, 2013, p. 13)

The teachers at Katoa Kindergarten are fortunate in that they work within He Whānau Manaaki o Tararua Kindergarten Association, which is committed to very high quality, culturally responsive practice, and provides multiple supports for their teachers. All their teachers are degree-level qualified, and are supported by senior teachers who visit regularly to oversee their practice and programmes, and the association provides regular professional learning opportunities for their teachers.

Kindergarten context

Public kindergartens in Aotearoa NZ have a particular history which has been well documented (May 1997, 2009; May & Bethell, 2017). They have long upheld a com-mitment to a child-centred philosophy, grounded in democratic origins. According to Helen May and Kerry Bethell, the early kindergarten movement in Aotearoa NZ:

> supported progressive education ideals and practices that recognised children as active rather than passive learners. Their vision was to influence and shape the education of young children as democratic citizens, in particular using the

teachings of Froebel, but also the newer ideas of John Dewey that were circulating amongst the educational elite.

(May & Bethell, 2017, p. 19)

An important commitment of the public kindergarten sector has been to staffing their services with fully qualified teachers, which in Aotearoa NZ means a minimum university undergraduate degree-level qualification. Public kindergartens belong to regional Kindergarten Associations, which oversee staffing and programmes of their constituent kindergartens. The Associations in turn belong to the national overarching organisation 'NZ Kindergartens Incorporated Te Pūtahi Kura Puhou o Aotearoa' (2018) which represents the collective interests of 25 regional kindergarten associations. The Associations receive bulk funding from the government towards staffing and other expenses.

Katoa Kindergarten is one of 85 kindergartens that belong to the not-for-profit organisation, He Whānau Manaaki o Tararua Free Kindergarten Association (2018). In addition to following *Te Whāriki* and other Ministry of Education and Teaching Council documents, teachers in He Whānau Manaaki Association utilise *Te Manawa: Criteria for Curriculum Implementation* (2011), which is intended to support their teachers to be 'collaborative, critical, reflective, and high performing' (Coulston, as cited in Wellington Kindergartens | Ngā Māra Tamariki, p. 7).

Overview of Katoa community

Katoa Kindergarten is in the Wellington regional city of Porirua. On the Katoa Kindergarten website, under the heading 'About Us and Our Programme', the description begins with the whakataukī of the famous Māori chief, Te Rauparaha, that is recited at mat-times every day at Katoa Kindergarten:

> Ka oho te wairua, ka matāra te tinana, he aroha ki te aroha, ka kā te rāma.
> When the spirit is awakened, when the body is alert, when the love is unconditional, enlightenment flows. Nā Te Rauparaha

The introductory statement goes on to recognise their location, around the corner from Takapuwāhia Marae, which is a prominent marae [traditional village and meeting place] of the local tribe, Ngāti Toa Rangatira:

> Ka oho te wairua, ka matāra te tinana, he aroha ki te aroha, ka kā te rāma. When the spirit is awakened, when the body is alert, when the love is unconditional, enlightenment flows. Nā Te Rauparaha
> This whakatauki has meaning to us as it was said by one of our chiefs, Te Rauparaha.
> Our kindergarten is based in beautiful Elsdon in Porirua, right in the heart of Ngati Toa iwi. We are fortunate to be close to our local Marae, Takapuwahia and visit the Marae weekly to read stories, sing songs and just hang out.

(He Whanau Manaaki, Katoa Kindergarten, 2019).

At the beginning of this study in 2015, the national museum Te Papa, located in the nearby capital city of Wellington, was hosting a prestigious exhibition of Ngāti Toa Rangatira history (Museum of NZ Te Papa Tongarewa, 2017), which serendipitously coincided with the theme of 'Ko wai ahau?' (Who am I?) that the teachers had chosen as their first focus for the year. The kindergarten did a field trip to view this exhibition, and children and their whānau with ties to this tribe were duly acknowledged for these important ancestral connections.

In 2015, the ERO report noted that the ethnic composition of the kindergarten was as follows:

Māori	35
NZ European/Pākehā	10
Samoan	4
Pacific	10
Other ethnic groups	3

Due to the urban migration of many rural Māori post World War II, encouraged by the government in order to remedy a labour shortage in the factory sector, many Māori live in urban areas away from their tribal lands. There is a distinction that is very clear in te ao Māori (the Māori world) between tangata whenua, literally 'people of the land', a generic term for the Indigenous people of Aotearoa, and mana whenua, those people who hold the mana, or authority over a particular tribal area, due to their whakapapa, their genealogical connections. A further caution is needed with regard to the Ministry of Education's tendency to aggregate diverse peoples from a range of different islands into the generic category 'Pacific Island'.

The following description of Katoa Kindergarten is provided by the ERO in its 2015 report:

Katoa Kindergarten's philosophy is highly evident in practice. The philosophy focuses on providing a welcoming, relaxed environment for all, which features whakawhanaungatanga [relationship building], kotahitanga [collectivity] and manaakitanga [caring, kindness, generosity, hospitality]. Developing strong relationships is a priority, and the role of the family in children's learning is valued, promoted and supported. Children and their whānau have a sense of belonging. The wellbeing of children and whānau aspirations are at the heart of decision making and planning. Teachers work collaboratively as a team. There is a sense of ako where children, whānau and teachers work together as a community of learners. Relationships between staff, parents, whānau and the community are supportive. Strong links with local iwi [tribes] and a marae [tribal meeting place] assists Katoa Kindergarten's commitment to bicultural practices. Children are viewed as capable and confident explorers and they are supported to problem-solve and take risks. They play cooperatively, learning to take turns and listen to each other. Careful consideration is given to supporting children when they start kindergarten. The kindergarten has developed positive links with local schools to support children and their whānau in transitions. Teachers attend local pōwhiri and hui [welcoming ceremonies and meetings] creating a collaborative culture with its community.

(ERO, 2015)

The kindergarten runs daily sessions from 8.30–2.30 for 40 children aged 2–5, with the additional service of a playgroup for younger children attending with a parent or caregiver who join in alongside the older children until 11.30am each morning. At the time of the study there were six full-time kindergarten teachers and one further part-time teacher whose role was to support the playgroup that runs alongside the kindergarten programme.

Teachers' pedagogical approaches

One of the key findings of our study was that young children's civic action, whilst often spontaneous, is encouraged when teachers pro-actively foster and model foundational dispositions such as co-operation, caring, kindness and empathy. When considering how the teaching team enhanced children's enactment of community building within the environment, it is important to contemplate the pedagogical planning and evaluative framework that is used. At Katoa Kindergarten there was a pre-established and embedded methodology for a 'community of learners approach' to group planning, that followed clear and directive systems. These provoked regular reflection and evaluation regarding the ways in which we plan our intentional teaching with regard to learning as a collective.

This community of learners approach to group planning was established in accordance with 'Te Manawa' (Wellington Kindergartens | Ngā Māra Tamariki, 2011). Te Manawa provides a set of 'criterion for curriculum development' developed by our association outlining quality practice in relation to the systems and processes that make up: intentional teaching, individual learning portfolios and a community of learners approach to group planning. It identifies the requirements for each section and provides indicators of what quality practice looks like. These criteria are used as a provocation for teaching teams to develop their own systems and processes for implementation.

The pre-established processes and systems that empowered the teaching team's community of learners approach to group planning at Katoa Kindergarten can be broken down into four main phases, with ongoing processes of reflection embedded into each. These phases are: observation, research, implementation and evaluation phase. This style of planning and implementation is grounded in values and processes conducive to fostering civic action, in that it is child-focused and supports teachers to uncover, unpack and channel learning that is occurring and significant to the kindergarten as a collective.

The process began with observations of our community of learners over a set period of time. We documented this by displaying an emerging learning template on our planning wall; each teacher contributed group learning that they had observed and identified as significant. For example, I (Jared) recall documenting Kaitiakitanga (guardianship, care-taking) on our emerging learning template when new children began at Katoa Kindergarten. I did this after observing a group of children welcome the new tamariki into the learning environment and teaching them about our kaupapa. Emerging learning sheets captured dispositions, as well as learning experiences such as children revisiting their learning in their individual portfolios, or groups of children constructing buildings together.

After the observational phase, the teaching team then came together to unpack trends by sharing what dispositions we had identified as being significant, along with examples of what they looked like in children's play. Unpacking these and identifying what learning is most predominant is where the enactment of civic action is made visible. As a focus is constructed from the interests and voices of all children, by tapping into what's current for children, we foster citizenship. In this way we demonstrate that children's words and actions influence their world. Once the focus is set, the team proceeds by establishing strategies and resources that empower tamariki to learn as a group, as one whānau.

Moving forward into the next phase of the group planning cycle, individual teachers take on and conduct their own areas of research related to the focus that has been identified. These areas included the following: theories, research, display, whānau voice, child voice, links to curricular documents and links to culture. Theories and research consisted of reading articles and theories and illustrating how a specific theory and article links to our focus. Display entailed designing and displaying our planning focus on a wall to demonstrate progression visibly to our community of learners. Links to curricular documents focused on demonstrating how our focus was represented within our national curriculum, along with other key publications, such as Tātaiako (NZ MoE & NZ Teaching Council, 2011). 'Child's and whānau voice' involved creating questions to capture our community of learners' thinking about our focus.

One key element of the research phase is cultural links, this included researching what our focus looked like in the many diverse cultures that made up the demographics of our kindergarten. When considering citizenship within an educational setting it is paramount to view the whānau and community as active citizens. Representation of the varying values within our diverse community empowers whānau to engage, role model and enact civic action within the setting.

Figure 5.1 is an example of a poster, which included an image of the source book's cover, that was produced by Trinity, the head teacher, and placed on the planning wall for whānau (families) and children to see.

To conclude the research phase of this cycle of teaching practice the teaching team would come together to share our findings and further develop a shared understanding

FIGURE 5.1 Head Teacher Trinity's poster 'Theory On Rangatiratanga'

of what our focus is. This strengthens how we plan to facilitate a learning environment that not only provokes collective learning relative to the focus, but more importantly empowers children to learn with their peers.

The final two phases, implementation and evaluation, work in association. The implementation phase begins immediately after the research phase and is essentially putting into practice the plan, teaching strategies and intentional pedagogy we have developed for our community of learners based on our focus. The evaluation phase consists of multiple reflection and evaluation templates developed to regularly review the effectiveness of our plan. The evaluation phase ensures that the focus stays relevant, continues to evolve and is conducted throughout the implementation of the plan. During the period of the study, focuses that were actioned included 'Ko wai ahau?', 'Social Competence', 'Exploration', 'Kotahitanga' and 'Rangatiratanga/Leadership'.

Here is an excerpt from a discussion between Jared and Jenny:

JARED: Okay so we had a goal it was part of our strategic teaching and learning goals and one of them was on the Treaty of Waitangi. So as a teaching team we split up and we took one of three principles and we had to read articles on it, do reflections on it and we had to go out and take photos of what we thought it looked like in action and so we created this wall display on the Treaty of Waitangi. What partnership looks like in action and it had pictures of children demonstrating partnership, and participation, and protection. From there we decided we would use our mat-times to create our own treaty based off this project. We sat down and had a hui with the children, they all feed in their ideas. We went over our 'good friend rules' you know kind words, safe hands, etc. So we stuck with those and then I think the children contributed their own. Created the treaty, made it look all beautiful and lay it out at a mat-time and invited the children to come up and sign it.

JENNY: Because I remember in one of my other research projects there was a kindergarten that did that every February. It's such a cool idea because it brings the treaty to be a living thing and children understand this is a relationship thing, this is how we work, how we live together and look after each other. It's not a big scary thing.

JARED: It helps the teachers as well because I think like it can be really easy to get caught up in the business of everyday teaching and learning and then when you get hit with all this additional paperwork and you have to learn this and you've got to unpack the treaty, which can be pretty scary if you don't.

JENNY: If you haven't been well schooled in it.

JARED: Exactly, it's like 'oooh!', you can't do it wrong.

JENNY: It can be intimidating, you don't want to cause offence.

JARED: It's very intimidating.

JENNY: Yes.

JARED: Especially in Katoa because it was in the pā [Māori community], and yeah it was good for the teachers because it took the intimidation away. It brought it into just what we do every day.

Māori values underpinning the philosophy and practice

Charles Te Ahukaramū Royal provides the following succinct explanation of six key te ao Māori constructs pertinent to this study:

A brief interpretation of the six concepts goes as follows: Rangatiratanga is concerned with leadership and defines leadership as the ability to bind (ranga) groups (tira) together. A rangatira binds groups together and a person who does not, can not be said to be a rangatira. Manaakitanga points to the mutual elevation of mana [power, prestige, esteem] in an encounter scenario. As one person or group encounters another, they go through some kind of process. If the outcome of that process sees the elevation of mana of both parties, then it can be said that manaakitanga has been expressed. Whanaungatanga denotes the interconnectedness of all things and this is shown in whakapapa [genealogical connectedness]. Tohungatanga concerns expertise and skill, particularly

with symbols, with interpreting them, with creating new symbols, with pre-
serving old symbols. Ukaipo are those spaces and places where one is nour-
ished. These spaces and places are likened to the mother's breast. Finally,
Kotahitanga denotes the unity of all things in the world.

(Royal, 1998, p. 5)

All of these values (except perhaps tohungatanga which was implicit rather than
referred to explicitly) are evident in the work of the Katoa Kindergarten teachers,
thoughtfully woven into their planning and learning stories.

Examples of civic action by tamariki

During the course of the data collection period for the study, many examples of
young children's civic action were identified, such as in the indicative list shown in
Table 5.1.

When reflecting on examples of civic action demonstrated in children's play, I
(Jared) categorised them into two domains: child-led, and intentional teaching.
'Child-led' signifies that the practice of civic action emerged spontaneously and
without the assistance or encouragement of teachers. Intentional teaching relates to
civic action that was empowered through the assistance or encouragement of the
teaching team.

   Child-led civic action is powerful in the sense that children are developing their
own understanding of citizenship and working as a collective without guidance and
through their own play. One significant example of child-led civic action was the
way in which our tamariki at Katoa Kindergarten responded to injured children.
As my educational brothers and sisters know in an early childhood setting, acci-
dents happen. Children fall over, graze their knee, obtain a cut, etc. At Katoa
Kindergarten when a child had an accident their peers would identify this and head
to the child-height fridge to get an ice-pack which was then offered to the injured
child with great care and attentiveness. They often shared what happened with a
teacher but took great pride in being the children who helped their injured peer.
Over time, this became an entrenched culture and a quality example of civic
action.

   Another example of child-led civic action that over time developed into an
entrenched culture was the kaupapa around kotahitanga te wā (group times), or
mat-times. When I first joined the teaching team at Katoa Kindergarten, I often
noticed teachers would ask the children before starting their mat-time, 'would you
like to do the karanga?' (call). This meant calling 'Haere mai ki te whāriki tamariki
mā' (come to the mat children). The children stood at the door calling as loudly as
they possibly could to gather our community together as one. This initially was
presumably an example of intentional teaching. However, over time I noticed that
this culture grew and evolved. It moved from being about one child calling the
karanga, to groups of children working as a collective to bring everyone together.
One morning I recall watching as nearly every child inside stood out the door and

TABLE 5.1 Some of the different kinds of civic actions observed at Katoa Kindergarten

Assisting with shared problem

Taking food scraps out to compost

Helping a child up when they have fallen

Walking over to help out (offer to help – can be non-verbal, making it a shared problem; solidarity)

Noticing someone is trying to reach out of reach object so walking over to help her

Noticing a friend has a bleeding nose and going and telling a teacher

Making suggestions to someone who is struggling to reach something

Overhearing that a child fell down and got hurt and then walking over to help them

Offering assistance to enable game to resume through relocation

Assisting with opening food packaging

Reminding of kindergarten eating practice

Noticing and return a piece of equipment that is in the incorrect space (to correct shelving)

Working together to obtain a hard-to-reach resource for other children to use

Passing the ukulele to younger child (non-verbal communication)

Noticing and offering to help when a resource (squab) is being taken away from a friend, that they were already using and offering to help

Noticing that someone is trying to open food packet and ask teacher for help

Noticing a child crying and leaning closer to see, mirroring a distressed child's body

Inventing a game to distract a distressed child and to get them to stop crying

Standing between someone on a bicycle and someone else coming at them with a stick and asking them to stop with their stick to ensure safety

Stepping in physically standing in the way to stop a possible incident

Inventing a collectively generated ball game non-verbally

Communicating rules

Reminding a child to sit down and eat

Standing alongside teacher who is calming a hurt child, silent communication of concern

Noticing messy playdough on floor and cleaning it up

Assisting others with serving meals and drinks

Opening food packets for others who are struggling and seeking help

Replenishing drinking glasses for others

Sweeping floor (own initiative)

Demonstrating patience

Waiting your turn by standing patiently and waiting if there aren't enough seats at the kai table

Ensuring others get a fair turn

Asking others not to harm the tree

Defending younger sister

Defending game from a perceived intruder

Caring for a hurt friend, such as assisting them to go inside and getting an ice-pack to place on injury

Asking someone if they feel okay

Giving up what you are doing to comfort a crying child

Showing a younger child how to do things

Putting out others' paintings to dry on rack

Offering to share each other's food

Showing someone how to accomplish a task

Enabling a friend to solve a problem

---

called 'haere mai ki te whāriki tamariki mā' as one. This is a powerful example of child-led civic action, in that it demonstrates a group of children working as a collective. To go deeper the collective were working together with the shared purpose being to gather their community.

One significant example of intentional teaching provoking civic action was our methodology when capturing children's voice to inform our planning. This supported us as a teaching team to reflect on and implement learning experiences as a direct response to what children shared. But, more importantly, it demonstrated to children that they are active citizens and participants in our community of learners, and that their voice is valuable and as a collective makes a difference to the construction and facilitation of their learning environment. Often the children's perspectives would be obtained by teachers during a mat-time. We would prepare our questions on a whiteboard beforehand. One teacher would ask the questions, another would record responses and the other teachers would be active participants in the discussion. We participated by unpacking concepts identified in the discourse. For example, at one mat-time child 'A' shared 'leadership means being a good friend', and one of the teachers replied, 'Great answer, and very interesting. What does being a good friend look like?' This approach to participation enabled children to share their thoughts and ideas in a safe and supportive environment. This is only one of the many ways the teaching team at Katoa Kindergarten purposefully empowered children to practise civic action.

Whanaungatanga – engaging whānau (families)

The weather today is very cold and wet and there is nobody playing outside. Inside the centre, four whānau members in the kitchen stand chatting to a couple of staff members who are preparing hot drinks and morning tea for themselves. The remainder of the staff are sitting at various tables supervising the children eating morning tea. The centre is filled with a wonderful aroma coming from the food cooking in the oven. I am invited to make myself some morning tea and encouraged to take some food from several covered plates on the bench in the kitchen. Jessie explains to me that Papa Barry (Emma and Carolina's grandfather)[1] has brought in some rolled pork for the staff to cook for lunch. She says that he often gets asked by hunters and whānau to bone out carcasses before the meat is taken to the butcher, and he always saves some meat for the centre.

[Fieldnotes, Katoa Kindergarten]

Empowering the whānau and community to be active participants and citizens is paramount as a key principle of Te Whāriki, and thus in the success of facilitating an authentic 'community of learners' approach to group planning. Three main practices are significant in this regard. Firstly, it is important that as teachers we are intentional in this approach and that our strategies are purposefully designed by the teaching team to support whānau engagement. Several examples from the Katoa approach include obtaining whānau voice, and the facilitation of information evenings and whānau days. Whānau were invited on the many excursions that took place, which during the period of the study included frequent visits to the local marae, a trip to Te Papa the national museum of Aotearoa NZ, a visit to the Wellington wildlife sanctuary Zealandia, to the nearby Tītahi Bay North School, and to Junglerama, an indoor adventure playground. Teachers' reflections after a pōwhiri (welcoming ceremony) for new teachers, children and families at Takapuwāhia Marae included the following:

What stood out for teachers?

- Families from other cultural backgrounds experiencing marae for the first time
- Really great feedback about karanga – feeling more confident
- Children's curiosity around carvings. Children did lots of touching. Great conversations
- Enjoyed being in the wharenui [meeting-house] with the children – let the children be free, let them touch. Brings it alive, children's mana into the energy of marae
- Great whānau turn out
- Lots of connections with Māori families who aren't Ngāti Toa
- We went through the process, taking shoes off at wharenui, eating at the end to close the time off. Some weren't too sure about hongi [traditional greeting] – maybe we practise it with tamariki
- Some families who were Ngāti Toa wanting their children to walk in and experience pōwhiri as manuhiri [guests] because they hadn't been on before
- Insightful conversations with whānau – observing children in action

What we would do differently?

- Empowering our Ngāti Toa families to be active tangata whenua
- Building relationships on our side – keep walking the roads, keep making the connections
- Maybe more kaumātua [Elders] morning teas, family hui
- We want our children to see old people singing old songs – how can we get that to happen?

During the research phase of our planning process, one of the key roles is researching the whānau voice. In a similar way to the focus on gathering examples of child's voice, it entails the construction of questions to elicit an understanding of the views of our whānau around our focus. This information is then used to inform our plan and support our whānau to deepen their understanding of the focus as well as participate in its implementation. Again, it demonstrates to our whānau that they are citizens in our learning community and that their voice is important.

At Katoa Kindergarten, information evenings and whānau days were held each term and involved providing information to our whānau and community about early childhood education and bringing our community and whānau together to participate in our programme through morning teas, shared lunches and much more.

One distinctive example of civic action that I (Jared) can recount was during a parent information evening. We had invited Jenny to share some valuable information acquired and the methodology of the research project on civic action. As part of the information sharing, Jenny displayed a video that captured children working as a collective. Immediately whānau begun to share their thoughts with one another expressing thoughts such as 'That's my child', 'Oh that is so her', 'He does that at home too', 'He always helps his sister too', etc., as they watched their children practise civic action. This demonstrates the enactment of civic action in that our whānau community were empowered to learn about how their children navigate play at Katoa Kindergarten. Their thoughts and ideas were then strengthened through the encouragement of sharing them with other members of the learning community, such as other parents and teachers. In this example whānau worked together with the shared purpose of learning about civic action in the context of early childhood education.

Parents were also engaged during the transitioning of tamariki from kindergarten to school. The teaching team worked hard to build and maintain the connections we held with the local schools; because of where we were situated we feed into five different local schools. When considering how to create a transition process that supports the individual child and fosters connections with these schools there was one thing that always stood out for me. That was the consistency and accessibility to a transition into school. Trinity talked to us about all children having the right to a quality transition and all children receiving the same process. So she established a procedure that would ensure children and teachers could connect with the local schools, acquire the information that school deems as essential for parents to know prior to starting and to display this so that is accessible for all whānau. From there we had a starting point to grow our relationships with the local schools. I can remember inviting representatives from each school to attend one of our whānau information evenings, so that they could meet the parents and answer any questions they may have. It also provided us a great opportunity to have discussions with the teachers and foster our growing relationships.

Rangatiratanga – leadership

Rangatiratanga operates at both the individual level as self-management and as leadership in service of the collective (Mead, 2003). Attributes of a rangatira include 'exhibiting nobility of character' (Benton et al., 2013, p. 325) and demonstrating 'leadership through exemplary action' (Vayda, 1960, p. 29, as cited in Benton et al., 2013 p. 329). The literal meaning refers to the capacity to weave (raranga) the group of people (tira) together, as expressed in the following extract:

> Te rangatira, he kai ranga i te tira: i te tira o te hapu o te iwi. Ki nga haere, ki nga mahi e pa ana ki te hapu ki te iwi. He kai arahi. He kai timata he kai whakatutuki i nga mahi, ka whai ai te iwi i raro. Ka kiia te tinana penei he 'rangatira' ko tenei kawai rangatira tonu tenei, e manaakitia ai, e piki ai, e mana ai, ki roto ki tetahi iwi ke. [Translation by Te Mātāhauariki]: The chief is someone who can bind the people at both hapu and iwi level in their endeavours. She is a leader. She starts and finishes tasks and is followed by the people. She is described as a chief whose chiefly lines are held in regard, increased and distinguished, by other tribes.
>
> *(Dr Wi Repa, 1926, as cited in Benton et al., 2013, p. 326)*

Furthermore, rangatiratanga is earned through demonstration of one's leadership capacities: 'Rangatira was people bestowed' (Te Rangihau, as cited in Benton et al., 2013, p. 329). It is also associated with autonomy and self-determination (Bishop, 2011).

Te rangatiratanga o te manaakitanga – collectively caring

> Good friends
> listen to each other
> use good words
> safe hands
> *(Good Friends poster on the wall at Katoa Kindergarten)*

Rangatiratanga is not only demonstrated through verbal pronouncements, it can be seen in non-verbal enactment, such as is evident in examples of manaakitanga (caring, generosity):

Johnny is lying face down on the ground crying. There are children playing tag-type games all around him. Layton steps over him, initially paying no attention to the fact that Johnny is crying. Having moved a few steps away from Johnny, Layton turns around, goes back to him bending down to check on him. Johnny responds to this concern by moving up onto his hands and knees. Layton imitates this position and they start 'barking' at each other. This attention diverts Johnny from crying and together, Johnny and Layton go to the building block area and start playing cooperatively.

[Fieldnotes, Katoa Kindergarten]

During the study we recorded numerous occasions of children showing manaaki (care) for others, as seen in the following example:

Jessica [teacher] has joined the kai table and notices Tama trying to open his yoghurt pottle. She demonstrates what he needs to do then encourages him to try to open the pottle himself. When he is successful, Jessica says 'Ka pai, Tama!' Jessica is now watching Calvin attempting to open a cereal bar with the child-size scissors that are attached to the wall beside the kai table. Calvin spends considerable time attempting to cut the packet and is eventually successful. Jessica then expresses her surprise and delight when Calvin takes the cereal bar and gives it to Zena. Jessica inquires, 'Were you being helpful to Zena? That's great leadership. You are very caring! Ka pai Calvin!'

[Fieldnotes, Katoa Kindergarten]

Usually when I (Jenny) arrived at the kindergarten, I would do the rounds, chatting to each teacher in turn as they became available. On one occasion, Sonya told me about a mat-time game she had recently facilitated, in which children had to recall an object from amongst those on a tray which she had covered over. Karena, a younger girl, had been having difficulty in recalling the particular object. The other children started to help her out by offering her clues, but Karena still didn't respond. So Sonya had asked children to put up their hands if they knew the answer and chose one of the older children, Ross, to respond, whereby he answered correctly 'Frog'. So Sonya called Ross over to duly collect the frog as per the structure of the game. Instead of keeping the frog for himself, Ross took the frog and gave it to Karena, the child who had struggled to name it. I also noted that at breakfast time Ross had been helping the other children on his own initiative by dishing out the rice bubbles and also by wiping the table as the bowls were removed.

Jared writes:

I remember this day very clearly, I had a great relationship with Ross and loved working with him around his social strategies to enter play, see kindergarten as a place he belongs (tūrangawaewae), but also to establish and maintain relationships. At the time we had the respect stone and book, it was a special stone that one child would be awarded each week. They would be invited to the front of the mat and a teacher would read the story behind why they had received the rock. They would then take it home with them along with a book where they would colour it in with their whānau. The children loved receiving the rock and it held a lot of social power among the peer group. I remember nominating Ross for the respect stone and book to celebrate his kaitiakitanga caringness for others at the mat-time with the frog he so generously gave to his peer he could see was struggling to articulate what they wanted to say. To helping others get their breakfast and cleaning up with them. I was so proud of Ross this day.

Te rangatiranga: kia mōhio ai rātou ki ō rātou mana ake – self-confidence and pride

One day Jenny observed how Vinnie, a two-year-old boy, had gone to retrieve his own bag, taken it into the bathroom, taken off his nappy, and got a clean nappy out of his bag. Sonya had been respectfully monitoring this from the kitchen, via the mirror. Eventually Maddie went into the bathroom to assist Vinnie to complete the exercise. She asked him 'Kua mutu?' [Are you finished?] and reminded him to 'Horoi o ringaringa' [Wash your hands]. Maddie then guided him to complete the exercise. Jared recalls this child's particular self-determining routine and elaborates:

> I (Jared) remember Vinnie and the rituals he had created around changing his nappy. I remember this significantly because it was one of the first times I saw the team at Katoa Kindergarten really valuing the uniqueness of the child. There was a consistent procedure we all followed when doing nappies, and all teachers followed it. It meant that children who had nappy changes knew what to expect and became comfortable with a familiar kaupapa. However, this one boy was not comfortable with it. He had his own way of changing his nappy and he needed his autonomy. Vinnie would not climb up on the changing table, he did not like being lifted up on the changing table. What Vinnie liked was independence, if someone was going to change his nappy it would be him. So slowly over time I watched as he rebelled against the pre-set kaupapa [procedure] until eventually Jess one of the teachers there called me into the bathroom to encourage me to observe how Vinnie changes his nappy and learn about his own nappy kaupapa. After my observations and a few discussion with Jess I worked out that Vinnie liked to

> 1   Be on the ground and on the floor
> 2   Be standing up – not lying down
> 3   He would remove his own pants, and nappy
> 4   The teacher would support him to clean himself with a wet wipe
> 5   He would then put his own nappy back on with the help of a teacher
> 6   Followed by his clothes
> 7   But no stickers or praise

It was a beautiful example of how the teaching team had created this purposeful kaupapa around routines to support children to be comfortable with a familiar process and the regular events of the day. But they were also open to a child-led curriculum when their kaupapa didn't quite fit the individual needs of the child. The Katoa team managed to do this in such a seamless and harmonious way.

Te rangatiratanga i roto i te whanaungatanga o te tuakana me te teina – looking after one's kin

> In the outside covered area, Bonnie calls out to her sister 'Come here Maia'. They sit together on the opposite side of the table from me. Bonnie explains that 'Maia is two. I am (holds up four fingers)'. Bonnie opens up her lunch box then runs off to the bag area by the entrance doorway. She returns to the table with Maia's lunch box and opens it up for her. They each start eating food from their respective lunch boxes, then Maia runs off. Bonnie pulls Maia's lunch box closer to hers, closes the lid and says 'I'll look after it here by me'. Bonnie eats some more food then takes the drink bottle from the side of Maia's box. She asks 'please open my drink' then drinks from Maia's bottle. After a few more mouthfuls of food, Bonnie closes up her box and the drink bottle, and makes two trips to return the containers to the bag area.
>
> *[Fieldnotes, Katoa Kindergarten]*

One afternoon during the study, in conversation with Jenny regarding the pairs of siblings attending, Jared listed nine sets of tuakana/teina [older/younger siblings], and pointed out that in addition to these siblings, there was a further number of cousins in attendance.

Jared writes:

> Reflecting on when I spoke about Holly and her brother Layton, I can see the same thing happened with Bonnie and her younger sister Maia. Bonnie took on a supportive role for her younger sister and taught her about our kindergarten kaupapa. Evidently, this also translated into her peer relationships and she was another natural leader. Looking back I wonder how much having a younger sibling empowered children at kindergarten, and if these roles demonstrated to their peers the kind of friends they could be. Perhaps this is why both Bonnie and Holly were strong leaders within the peer culture. I can't say for sure, but I do know both had younger siblings, both actively cared for them, and both held power within the peer group.
>
> When I (Jared) started at Katoa Kindergarten I remember Trinity and Anne (the administrator) talking to me about the whānau approach to enrolment. This meant that when admitting children into Kindergarten, their connections to the kindergarten were valued first before age order. This also meant that the needs of the local whānau and community were met. But it also created a stable and consistent peer culture. This is evident in the listed siblings within the centre, and multiple cousins and relatives that attended Katoa Kindergarten.

JARED: It's interesting because what I talked about quite a bit was the children that had siblings in the centre. I found that the older siblings took on that supportive role. You know how there's children and in the peer culture there's the core peer group and other children on the peripheries. The older siblings were never on the peripheries they never had to fight to the top. But they were natural leaders and I talked about not really knowing but identifying both the two older sisters I mentioned who took on this supportive role and whether other children saw these values and these dispositions and whether that showed.

JENNY: It modelled it for them.

JARED: Yeah and that these values easily translated into their peer relationships.

JENNY: Just seeing that growth over time of children being really shy and introverted to suddenly being the ones that you know, who were going out and getting the ice-packs, or whatever it was.

JARED: I just feel like it was a really clear kaupapa [philosophy], the peer group was stable, you know, there was always a set, like the younger ones would move up and then the older ones would go to school. But the kaupapa always stayed the same, so it was really easy for the younger children to transition into leadership roles. Because they knew, you know, go get the ice-pack when someone's hurt.

Te rangatiratanga me te kotahitanga – collectivity

One of the functions of rangatiratanga is to generate a sense of collective and unity of purpose. This is illustrated in the following learning story, written by Jared:

Kia ora Mariana

Looking back through your learning profile I (Jared) can see that you are a bright and confident learner. This is highlighted throughout your learning profile. Recently at Kindergarten we have decided as a teaching team that we would focus on children's sense of kotahitanga (unity and togetherness) as our planning story, and today you showed some outstanding leadership skills and a real sense of Kotahitanga in the sand pit. Mariana over the past week I have noticed that you have been an active part of engaging in pretend play at the sandpit with your peers. This is clearly a strong interest of yours, so today I decided I would come and talk to you and asked 'what are you making?' and you turned around straight away with a big smile on your face and said 'chocolate soup, would you like some?' I quickly replied 'of course I would, who wouldn't want to try chocolate soup?' While you were preparing my soup I noticed how well your group operated as a team, each person had their own individual role but you were all still communicating and working collaboratively. Malia and Alan were collecting water and bringing it back to the sandpit, Natalie was filling up buckets of sand and bringing them over to you, and you were mixing all the ingredients together in a cake tin. Mariana, I loved the way that you encouraged everyone to work together and ultimately created some beautiful pretend dishes for your peers to share. Te Whāriki highlights the importance of kotahitanga and establishes this as a principle that underpins the curriculum, it suggests that kotahitanga is about having respect for the holistic way in which children grow and learn. Mariana I could see that you were able to lead the group today and did it with respect for the way in which everyone worked, this shows robust leadership skills. (Kaiako Jared)

(Learning story, Katoa Kindergarten)

I (Jenny) recall four-year-old Mariana as demonstrating her deep concern for others on several occasions. In one of the videos that was shared with teachers across the project, Mariana is the child who gently responds when another, young girl, Zena, is accidently knocked over by Natalie. Mariana moves over to Zena and tends to her, leading her inside, whilst Natalie rushes ahead to get an ice-pack. Zena recovers. However, on returning from replacing the ice-pack in the fridge, Mariana trips over a chair leg, falling heavily to the floor and this time the younger child Zena reciprocates and sits Mariana down, and in turn fetches the ice-pack for her.

Annabel was a very shy two-year-old who constantly shadowed her older brother David. One afternoon Annabel had injured her toe and was crying inconsolably, despite being carried by a teacher who had sent another child out to bring David in to offer Annabel some comfort, although to no avail. David returned outside, and meanwhile Mariana came and stood alongside the still sobbing Annabel, resonating her empathy for such misery. Some months later after Annabel's older brother David had left for school, some of the older girls took over his role in supporting Annabel, forming a community of care for this younger child. Rolene recorded the following:

Annabel and Martha are playing at the entrance way with some blocks. They run off to the climbing frame. Annabel says 'let's play on the swing'. They climb onto separate swings, side by side, laughing and smiling at each other. Annabel only stays a few moments then runs back to the climbing frame. Martha goes to join her after about a minute but trips up in the process. Jarrod sees this, waits a moment, then goes over to check on Martha who is still lying on the ground clutching her knee and whimpering. Annabel joins them. Jarrod says 'Annabel, can you help Martha get an ice-pack?' Annabel doesn't say anything but starts to head inside; Martha follows her. There is no verbal interaction between the girls. Annabel goes to the bench-high fridge and gets out the ice-pack, gives it to Martha then also fetches and gives her a paper towel. She helps Martha hold it on her knee. This action lasts less than a minute before they tidy up together, putting the paper towel in the bin and ice-pack back in the fridge. The only conversation occurs when Annabel asks 'You okay now?' The girls run back outside, play briefly on the climbing frame then run back inside.

(Fieldnotes, Katoa Kindergarten)

What we came to know about young children's community building at Katoa Kindergarten

In our study we learned from carefully observing young children's ways of being, knowing, doing and relating. This led us to identify ways in which we might shift away from 'adultist' views of citizenship such as having the right to vote, to instead view young children's community building as their way of enacting civic concern and responsibility. Not all of the expressions of civic action were bold and visible, many were more subtle and embodied, such as the child positioning herself alongside a hurt friend, her or his physical presence resonating concern, solidarity and empathy. We also recognised the importance of teachers' intentional, thoughtful and collective processes to enacting their pedagogy, which was grounded in the careful noticing of children's expressions of feelings and needs, and which also deliberately included whānau through a range of daily, weekly and annual means of engagement. The sociocultural, collective approach of the teachers in their planning, teaching and evaluation process enabled a shared philosophy to be enacted in consistent ways that reinforced young children's civic action, hopefully laying foundations for life-long caring and concern for their communities.

What I (Jared) learnt from participating in this project

Reflecting on what I've learnt over the time I have been involved in this research project is difficult. It's difficult to separate personal growth, and life lessons from professional growth, and the acquisition of new knowledge. I write this because during this time frame a lot has happened for me professionally as well as personally.

From when I first started at Katoa Kindergarten being a full-time qualified teacher to growing and developing my practice, pedagogy and leadership. I have since moved into a Head Teacher role, and continue to grow and learn from it.

From my first discussion with Jenny about what civic action meant, because in the beginning I had no idea. To having ongoing conversations with her about what civic action looks like for an adult and how to reconceptualise this into the context of Early Child Education – with the emphasis of community building.

There is one intersection between what I have learnt both personally and professionally and that is to not take life for granted. Professionally I learnt about the importance for challenging societal norms that trap us in a outdated perspective of what an active citizen looks like. Professionally I learnt about speaking up for what matters and taking my role as an educator as a position of significance. As I have the opportunity to challenge bias or stay silent and contribute to New Zealand's collective sense of amnesia as discussed in Chapter Seven and inadvertently empower the common misconception of westernised superiority. Personally I experienced loss and grief, as I lost my twin brother. This is where the two intersect, professionally I now know what is just, and I know I need to advocate. Personally I now know that life is for living, that we are all given a voice and that we decide what we use it for – advocacy, or suppression.

I have learnt about what it means to be a citizen as an adult, and I have learnt how to translate that into community building for young children. I learnt how to use my voice and so, my challenge to all teachers who read this piece of work is this: how will you contribute to building citizenship? and how will you use your voice for the Indigenous people of your land?

Note

1 All children's and family members' names have been changed to pseudonyms.

References

Benton, R., Frame, A. & Meredith, P. (2013). *Te Mātāpunenga. A Compendium of References to the Concepts and Institutions of Māori Customary Law*. Wellington: Victoria University Press.

Bishop, R. (2011). *Freeing Ourselves*. Rotterdam: Sense.

Bruner, J. & Haste, H. (1987). *Making Sense*. London: Methuen.

Carr, M. & May, H. (1991, 8–12 September). National curriculum guidelines for early childhood in Aotearoa/New Zealand: a philosophical framework for development. Paper presented at the Fifth Early Childhood Convention, Dunedin.

Education Council Aotearoa NZ. (2017). *Our code our standards*. Wellington, NZ: Education Council. Retrieved from https://educationcouncil.org.nz/content/our-code-our-standards

Education Review Office. (2013). *Working with Te Whāriki*. Wellington, NZ: ERO. Retrieved from http://www.ero.govt.nz/publications/working-with-te-whariki/

Education Review Office. (2015). *Evaluation of Katoa Kindergarten*. Wellington, NZ: ERO. Retrieved from http://www.ero.govt.nz/review-reports/katoa-kindergarten-17-06-2015/

Education Review Office. (2018). *Engaging with Te Whāriki*. Wellington, NZ: ERO. Retrieved from https://www.ero.govt.nz/publications/engaging-with-te-whariki-2017/

Erikson, E. H. (1950). *Childhood and Society*. New York: Norton.

He Whānau Manaaki o Tararua Free Kindergarten Association. (2018). *Kindergarten – Education & Care. Whānau Manaaki*. Retrieved from http://www.wmkindergartens.org.nz/

He Whānau Manaaki o Tararua Free Kindergarten Association. (2019). *Katoa Kindergarten*. Retrieved from http://www.wmkindergartens.org.nz/Find-Kindergarten/Porirua/Katoa-Kindergarten-__I.1826__C.1456__N.135

Katz, L. G. (1975) Early childhood education and ideological disputes. *Educational Forum*, 38 (3), 267–271.

May, H. (1997). *The Discovery of Early Childhood*. Auckland: Bridget Williams Books, Auckland University Press.

May, H. (2009). *Politics in the Playground: The World of Early Childhood in New Zealand* (2nd edn). Dunedin: Otago University Press.

May, H. & Bethell, K. (2017). *Growing a Kindergarten Movement in Aotearoa New Zealand: Its People, Purposes and Politics*. Wellington: NZCER Press.

Mead, H. M. (2003). *Tikanga Māori. Living by Māori Values*. Wellington: Huia.

Museum of NZ Te Papa Tongarewa (2017). *Whiti te Rā! The Story of Ngāti Toa Rangatira*. Retrieved from https://www.tepapa.govt.nz/about/past-exhibitions/2017-past-exhibitions/whiti-te-ra-story-ngati-toa-rangatira

NZ Kindergartens Inc. Te Pūtahi Kura Puhou o Aotearoa (2018). *These are the wonder years*. Retrieved from https://nzkindergarten.org.nz/

NZ Ministry of Education (1996). *Te Whāriki. He whāriki mātauranga mō ngā mokopuna o Aotearoa: Early Childhood Curriculum.* Wellington, NZ: MoE. Retrieved from https://education.govt.nz/assets/Documents/Early-Childhood/Te-Whariki-1996.pdf

NZ Ministry of Education (2004–2009). *Kei Tua o te Pae/Assessment for Learning: Early Childhood Exemplars.* Wellington, NZ: Learning Media. Retrieved from http://education.govt.nz/early-childhood/teaching-and-learning/assessment-for-learning/kei-tua-o-te-pae-2/

NZ Ministry of Education (2004). *Bicultural Assessment. He aromatawai ahurea rua.* Wellington, NZ: Learning Media. Retrieved from https://education.govt.nz/early-childhood/teaching-and-learning/assessment-for-learning/kei-tua-o-te-pae-2/bicultural-assessment-he-aromatawai-ahurea-rua/

NZ Ministry of Education (2009a). *Ka Hikitia. Managing for Success. Māori Education Strategy 2008–2012.* Wellington, NZ: MoE. Retrieved from http://www.parliament.nz/resource/en-nz/49SCMA_EVI_00DBSCH_INQ_9064_1_A14037/0449a92c3574c1e5b0f850ae1fdb155b155fe3aa

NZ Ministry of Education (2009b). *Te Whatu Pōkeka. Kaupapa Māori Assessment for Learning. Early Childhood Exemplars.* Wellington, NZ: Learning Media. Retrieved from https://www.education.govt.nz/early-childhood/teaching-and-learning/assessment-for-learning/te-whatu-pokeka-english/

NZ Ministry of Education (2013). *Ka Hikitia. AcceleratingSsuccess. 2013–2017. The Māori Education Strategy.* Wellington, NZ: MoE. Retrieved from https://education.govt.nz/ministry-of-education/overall-strategies-and-policies/the-maori-education-strategy-ka-hikitia-accelerating-success-20132017/the-maori-education-strategy-ka-hikitia-accelerating-success-2013-2017/

NZ Ministry of Education (2017). *Te Whāriki. He whāriki mātauranga mō ngā mokopuna o Aotearoa. Early Childhood Curriculum.* Wellington, NZ: MoE. Retrieved from https://www.education.govt.nz/early-childhood/teaching-and-learning/te-whariki/

NZ Ministry of Education & NZ Teachers Council (2011). *Tātaiako: Cultural Competencies for Teachers of Māori Learners.* Wellington, NZ: MoE & Teachers Council. Retrieved from https://educationcouncil.org.nz/required/Tataiako.pdf

Piaget, J. & Inhelder, B. (1969). *The Psychology of the Child.* New York: Basic Books

Ritchie, J. (2012). An overview of early childhood care and education provision in 'mainstream' settings, in relation to kaupapa Māori curriculum and policy expectations. *Pacific-Asian Education,* 24(2), 9–22.

Roopnarine, J. L. & Johnson, J. E. (1987) *Approaches to Early Childhood Education.* Columbus Ohio: Merrill.

Royal, T. A. C. (1998). Te Ao Marama – a research paradigm. *He Pūkenga Kōrero,* 4(1), 1–8.

Te One, S. (2003). The context for Te Whāriki: contemporary issues of influence. In J. Nuttall (Ed.), *Weaving Te Whāriki* (pp. 17–49). Wellington, NZ: NZCER.

Vygotsky, L. (1968). *Mind in Society.* Cambridge MA: Harvard University Press.

Wellington Kindergartens | Ngā Māra Tamariki. (2011). *Te Manawa. Criterion for Curriculum Implementation.* Wellington, NZ: Wellington Kindergartens.

6

ENVIRONMENTS AND PEDAGOGIES FOR CHILDREN'S COMMUNITY BUILDING

Our critical ethnographic and decolonising methodological approach as outlined in Chapter Three involved working closely with teachers in the two research sites documenting and discussing children's engagement in the daily life of the centres. As one aspect of data gathering we employed the use of video as a means of data recording. On two occasions during the course of the study, edited videos were shared with educators and children between sites, drawing from Joe Tobin and colleagues' video-cued multivocal ethnography to create transnational/intercultural dialogues about pedagogical ideas (as discussed in Chapter Three). In our project, the focus of these video-cued discussions was on young children's civic action which we came to view as community building.

Early on in the study we shared a three-minute video from each site of children engaging in what we recognised as civic action. From Gundoo, we shared a video clip of Ezra and Talia catching a bee (detailed in Adair, Phillips, Ritchie & Sachdeva, 2016). Katoa shared a video of one child caring for another who had bumped her knee and another group climbing on and in and wheeling around a wheelie bin with a child inside it. In order to have a three-site discussion of these preliminary videos, the educators from each site in Australia, New Zealand and the USA were linked together through google hangout. On seeing Gundoo's video of bee catching, educators in the US were immediately alarmed by the children's bare feet and the risk of the bee stinging the children. The readily accepted practice at Gundoo was recognised as highly risky in the US. Bena from Gundoo explained that:

> It's up to the children whether they want to wear shoes. It helps us to connect to country. We feel more connected to country. Nothing in our regulations

says our children have to wear shoes. It's the children's choice. It's how children move around in community.

The Katoa teachers agreed, as children are generally trusted to choose whether or not they wish to wear shoes. Doctrines of childhood innocence and thus the need for protection that are strongly apparent in the litigious society of the USA have yet to severely impact early childhood care and education discourses in Aotearoa via restrictive safety rules and regulations. (In Australia, emphasis has been on injury prevention placing strict regulations and standards on equipment (Little, 2006)). Sonya appreciated that there was no teacher intervention and the respect for children to explore freely in connection with nature, to which Bena replied 'it comes natural to us. We are Aboriginal people. We teach the children that the land owns us, we don't own the land'.

In a subsequent discussion about the day in the life video, the bare feet of the Gundoo children were again noted, with one of the Katoa teachers saying 'I like the bare feet'. Scott responded:

> That was a comment that the Americans had when they were watching the video. They had a safety concern. And the Australians said it is about connecting to the earth, grounding themselves. I was barefoot in England and someone said 'Can't you afford shoes?'

This remark stems from social class delineations, whereby the capacity to afford shoes is deemed to signify belonging to a superior social class than those who can't. The teachers at Katoa were very comfortable in the working-class community setting in which they worked, many of them living locally. Rather than judging families for inadequate provision of clothing or food for their children, they supported children and their families as they were. Breakfast was available for children in the first part of the day at both sites, with cereal and milk, bowls and spoons set out on the table so that children could help themselves and each other, with no judgement attached.

On viewing the video from Katoa Kindergarten, Tracey from Gundoo appreciated how the older child looked after the little one, taking her inside and asking her which knee had been hurt. Katrina explained that their teaching philosophy is on actions rather than simply saying sorry – so children can get ice-packs from the child accessible fridge.

JARED: Katrina mentions that the focus was not on the word 'sorry' but the actions. I recall many discussions around this approach to education. There was a shared pedagogical approach to supporting children's understanding of concepts. The focus was always on actions – what it looked like in practice, it was never about how well the child could articulate a point, as this can be restrictive, it was more about how their choices and actions demonstrated the concept of being 'sorry' or the concept of kaitiakitanga, etc.

BENA: I liked how the children initiated their own play [at Katoa]. They do it here too. It's their play. Not much direction or assistance from the educators. I like that the children have a choice about what they want to do and how they want to play.

In the discussion after viewing all three short videos, Sonya (Katoa) commented that across the three totally different countries 'we all focus on supporting children to show empathy and care for others'. Trinity, the Head Teacher at Katoa, elaborated on this, saying 'We are all trying to empower children, not to shame them, letting them have a sense of belonging and ownership of their environment and their learning'. Jacqui (Gundoo Director) added: 'And all the children are being taught powerful leadership when the educators stand back and teach respect, empathy and caring for one another. When they see a child being hurt they all want to help each other.'

One of the differences between Gundoo and Katoa's video clips was that educators were present in the Katoa video providing verbal affirmations (e.g., 'wow you did it by yourselves'), explanations (e.g., 'if you touch the bugs you can still hurt them, like if you punched me, I wouldn't die, but it would still hurt') and encouragement to children's actions (e.g., 'give it a rub'). The team of all degree qualified teachers collaborated through a 'community of learners approach' to plan term foci, and then collectively enact clear and directive approaches to teach the focus within child-initiated and directed play, as explained in Chapter Five. They also regularly reflected and evaluated on the ways in which they planned and enacted intentional teaching with regard to learning as a collective. At the time of the video the teachers' planning focus was 'Kotahitanga' (unity, solidarity, collectivity), therefore much of the teachers' verbal commentary was directed to highlighting children's awareness of being part of the collective. This approach presents a practice of well-qualified teachers who communicate well as a team to ensure a shared philosophy of holistic development, relationships and community, through clearly expressed pedagogical goals and strategies articulated through national curriculum documents and enacted with a commitment to sociocultural equity.

Gundoo operates under a very different national early childhood education and care framework, whereby the centre of 81 is only required by legislation to have one full-time degree qualified early childhood teacher and one half-time degree qualified early childhood teacher, with lead educators in each age-grouped room (either enrolled in or completed a diploma in early childhood) for each age group accompanied by another educator (enrolled in or completed a Certificate III in early childhood) (State of Queensland, 2018). Lead educators are responsible for planning, teaching and evaluating for their own group. There is not the same opportunity to plan as a whole team, nor does the physical environment enable a collective 'community of learners approach', with the regulatory requirement for separate indoor and outdoor spaces for each age group. Further, words are used sparingly by many Aboriginal people, meaning is much more communicated through actions and relationality as Kerryn shared in Chapter One.

The transnational online dialogue between sites continued with the teachers posing the question to one another: 'How do you foster belonging?' This question provoked reflection of their practices and how these may support children's civic agency. And that perhaps by modelling building community, the children learn to build communities themselves.

Belonging

Attention to belonging invokes a connection with a feminist perspective of citizenship, whereby, as noted earlier, that Werbner and Yuval-Davis (1999) define citizenship 'as a sense of belonging' (p. 4). Belonging features strongly in the early childhood curricula for both Australia and Aotearoa. The subtitle for the Early Years Learning Framework for Australia (Australian Government Department of Education Employment and Workplace Relations, 2009) is Belonging, being and becoming, acknowledging that children's lives are characterized by belonging, being and becoming. 'Belonging acknowledges children's interdependence with others and the basis of relationships in defining identities … Belonging is central to being and becoming in that it shapes who children are and who they can become' (p. 7). And as noted in Chapter Four, belonging was a core understanding of children in Gundoo philosophy. Table 6.1 from Te Whāriki (2017) shows the goals and learning outcomes for the Belonging | Mana Whenua strand of the curriculum.

TABLE 6.1 Belonging strand goals and learning outcomes (NZ Ministry of Education, 2017, p. 24).

Belonging Mana whenua	Children and their families experience an environment where:	Over time and with guidance and encouragement, children become increasingly capable of:
	>> Connecting links with the family and the wider world are affirmed and extended	>> Making connections between people, places and things in their world | te waihanga hononga
	>> They know that they have a place	>> Taking part in caring for this place | te manaaki i te taiao
	>> They feel comfortable with the routines, customs and regular events	>> Understanding how things work here and adapting to change | te mārama ki āhua o ngā whakahaere me te mōhio ki te panoni
	>> They know the limits and boundaries of acceptable behaviour	>> Showing respect for kaupapa, rules and the rights of others | te mahi whakaute

In reflecting ón how they facilitate a sense of belonging for their children and families, Bena, Jacqui and Tracey responded with:

> We find out family values, encouraging family input, to build a community of shared values. Educators are called Aunty or Uncle, or Nan/Pop following kinship protocols for building relations. Children's names, photos and learning feature in room displays and portfolios. Family names are respected. Each grouping becomes a family.

As long-term mentor for Gundoo, Kerryn added:

> we communicate a sense of who we are and what country we walk on through language. English is a second language. It's about reaching out to the whole community, like Uncle Jeffrey having a men's yarning circle with the Dads.

Educators respect children's preferences. A recent study of Gundoo's practices pertaining to belonging note that the educators cultivate 'a strong culture of acceptance; a willingness to allow the children to engage with others and the learning environment to whatever extent they want at any given time' and 'it's about sharing, teaching sharing, and looking after one another and that helps them belong' (Sumsion, Harrison, Letsch, Bradley & Stapleton, 2018, p. 347).

Co-sleeping is a commonly accepted family practice, so to follow family practice and reassure young children by being in the company of others, babies sleep on mattresses on the floor, rockers or cots near educators and other children doing daily activities in the playroom. Cots in separate sleeping rooms isolate, and fence bodies from touch, warmth and community. Belonging is fostered through trust. Educators have trust in children's competence to explore the environment (to work through risks), to look out for each other and work together. Mostly such encouragement and assurance is not communicated explicitly, but through a watchful presence.

In response to the provocation as to how they foster a sense of belonging, the Katoa educators offered that in their setting belonging is similarly fostered by the use of portfolios. They also: utilise a whānau (family) tree; have children's photos with names on laminated cards on a low wall where children can reach these; there is their 'planning wall' display of planning and learning stories; and their whānau participation wall that documents families' engagement in and responses to the kindergarten programme. Trinity explained that their programme is strongly influenced by a commitment to Tiriti o Waitangi and their connections to local iwi [tribe/s]. They constantly try to find ways of bringing those tribal connections into the kindergarten, and try to have a Māori lens to everything that they do. At the beginning of the study, the focus for the programme had been 'Ko wai ahau?' (Who am I?) and this featured on a wall display which included photos and maps

FIGURE 6.1 Wall display at Katoa Kindergarten, during 'Ko wai ahau/Who am I?' focus

of Aotearoa and the world (Figure 6.1), so that children and families could make links to their places of origin.

In *Te Whāriki*, the Māori construct alongside the 'Belonging' strand is 'Mana Whenua', which refers to local tribal connectedness. The two terms are summarised as follows:

> Belonging | Children know they belong and have a sense of connection to others and the environment
>
> Mana whenua | Children's relationship to Papatūānuku [Earth Mother] is based on whakapapa [genealogy], respect and aroha [love, compassion, empathy]
>
> *(NZ Ministry of Education, 2017, p. 31)*

The notion of belonging links to whanaungatanga [relationships, family connectedness] which is a core Māori value. Another example during the study was when Trinity liaised with Elders from the local marae in getting a kākahu, a traditional woven cloak, made for the kindergarten, so that when a child turned five and was about to leave for school, she or he would be seated wearing this kākahu as a badge of honour during the farewell ceremony which would be attended by family members.

To further identify how educators may support young children's community building and agency, we involved educators and children from both sites in collective reflection and interpretation of a typical day at the site video that captured children's community building and agency. Educators responded to their own site's video and each other's. Across their dialogues relationality, freedom to choose and move, confidence and cultural pride were jointly consistent principles that informed the environments and pedagogies educators provide for children's community building and agency.

Relationality

Whenever we shared videos with the children, they were so excited to see themselves and their friends, naming their friends as they appeared on the screen, laughing and naming what they were doing. And when educators viewed the videos they too immediately identified children by name and their achievements. Such as: 'See how Holly is standing back there, she's not like that now.' Educators at each site know all the children regardless of age group and who they may be directly responsible for. They know the children – who they are, their personalities, interests, backgrounds and learnings. Relationships are foregrounded. Responsibility is shared.

As noted in Chapters One and Four, kinship is at the core of Aboriginal lore, so that children grow up knowing their kinship relations, behaviours, rights and responsibilities (Daylight & Johnstone, 1986). Children refer to Educators as Aunty and Uncle or Nan and Pop as part of the kinship practice. Katoa educators notice the calling of educators Aunty in the Gundoo day video appreciating the respect and relationality such conveys, along with recognising similar practice in Pasifka communities. As noted earlier in Chapter Four, Gundoo's community is a small town of approximately 2,000, predominantly Aboriginal and Torres Strait Islander people, so most everyone knows each other. There is the acknowledgement of one blackfella to another – as community.

Knowing each other is nurtured from birth. In the Gundoo babies room, educators welcome family members to stay and talk, so children's preferences are learnt and followed through. Children's photos are placed on the wall in displays at children's height that celebrate their learning. In the Gundoo day in the life video, toddlers were standing by the wall, looking and patting the photos. On viewing this, one of the Katoa teachers commented: 'it's the faces they recognise, showing that they recognise themselves'. The scene from the video continues with the nurturing acceptance story from Chapter Four, a scene that illustrates how relationality is welcomed and nurtured at Gundoo across different ages and generations. Bena projects a strong sense of comfort and foundations for children to feel secure and belong, and as she shared in Chapter Four her intentionality all stems from a pedagogy of love.

Relationships are nurtured through doing together, for example through shared meal time. At Gundoo the children sit around a table and share a cooked meal prepared by a cook on site.

BENA: That's why we have it [mealtime] together so they share together, with the other children at mealtimes talking to them.

When Katoa educators saw the video of the Gundoo mealtime they appreciated the circular tables so all the children were facing in to each other. Educators and children take turns to serve the food for each other. The Gundoo children all sit together talking and eating. The tradition of sharing and serving each other is embodied daily practice, so if a child wanted something, say a cup of water, they would get one for each of the children then his or herself.

Katoa was purpose built, it was made to meet the needs of the local community, and a playgroup was provided as an extension of that. It was set up to support community and family engagement. Typically, playgroups are in a separate building to the kindergarten in New Zealand. When they were establishing the playgroup at Katoa, they questioned 'how do we get the community in so that they can participate but also become familiar with the Kindergarten environment?' In foregrounding community connectedness, an extension of the building was built rather than a separate building, so that families with young children initially come to the kindergarten for the playgroup building relations with staff, children and the physical space.

JARED: Community connectedness to children's sense of identity was a key aspect of Katoa Kindergarten, this was because of where the Kindergarten was established. Katoa was a purpose built kindergarten located in a pā – an area where the community is predominately Māori and is connected to their Marae. When I first started at Katoa, the teaching team had created connections with the local Marae and visited weekly. This is a fantastic example of how community connectedness fosters children's sense of identity, as many of the children that attended belonged to this Marae and had the opportunity to explore their cultural and spiritual identity when walking onto the marae. They were also offered stories about their local community and the kaitiaki [spiritual guardians] that watch over it. Katoa engaged in other community events, their relationships with the kōhanga reo were also fostered in communal events. I recall being invited to a community hall where the kōhanga had thrown a gathering for children to engage in physical education. The hall belonged to a local health centre and they had invited us to connect with the centre to learn about physical health and have access to other services. For as long as I can remember, it was always important for us to take part in these communal events. They provided connections to the local community and opportunities for children to learn about what is available to them in their wider community. We also attended many school events with the local schools including walks to the school for children to experience the learning environment and develop their own sense of tūrangawaewae [a place to stand, sense of belonging] in the primary setting. It was important for us to support children to see their school as a place they have place in and belong.

Educators at Katoa commented on children's interactions with each other, signposting social skills, especially those that they were focussing on in their current community of learners teaching approach. We see in the Katoa day video children caring for each other, by inviting them into their play, including others by getting another play item, through a gentle pat on back.

BENA: I like the care.

LOUISE: So the ice-packs are in a little bar fridge that the children can reach. See? [a child in the video takes another injured child to the fridge to get an ice-pack.]

BENA: I like that it's giving them some independence and responsibility. Capable learners. And how everything is at the children's level.

In a discussion with the Katoa teachers with regard to choosing what they felt would be important to include in the 'day in the life' video, the teachers' responses included an array of relational priorities, which included advocacy on behalf of others, empathy, accepting others, and communication and negotiation skills, as outlined in the dialogue in chapter three, pages 72–74.

The teachers intentionally sought to prioritise their focus on supporting children's capacities as relational, responsible members of the kindergarten community. Rituals of spiritual relationality were also purposefully and respectfully woven into the programme at Katoa, as illustrated in the following story of Katoa practice.

During the morning wā kotahitanga [literally collective time, or mat-time] a taonga [treasure] – a large paua shell within a woven flax basket – is passed from teacher to teacher. Each teacher responds by saying 'Morena [Good morning], my name is ....'. Jerome reaches up and takes it from Maddie's hands and says 'Morena, my name is Jerome'. This surprises all the teachers and Scott says 'It looks like we are all going to join in – ka pai Jerome, that's great leadership'. The other teachers offer their affirmations of good leadership. The process of sharing the taonga and introductions continues smoothly for part of the circle ... Mat-time finishes with the children standing to say the whakatauākī before being dismissed to have morning tea.

Whilst the general consensus in the preponderance of early childhood care and education settings in both Australia and New Zealand is that the majority of the children's time should be spent engaging in 'free play' or play-based programmes, questions can be asked as to the nature of the 'freedom' to choose between teacher provided activities and resources. There is less of a consensus on the role of the teachers in making visible the values and cultural practices of the local Indigenous peoples as well as those of the other children and families who attend that service. Another focus worthy of attention is the extent to which teachers actively build a sense of community amongst the attending children and families. One means of doing so is to have daily rituals such as the one described above. The whakatauākī recited daily at mat-times at Katoa Kindergarten is a short repetitive tribal saying originally composed by a famous Ngāti Toa chief, Te Rauparaha. For Māori, such rituals are regularly 'performed and people are brought together to make the transition from one state of being to another a peaceful and settled process' (Smith, 1999, p. 103). They underpin a sense of collective spiritual wellbeing and relationality.

Freedom to choose, move and do

In a similar way to the feminist citizenship project (Lister, 2003), we see that the children's citizenship project is about giving due accord to children's agency both individually and collectively, recognising and countering the ongoing discrimination children endure and doubly so for Indigenous children. To support children's civic agency, that is opportunities for them to make choices that affect their lives and the belief that they have capacity to address collective challenges and initiate new ideas and actions for common good, varying pedagogical strategies were evident at both Gundoo and Katoa.

At Gundoo, Bena explains that enacting children rights is about:

> culture and rights in making choices and setting up areas for choice of where they want to go and play ... and talking to them and they talking back to get self-confidence to talk and voice their opinion and be understood, knowing what they are interested in, what they are saying to us and listen to what they're saying to us too.

Educators at Gundoo provide children with time, space and freedom to explore the place in ways that they prefer. Children have freedom to explore and experiment while educators discreetly monitor their play at a distance (Sumsion et al., 2018). The educators' presence provides reassurance to children for their explorations. Such practice sustains traditional Aboriginal cultural values to ensure Aboriginal children are bestowed with freedom to explore their surrounds and to learn caring and protection responsibilities for one another (Daylight & Johnstone, 1986). All educators feel collectively responsible for all children, as do older children for younger children.

At Gundoo, their outdoor space is more than a hectare (about four times the outdoor space at Katoa), providing ample space for running around. There is a slight decline offering a thrilling speed boost as you run downhill. The Katoa teachers noticed this asset in the Gundoo day video: 'I like the outdoor space, lots of room for running around. Freedom!' After months of being with the children at Gundoo and taking up Bronwyn Davies' (2014) methodological approach of emergent listening, by listening intently to children, educators, families and community members to glean multi-directional layers of meaning, to notice what emerges as mattering (Barad, 2007) to these children, we understood that much of the listening was not verbally focussed; we read bodies engaged with environments, and noticed children's insatiable desire to move. The children were happiest when outside where there were less physical obstructions and their movement could be more boundless. They resisted practices of corralling such as group time, sitting at tables and chairs, lying on beds. The furniture in the centre is purchased from catalogues following regulatory standards. They are western inventions/structures designed for set singular purposes. The children desired to move in, with, over and under – their bodies entangled with the matter of these structures. They diverged from colonising conventions of usage. This was also illustrated in Chapter Four in the stories of their interactions with fences. These children were not disembodied as is required in western education. They were very much embodied – it seemed they were driven by 'what can my body do in this space?

To really listen to children's civic agency, we feel we need to listen to their bodies. The desirable agency that we witnessed at Gundoo was resoundingly the freedom to move. Before colonisation this would have been common practice. And such boundless play continues in community outside of regulated institutions (child care and school) (Kreutz, 2015). It is through exploring in and as part of environments, that learning occurs. A key principle, as Aboriginal education consultant Denise Proud explains with colleagues, is 'the notion of relatedness, and in particular environmental relatedness' so that 'learning is seen as a process of experiencing, absorbing and sharing ways of coming to know' (Proud, Lynch, á Beckett & Pike, 2017, p. 85). Western research also recognises how children's free play enables environmental competence and a sense of self separate from caregivers (e.g., see Chawla, 1986; Sobel, 1993). The provision of the freedom to move builds children's civic agency. By doing and exploring, children come to know what they can do in the world.

The Katoa teachers recognised this in the Gundoo day video, commenting: 'Having lots of space but less resources equals more learning.' And they also acknowledged that freedom also builds independence, as Jared appraised: 'I like how children are going off and doing that by themselves. At Katoa they did that. I like it when children have the freedom and independence to do that.' As Garth and Katrina had explained as important to be included in the Katoa video:

GARTH: I'd like to see something about how the space is used for running and, you know, the speed that children sometimes go through our environment cos I think that's a really important thing for kids to be able to do. Is to run freely and, you know, it's not the perfect environment that they still can and they negotiate the bumps …

KATRINA: And the hills. They love those hills and those bumps and we had some great play out there the other day with the mud. It was so cool. The mud and the water and the trucks.

Video footage of the stories of the children initiating packing away the beds and collectively getting the rope ladder down as described in Chapter Four was included in the Gundoo day video and are illustrative of the freedom to move nurturing independence and enhanced sense of civic agency. The Katoa teachers also saw great value in these opportunities, as they watched the Gundoo children putting beds away and working together to take the ladder down: 'Love it – those self-help stuff and taking care of themselves. Awesome group learning.'

At Katoa, for most of the day the children have freedom to choose what they do either inside or outside. This includes when they drink and eat, with all the necessary equipment (fridge, drinking glasses, scissors, spoons, bowls, bins, compost bin) accessible for children to self-access the food and drinks they bring from home as needed. Children were observed assisting one another, serving the breakfast cereal and pouring milk, getting glasses of water, opening food packaging, clearing dishes away and putting them in the dishwasher, taking leftover food out to the compost bins, wiping tables and sweeping the floor. These were commonly spontaneous initiatives to the situation rather than responding to requests from teachers.

At breakfast time, in the Katoa 'day in the life' video you can see the children scoop the cereal from the large container of rice bubbles and milk is available in a large drinking bottle with a small pouring spout (see Figure 6.2).

BENA: So like instead of the big bottles they just poured them in the bottles and let them pour out of that. Instead of saying, telling them to stop.

It is evident that the Katoa educators have carefully thought through and selected equipment to support children's independent management of routine care tasks. On finishing breakfast, in the video, we see a three-year-old girl take her bowl and spoon to the kitchen and place these into the dishwasher.

BENA: And I see when that girl goes into kitchen to put her spoon in the dishwasher, I'm thinking about the supervision 'cos the kitchen is always closed off here – for safety. But when they're at home the kitchen is an open space and it's part of their environment.

LOUISE: Yeah, so by cutting off access we kind of cut off that independence.

BENA: Yeah. Independence. And, their rights. They're [Katoa] saying day care should be like the children's home. At day care there a lot of rules. The children are not allowed in the kitchen here. There are a lot of rules that stop them from doing things, but they do it at home. So they're in the kitchen at home, helping with the cooking, washing, stacking the dishwasher. And just

FIGURE 6.2 Breakfast table set-up

being in the kitchen 'cos sometimes that's the only time you get to talk to them. With parents, they're cooking and you're sitting there and talking to them. But at day care there's rules and regulations. It's like, it really is the difference. It makes the difference between day care and home.

LOUISE: Do you think sometimes that some of those rules we could rethink and question are they necessary? And is there are a way we can still support their independence.

BENA: Yes. Their independence. Yes. We could just teach them about safety, talking to them. It's obvious at Katoa they're just walking in and out that they already know it all but what do they do when they have new children that starts at kindy? What are their routines for the children to know? And how do they teach them?

JARED: I recall learning about the ways that we supported new tamariki to transition at Katoa Kindergarten when I first started. We talked about our non-negotiables, the rules that were put in place to ensure the environment was holistically safe. But we also identified through team discussions where to make changes to support the individual needs of each child. For example, Kotahitanga te wā (mat-time) was a time of the day where all children came together to learn as one group. However, for transitioning children there was no expectation that they would join in straight away, we provided opportunities where they could play alongside the mat and watch what was happening. Over time those children became active participants because we worked with them at their own pace. When reflecting on expectations and routines for bringing children into our learning community this same practice was applied to almost all expectations and routines to empower children to make their own choices and independently engage when they decide. But one of our main strategies was to empower the peer group to learn about the kaupapa at Kindergarten and understand how to navigate not only the environment but also the peer culture. So, when new tamariki joined our community we empowered children to show them around the Kindergarten (e.g., where they can go to toilet, how they can access water, where to put their lunch boxes, and how to play as a 'good-friend', etc). Overall I would say our approach to welcoming new children into the kindergarten and empowering their independence was about giving our children leadership opportunities to take on a tuakana role and teach their teina about the ways of being at Katoa Kindergarten.

Just as with careful selection of a bottle with a narrow spout to support competence with pouring, Katoa educators carefully select equipment throughout the whole kindergarten for the children to build competence with navigating the real world, such as real glasses to drink from, that are accessible for children to reach and bring to the tables, metal shovels and real strollers (see Figure 6.3). Trinity, the head teacher, highlighted the care and thought that went into planning a responsive environment, with regard to the flexible uses of space, how teachers utilise the environment, prioritising clear spaces that are not full of stuff, that offer room for children to create their own playworlds. The kindergarten featured a mixture of standard equipment such as blocks, water, sand, musical instruments and paint, along with an ever-changing array of purposeful resources that are provided in response to children's interests.

On viewing the breakfasting scene in the video, Bena from Gundoo remarked:

BENA: I love this kind of school. I like the life-like settings. And the toys. They're little toys but they look so life-like. Like, the pram and I was looking at the shovel and that before.

LOUISE: That also communicates to children that 'you are a serious, capable person'. That they can handle the real things. Not just these plastic versions.

JARED: As a teaching team member we shared the teaching philosophy that children should have access to quality resources, this is where steering away from cheap plastic toys came in. We believed that our tamariki deserved the best, so if we were going to purchase resources it was worth investing additional money to provide quality resources for quality learning. What sat alongside this was the belief that resources can be a provocation to empower a robust understanding of the concept of responsibility. I remember when we would

FIGURE 6.3 Katoa children's photo of stroller

purchase new resources it was important that we introduced the resources at a mat-time. There we could acknowledge that this new thing is coming into our environment and discuss ways to look after it. For example, I recall one morning there were some new dolls and dolls clothes that had just been delivered to Kindergarten. Instead of setting them up and showing tamariki as they came through the door Scott waited until mat-time, so that all children could be introduced at the same time and as one group. He demonstrated how to put the clothes on the doll and opened up the floor for children to ask any questions that they had.

JENNY: I remember a mat-time shortly after this where you talked about how the tamariki could keep the new dolls clothes safe, responses from the tamariki included: 'no breaking them'; 'no cutting them with scissors'; 'no putting them in the bin' and 'don't throw them on the road'.

JARED: As for the real-life resources, they were intentional. We believed in facilitating a learning environment that replicated places in the child's wider world such as home, or even places out in the local community. Often these two guiding philosophies (resources as a provocation for responsibility and resources replicating the child's wider word) worked harmoniously. The best example I could provide of this is the use of actual drinking glasses. Because they represented the glasses used at home and other places in the community that the child may visit (e.g., a cafe, a friend's house, etc). But they also supported children's sense of belonging. When they weren't cared for they would break. Children quickly learnt how to associate the natural consequences with their actions. For example, if I chose to use one hand and skip around the room holding my glass it may result in the glass dropping and breaking. The glasses replicated the child's wider world and taught them about how to take care and look after our things.

This high-trust, high quality approach to resources emanates a respect for the children, that they are entrusted with the care of valuable equipment, with real tools, cups, bowls and cutlery. This was intended to resonate with children's own homes. If on occasion a glass was dropped and broke, there would be no fuss made, as the broken shards would be quickly cleared away by a teacher, whilst the child would go to the shelf and get another glass to replace the one that had been broken. At Katoa, children were free to physically re-position large items such as large mats and bolsters, and outdoor large wooden cubes and ramps to arrange these to suit their agendas. Routines are gently introduced to new children, respecting children's own preferences, attendance at mat-times expected but not required. Neither site included a surfeit of plastic toys. Natural resources such as sand, water, dirt feature strongly in children's preferences, offering great scope for freedom of usage.

Cultural pride and confidence

Cultural pride, as a culturally relevant and necessary resource, was nurtured as a core pedagogical practice at both Gundoo and Katoa. Cultural pride is seen as core for Indigenous peoples asserting community membership and Indigenous cultural rights.

> Indigenous peoples have the right to practise and revitalize their cultural traditions and customs. This includes the right to maintain, protect and develop the past, present and future manifestations of their cultures, such as archaeological and historical sites, artefacts, designs, ceremonies, technologies and visual and performing arts and literature.
>
> *(United Nations, 2007, Art. 11)*

At Gundoo, we witnessed the practice of honouring kinship relations (discussed earlier under Belonging and in Chapter Four), using Aboriginal English, and local languages (Wakka Wakka and Gubbi Gubbi), and sharing Aboriginal and Torres Strait Islander knowledges through Aboriginal and Torres Strait Islander children's picture books, play materials, displays, staff shirts with Aboriginal art designs and celebrating key Aboriginal and Torres Strait Islander events with community. As Gundoo is one of the Aboriginal governed services in the community, it is very much a community hub and gathering site for Aboriginal and Torres Strait Islander events. Key annual events include National Sorry Day (to acknowledge and recognise members of the Stolen Generation), NAIDOC (National Aborigines and Islander Day Observance Committee) week and National Aboriginal and Islander Children's Day. These events emerged across the last 100 years out of the counter colonising movement to assert Aboriginal rights, mourn the devastating struggles and grief inflicted by colonisation and celebrate Aboriginal culture.

BENA: We have Sorry day and in this room, we have family who are members of the stolen generation. It's something big for our parents and my Dad passed away at this time and same thing stolen generation and stolen wages and sorry times [a time of grieving for loss]. We are giving children this understanding – why we do these things. I think it helps them know who they are. It teaches you to think differently along the way because being an Aboriginal person and being distinguished because you're black. There's things that come with it and the turmoil our Elders went through and it affects us and our children. I feel our children have to be made aware of what happened back then.

At Katoa a sense of Māori and to a lesser extent Pacific Islands' cultural locatedness was pervasive throughout the geographical location in the same street as the local marae, Takapūwāhia, and the historical and ongoing relationship with the marae community which assisted in learning the culture, language, history, whakapapa and stories of Ngāti Toa Rangatira. The kindergarten had an 'open door' policy whereby families/whānau are invited to share food, stories, dances, with children/tamariki from the home cultures of all participating families. There were regular 'grandparents morning teas'. The teachers use an introductory 'Ko wai au?' sheet which has a set of questions to encourage whānau to share their cultural and iwi connections. It was also evident in the physical environment and teachers' pedagogical interactions and documentation. There was a 'Ko wai ahau?' notice-board/wall which contained provocations, maps, and imagery representing Ngāti Toa Rangatira. As discussed in Chapter Five, the first planning focus during the period of the study was 'Ko wai ahau?' (Who am I?). This included a visit to the national museum, Te Papa Tongarewa, to see the exhibition celebrating the history and presence of Ngati Toa Rangatira, the tribe local to the Katoa community. At each mat-time, the pepeha (tribal saying) of a prominent ancestor of the tribe was recited. The learning stories that teachers wrote and displayed on the planning wall included frequent reference to children's ethnic affiliations, as well as to key Māori values. As described in Chapter Five, Māori values such as manaakitanga, rangatiratanga and kaitiakitanga underpinned the curriculum, and older siblings were encouraged to care for younger ones. Jared also noted the challenges involved in maintaining relationships with the marae community.

JARED: Trinity worked really hard to get relationships in the Marae, to do weekly visits.
JENNY: Yeah I know, she did.
JARED: But like she also talked about how challenging that can be as a Pākehā, and the only real way that she could get that relationship was by having teachers within the team that had connections.

This signals the importance of further attracting and retaining Indigenous student teachers in teacher education programmes through authentic culturally safe initiatives that affirm Indigenous values, histories and knowledges.

The children's citizenship project is not just about children having choice to explore and build independence, but also children having confidence in being in and contributing to the world. Educators at both Gundoo and Katoa shared the pedagogical goal of building children's confidence. Illustrated above (under Relationality) when viewing children in videos, Holly's growth confidence in taking part was immediately acknowledged.

Being Indigenous is a life of being marginalised. In Australia, the Aboriginal and Torres Strait Islander population was recorded at 2.8% of the total population in the 2016 Australian Census (Australian Bureau of Statistics, 2017) and in New Zealand Māori account for 14.9% of the total population (NZ Ministry of Social Development, 2016). In most mainstream social contexts, as an Indigenous person you will be in the minority, so not only do you have to wear that point of racial difference, but broader society also circulates a plethora of deficit discourses about your kind that with which you are assaulted every day.

At Gundoo to prepare the children for an unwelcoming and unkind world, Bena asserts:

That's our responsibility in our role, along with their parents to teach them that they are active citizens with rights. It's important to raise children to have that confidence to be heard ... We teach them about who they are and their real name and that they are part of a family and a community who want them.

Knowing your identity and that you have a community in which you belong are foundations for confidence. Children's achievements, and caring of others, were also regularly verbally and nonverbally affirmed. Each year at the end of the year, a family and community celebration is held at the centre to acknowledge those children going off to school the next year providing a ceremony for this rite of passage into mainstream society. The community gathering communicates 'we are here with you'.

The work of the teachers at Katoa reflects the importance of the Te Whāriki principle of Whakamana | Empowerment, and the planning wall is covered with an array of learning stories which celebrate children's achievements, and their growing confidence grounded in their cultural identities, as seen in this excerpt from a learning story by Kaiako Scott for Bonnie:

> Taking responsibility like that shows you have spirited initiative. Tino pai to mahi! You showed ma'afafaioi – responsibility – by telling other tamariki what was expected as you all worked together to reach a shared goal. In the end, everyone managed to create a well-formed snake that extended the entire way around the table. Kia ora for helping everyone be successful. Bonnie, you demonstrated kotahitanga – unity, and ako – teaching and learning alongside others. You also clearly showed rangatiratanga – an ability to lead. This term we are focusing on thinking. Te Whāriki talks about children developing an 'awareness of their own special strengths, and confidence that these are recognised and valued'. You are showing your ability to be a clear thinker. He rawe!

The collective reflections of the teachers' planning stories contain questions considering the ways their work has contributed to the empowerment of children and their families. They contain reflective questions, and links to the various supporting documents, such as the following list of Samoan dispositions recorded in one of their reflections during the Rangatiranga (Leadership) focus: Loto toa (courageous and confident); Tauivi (persevere); Naunau (willingness); Fa'amalosia (empowerment); and Ma'fafaioi (responsibility). During the study the teachers particularly enjoyed and celebrated the growth in the confidence of children as they viewed previous videos from the project.

Cultural pride and confidence are necessary tools for participation in wider society (that can be racist, exclusionary and very white). Educators at Gundoo and Katoa passionately advocated for and promoted young children's cultural pride and confidence through foregrounding knowing country and kin and doing together, and showing rangatiranga (leadership) through manaakitanga (caring) for others.

Discourses, curriculum and policy influences

Practising these cultural and community pedagogical principles with young Indigenous children is not always welcomed and given free reign. Discourses of colonialism, neoliberalism and racism perpetuate and intervene, block and hinder progressivist and counter-colonialist agendas. Both Gundoo and Katoa operate within national early childhood education and care legislation, standards and policies, along with national and local politics. Being an Indigenous person is political.

KERRYN: In my view Aboriginal and Torres Strait Islander people deal with the notion of civic agency on a daily basis, with Australia's first nations people being a highly politicised identity, with effects often arising from deficit lens and affecting the lives of Aboriginal and Torres Straits Islander people in one way or another. The national conversation is ongoing in this nation regarding citizenship and agency of this right for Aboriginal and Torres Strait Islander people identities and are we hearing children's voices in this conversation?

Kerryn and Bena acutely felt this difference when watching the Katoa video.

BENA: I think what I like about New Zealand, is they've got their Māori culture and they seem to acknowledge and accept it. It's taught to everybody. Whereas in Australia, they don't. The Aboriginal culture is only there for Aboriginal people they say. In New Zealand, I like how it's open for everybody. The sharing. It's open for everybody. It's not excluding anyone.

LOUISE: There's much more support for biculturalism there. I mean, we do have some foregrounding in our Australian Curriculum, with Aboriginal and Torres Strait Islander Histories and Cultures as a cross-curricular priority, but there still hasn't been much uptake has there?

BENA: And you try to bring them together but there's always someone fighting it. I think we're seeing more disrespect for Aboriginal and Torres Strait Islander peoples. We're seeing white men playing the didgeridoo. We're seeing the tourism of us. Playing the didgeridoo we get laughed at by another culture. We were standing around watching them. We were shocked ourselves. And we get laughed at by another nationality, saying 'What are you doing? The blackmen play that, that's yours.' 'You should be there', they question. But just that sharing, the sharing of the culture and the children growing up with that respect. To respect and acknowledge and accept Māori culture.

Australia and New Zealand were colonised (as discussed in Chapters One and Two) in different eras framed by different thinking. Australia was colonised without treaty making or constitutional recognition of its Indigenous Peoples (MacDonald & Muldoon, 2006). Aboriginal people were believed to be a dying race (Power & Somerville, 2015; Harris, 2003). 'In the first century of colonisation and beyond, it was a convenient and widespread assumption that their extinction was irreversible' (Harris, 2003 p. 81).

And white Australians (in the most) were/are quite willing to accept such fate for the oldest living culture, 'blinded by their confident belief in their own racial superiority and their arrogant perception of the inferiority of all other races' (Behrendt, 2016). In contrast, the British were obliged to create a treaty with the Māori peoples in 1840 (Te Tiriti o Waitangi/the Treaty of Waitangi) since they had already acknowledged New Zealand was under Māori control in the 1835 Declaration of Independence. The naming of Indigenous peoples in each nation by the British capture the differing agendas and interactions between the British and Indigenous peoples in each nation.

On watching the Katoa 'day in the life' video, Louise shared the meaning of the word 'Māori' to Bena.

LOUISE: The word Māori means 'normal'.
BENA: Oh wow.
LOUISE: They were asked, 'What's the name for yourself?' and they replied in language 'Normal' – like 'we just are'.
BENA: And the word 'Aboriginal', it's abnormal.
LOUISE: It's warped thinking happening at that time.
BENA: Yeah 'cos 'Aboriginal' means abnormal. And 'Māori' means normal.

The Latin root prefix 'ab' means 'away; from'. The English word 'Aborigine' originates from the Latin phrase 'ab origine', literally meaning 'from the beginning' (Harper, 2018). Records indicate that from 1922 white Australian slang shortened the reference to 'Abo' (Harper, 2018), thus focussing on the 'away; from' point of difference feeding and aligning with constructions of 'abnormal' and less than ('backward') that have perpetuated British constructions of Australia's first peoples (Harris, 2003).

BENA: It's very hard to be accepted and acknowledged for the Aboriginal culture. Without someone whinging and saying 'They're looking for attention' and stuff like that when it's not. It's looking for recognition.
LOUISE: Yes sovereignty.
BENA: The others get that recognition, with respect. They get that recognition.

The widespread racist deficit discourses of Aboriginal and Torres Strait Islander people across Australia make every day challenging and challenged, requiring a steel suit to shield the persistent jabs of overt and covert racism. Cultural pride, a strong sense of belonging, confidence and spiritual understandings of relationality are resources that many Aboriginal and Torres Strait Islander people (regardless of age) draw from to assert civic agency – rights – rights to freedom to choose, do and move and build communities.

Since we gathered data at Gundoo of young children's community building, the Queensland Government has published a curriculum for Aboriginal and Torres Strait Islander children titled *Foundations for Success* (The State of Queensland (Department of Education), 2016) that showcases the strengths and good practice that occurs in community governed Aboriginal early childhood education and care (see Table 6.2). It was

TABLE 6.2 Comparison between Foundations for Success learning areas and principles of community building pedagogies and environment

Principles	Foundations for Success learning areas
Belonging	Being proud and strong
Relationality	Being an active participant
Freedom to choose, do and move	Being an active participant
Building confidence	Being proud and strong
Cultural pride	Being proud and strong

felt there needed to be a specific guideline to teach Aboriginal and Torres Strait Islander children. The primary focus for the curriculum was the early childhood education and care services in the 35 discrete Aboriginal and Torres Strait Islander communities (bounded by physical and legal boundaries, and inhabited predominantly by Indigenous people, with housing or infrastructure that is either owned or managed on a community basis (Australian Institute of Health & Welfare, n.d.)) across Queensland, of which Gundoo is located within one. Slowly over time with Kerryn's and others' sway in the Department of Education, *Foundations for Success* is now being promoted as a tool for all – so that all children's lives can be enriched with Aboriginal and Torres Strait Islander knowledges and pedagogies. As Kerryn claims:

> A curriculum is a dead tree unless we have the pedagogy. Educators need to analyse their own biases attitudes and barriers. And we need to ensure that we have a future generation that knows the whole history of this nation. We are denying our future if we don't show where we have been. We don't know where we are going, if we don't know where we have been.

Foundations for Success offers a positive curriculum and policy step forward that counters colonialism through showcasing strengths of Aboriginal and Torres Strait Islander early childhood curriculum and pedagogy that counters deficit narratives. And two key learning areas particularly align with the principles of community building pedagogies and environment discussed in this chapter: being proud and strong; and being an active participant.

The other three learning areas – being healthy and safe; being a learner; and being a communicator – are more focussed on individual health and academic achievements. In many ways these three learning areas respond more to Closing the Gap data and policy agendas. Closing the Gap is an Australian Government strategy to improve the lives of Aboriginal and Torres Strait Islander Australians, with set targets for life expectancy, early childhood education enrolment, school attendance, reading, writing and numeracy achievements, Year 12 attainment and employment outcomes (Australian Government, Department of the Prime Minister and Cabinet, nd). The gap and targets are all defined through comparison of Aboriginal and Torres Strait Islander Australians against the achievements and outcomes of non-Aboriginal and Torres Strait Islander Australians – a deficit framing – positioning white and other migrant Australians' achievements and outcomes as what is desirable. All of the targets are based on western ways of knowing: colonialism and neoliberalism in united force. Progress of counter-colonialist agendas are constantly compromised in negotiating a colonised landscape that feeds racism and neoliberalism.

Despite mandated aspirations in the New Zealand policy and curriculum environment, progress in enacting educational expectations about obligations to Māori has been slow. The Auditor General (Provost, 2013) has made public her office's critique of the under-supported roll-out of the Māori education strategy *Ka Hikitia – Managing for Success: The Māori Education Strategy 2008–2012* (New Zealand Ministry of Education, 2009), as mentioned in Chapter Two. This policy had aimed to shift the deeply ingrained deficit discourses held by teachers and educational administrators, and to ensure that being Māori was viewed as a source of cultural advantage and of potential for success. *Ka Hikitia* was rehashed in 2013 and ironically, given its lack of influence to date, re-subtitled to become *Ka hikitia. Accelerating success: 2013–2017 Māori education strategy* (New Zealand Ministry of Education, 2013). However, the progress of such strategies was impeded at the policy level by the National Party led government of 2008–2017 which was very much influenced by global neoliberalist ideologies, as demonstrated in their implementation of compulsory national standards for numeracy and literacy in primary schools and the introduction of charter schools. (NB: Both of these initiatives have recently been revoked by the incoming Labour led government).

National evaluations by the Education Review Office have highlighted that in early childhood education, despite the intentions of numerous documents that signal the importance of the mandated 'bicultural' approach, the implementation of this is too often lacking. As discussed in the previous chapter, a 2013 report concluded that whilst:

> Many services made reference to Te Tiriti o Waitangi and to New Zealand's dual cultural heritage and bicultural practice in their philosophy statements ... *only a few services* were fully realising such intent in practice by working in partnership with whānau Māori and through the provision of a curriculum that was responsive to the language, culture and identity of Māori children.
>
> *(Education Review Office, 2013, p. 13, emphasis added)*

This signals the need for an urgent reconsideration of the underlying causes for this continuing lack of delivery of this key aspiration of Te Whāriki, 21 years on.

Challenges in this regard are the focus of the following, final chapter of this book.

Pedagogical and environmental foundation (or Mauri) stones for young children's community building

From being with the children, educators and community members of Gundoo and Katoa, over time we came to better understand what matters in enabling young children's participation in communities. For Māori, a whatu mauri or mauri stone represents the life force entrusted from the Atua (gods) and ensures the spiritual wellbeing, mauriora of the people, rivers, forests and lands.

> Immanent within all creation is **mauri** – the life-force which generates, regenerates and upholds creation. It is the bonding element that knits all the diverse elements within the Universal 'Procession' giving creation its unity in diversity. It is the bonding element that holds the fabric of the universe together.
>
> *(Marsden, 2003, p. 44)*

We draw from this concept of foundation (or Mauri) stones to symbolise life-force, contained within stones which are laid to define and give purpose, such as has been long held cultural practice on the lands that we inhabit. The stone of belonging is necessary, for identity to be grounded in the collective, from whence is drawn strength, wellbeing and security. The stone of relationality lays out how we live, work, and play together. The stone of freedom offers choice and movement and scope to explore, to find out, to share and to learn with others. The stone of cultural pride and confidence adds further integrity to being part of a community that can move forward and look outwards. We invite you to consider carefully where you place and how you pedagogically use these stones with your communities.

References

Adair, J. K., Phillips, L., Ritchie, J. & Sachdeva, S. (2016). Civic action and play: examples from Māori, Aboriginal Australian and Latino communities. *Early Child Development and Care*, 1–14.

Australian Bureau of Statistics (2017). *Census: Aboriginal and Torres Strait Islander Population*. Retrieved from http://www.abs.gov.au/ausstats/abs@.nsf/MediaRealesesByCatalogue/02D50FAA9987D6B7CA25814800087E03

Australian Government Department of Education Employment and Workplace Relations. (2009). *Belonging, Being and Becoming: The Early Years Learning Framework for Australia*. Canberra: Australian Government Department of Education, Employment and Workplace Relations for the Council of Australian Governments. Retrieved from https://education.gov.au/early-years-learning-framework.

Australian Government, Department of the Prime Minister and Cabinet (n.d.). *Closing the Gap*. Retrieved from https://www.pmc.gov.au/indigenous-affairs/closing-gap

Australian Institute of Health & Welfare (n.d.). *Discrete Indigenous Community – Indigenous Community Identifier*. Retrieved from https://meteor.aihw.gov.au/content/index.phtml/itemId/269732

Barad, K. (2007). *Meeting the Universe Halfway: Quantum Physics and the Entanglement of Matter and Meaning*. Durham: Duke University Press.

Behrendt, L. (2016, 22 September). Indigenous Australians know we're the oldest living culture – it's in our Dreamtime. *The Guardian*. Retrieved from https://www.theguardian.com/commentisfree/2016/sep/22/indigenous-australians-know-were-the-oldest-living-culture-its-in-our-dreamtime

Chawla, L. (1986). The ecology of environmental memory. *Children's Environments Quarterly*, 3(4), 34–42.

Davies, B. (2014). *Listening to Children: Being and Becoming*. Abingdon, Oxon: Routledge

Daylight, P. & Johnstone, M. (1986). *Women's Business: Report of the Aboriginal Women's Taskforce*. Canberra: Australian Government Publishing Service.

Education Review Office. (2013). *Working with Te Whāriki*. Wellington, NZ: Education Review Office. Retrieved from http://www.ero.govt.nz/publications/working-with-te-whariki/

Harper, D. (2018). Aborigine. *Online Etymology Dictionary*. Retrieved from https://www.etymonline.com/word/aborigine

Harris, J. (2003). Hiding the bodies: the myth of the humane colonisation of Aboriginal Australia. *Aboriginal History Journal*, 27, 79–104. Retrieved from http://press-files.anu.edu.au/downloads/press/p73641/pdf/ch0550.pdf

Kreutz, A. (2015). *Children and the Environment in an Australian Indigenous Community*. Abingdon, UK: Routledge.

Lister, R. (2003). *Citizenship: Feminist Perspectives* (2nd edition). Basingstoke: Macmillan.

Little, H. (2006). Children's risk-taking behaviour: implications for early childhood policy and practice. *International Journal of Early Childhood*, 14(2), 141–154.

MacDonald, L. T. A. O. T. & Muldoon, P. (2006). Globalisation, neo liberalism and the struggle for indigenous citizenship. *Australian Journal of Political Science*, 41(2), 209–223, doi:10.1080/10361140600672477

Marsden, M. (2003). *The Woven Universe. Selected writings of Rev. Māori Marsden*. (Ed. T. A.C. Royal). Wellington: The Estate of Māori Marsden.

New Zealand Ministry of Education. (2009). *Ka Hikitia. Managing for Success. Māori Education Strategy 2008–2012*. Retrieved from http://www.parliament.nz/resource/en-nz/49SCMA_EVI_00DBSCH_INQ_9064_1_A14037/0449a92c3574c1e5b0f850ae1fdb155b155fe3aa

New Zealand Ministry of Education. (2013). *Ka Hikitia. Accelerating Success. 2013–2017. The Māori Education Strategy*. Retrieved from https://education.govt.nz/ministry-of-education/overall-strategies-and-policies/the-Māori-education-strategy-ka-hikitia-accelerating-success-20132017/the-Māori-education-strategy-ka-hikitia-accelerating-success-2013-2017/

New Zealand Ministry of Education. (2017). *Te Whāriki. He whāriki mātauranga mō ngā mokopuna o Aotearoa. Early Childhood Curriculum*. Retrieved from https://www.education.govt.nz/early-childhood/teaching-and-learning/te-whariki/

New Zealand Ministry of Social Development. (2016). *The Social Report*. Retrieved from http://socialreport.msd.govt.nz/

Power, K. & Somerville, M. (2015). The fence as technology of (post-) colonial childhood in contemporary Australia. In V. Pacini-Ketchabaw and A. Taylor (Eds), *Unsettling the Colonial Places and Spaces of Early Childhood Education* (pp. 63–77). New York: Routledge.

Proud, D., Lynch, S., á Beckett, C. & Pike, D. (2017). 'Muck-about': Aboriginal conceptions of play and early learning. In S. Lynch, C. á Beckett & D. Pike (Eds), *Multidisciplinary Perspectives on Play from Birth and Beyond*. Singapore: Springer Nature.

Provost, L. (2013). *Education for Māori: Implementing Ka Hikitia – Managing for Success*. Wellington, NZ: Office of Controller and Auditor-General. Retrieved from http://www.oag.govt.nz/2013/education-for-Māori

Smith, L. T. (1999). *Decolonizing Methodologies. Research and Indigenous Peoples*. London and Dunedin: Zed Books Ltd and University of Otago Press.

Sobel, D. (1993). *Children's Special Places: Exploring the Roles of Forts, Dens and Bush Houses in Middle Childhood*. Tucson, AZ: Zephyr Press.

State of Queensland (2018). *Education and Care Services National Regulations*. Retrieved from https://www.legislation.qld.gov.au/view/pdf/inforce/current/sl-2011-ecsnr

Sumsion, J., Harrison, L., Letsch, K., Bradley, B.S. & Stapleton, M. (2018). 'Belonging' in Australian early childhood education and care curriculum and quality assurance: opportunities and risks. *Contemporary Issues in Early Childhood*, 19 (4), 340–355.

The State of Queensland (Department of Education), (2016). *Foundations for Success*. Retrieved from http://www.foundationsforsuccess.qld.edu.au

United Nations (2007). *Declaration on the Right of Indigenous Peoples*. Retrieved from https://www.un.org/esa/socdev/unpfii/documents/DRIPS_en.pdf

Werbner, P. & Yuval-Davis, N. (1999). Introduction: Women and the new discourse of citizenship. In P. Werbner & N. Yuval-Davis (Eds.) *Women Citizenship and Difference (Postcolonial Encounters)* (pp. 1–38). London: Zed Books.

7

CHALLENGES FOR POLICY AND PRACTICE FOR YOUNG CHILDREN'S COMMUNITY BUILDING

This chapter begins with a critique of the hegemonic pervasiveness of the assumption of white superiority that has perpetrated the project of colonisation and which continues to this day. Next racism is highlighted as a key mechanism that reinscribes such oppressive relations on a daily basis, simultaneously reinforcing the ongoing impacts of longstanding intergenerational trauma. We then describe how working within collectives of children, families, Elders, teachers and more-than-human entities challenges individualist western modes of operating. We consider how our learnings challenge universalising early childhood discourses, policies and pedagogies. We highlight key pedagogical learnings in relation to foregrounding Indigenous wisdom, recognising the power of silent pedagogies, valuing community contributions and embracing relationality with the wider community including the more-than-human realm. The chapter concludes with a discussion of how our study contributes to reconsiderations of notions of citizenship.

Challenging the assumption of western superiority

'Civil', 'civilised' and 'civilisation' are terms that have a history of association with the western construct of citizenship. The word 'civil' originated in the late 14th century 'relating to civil law or life; pertaining to the internal affairs of a state', from the Old French word *civil* 'relating to civil law' (circa 13th century) and directly from the Latin word *civilis* 'relating to a society, pertaining to public life, relating to the civic order, befitting a citizen' (Harper, 2019). From about the 1550s, the meaning of civil as 'not barbarous' emerged (Harper, 2019), aligning with the creation of the modern world through invasion and colonisation, when European colonisers were measuring their versions of society and governance against what they read of the societies they colonised. This is the origin of the meaning of 'civil' as courteous and polite which emerged in the late 16th century.

The civil element of citizenship developed largely in the 18th century, and is concerned with 'the rights necessary for individual freedom, such as the right to freedom of speech and the right to own property' (Chesterman & Galligan, 2009, p. 5). In everyday English, reference to being civil or civilised indicates being courteous and polite framed by Victorian societal standards. Such a discourse lingers and dominates, whereas civil rights assert the right to freedom of speech and the right to have a voice on matters that affect you. These are quite contrasting meanings that are messily entangled in the citizenship project for Indigenous Peoples who have been defined by colonisers as 'uncivilised' 'primitive' or 'savage' 'races' where Aboriginal Australians were placed at the bottom of the scale of civilisation with western societies monopolising the highest position (Sabbioni, 1998). This biased ranking is of course performed by those who have allocated themselves the highest position, and categorisation has been defined through comparison to self, noting difference by misguided, ill-informed perceptions as to what is missing, what is lacking, such as writing, religion and agriculture (Kowal, 2015).

The Oxford dictionary defines *civilisation* as 'The stage of human social development and organization which is considered most advanced' (2019a, para 1). Indicators of 'advancement' have been viewed from a western perspective which is detached from nature and is framed by materialistic, individualistic and hierarchical measures, with white males at the top and insidiously embedded structures that protect these hierarchies of privilege. What needs to be questioned is: what are the indicators of advancement, for what goal, for what purpose, who is defining these and who is benefitting from them? A society that writes has come to be understood as an advanced civilisation, along with agricultural societies. The widely held perception is that pre-colonised Aboriginal Australians did not engage in agricultural practices. For example, Australia is left empty on the mapping of the centres of origin and spread of agriculture in wikimedia commons, and this is then cited in the Khan Academy (2019) webpage on early civilisations. So the popular perception of Aboriginal Australians as 'uncivilised' continues, even though there are vast bodies of evidence to prove otherwise (e.g., see Pascoe, 2014). The Oxford dictionary further defines *uncivilised* as 'not socially, culturally, or morally advanced', and gives as an example: '*children are basically uncivilized*' (2019b, para 1). Hence both Indigenous peoples and children are placed on the lower ladders of a hierarchy of being (un)civilised as per the 'Great Chain of Being' discussed in Chapter Two.

The assimilationist project of the British colonials was intended to replace whatever had previously existed in the 'new' country, both Indigenous peoples and biodiversity, with a replica of the 'mother' country grounded in an inherent assumption of the superiority of western, and in particular British, 'civilisation'. Tuck and Gaztambide-Fernández (2013) define settler colonialism as 'the specific formation of colonialism in which the colonizer comes to stay, making himself the sovereign, and the arbiter of citizenship, civility, and knowing' (p. 73). However, as pointed out by Skerrett and Ritchie (forthcoming), colonisation sets up a system of privilege (the descendants of the settlers) and oppression (of the original Indigenous inhabitants of the land). British settler colonisation is a particular type of colonisation. It has nothing to do with 'civilisation' (one of its fake narratives), but all to do with access to land or territory.

(p. 2)

Patrick Wolfe (2006) describes this most succinctly: 'Settler colonialism destroys to replace' (p. 388). As Aboriginal Australian lawman and elder Hobbles Danaiyarri often said 'Captain Cook was the real wild one. He failed to recognise law, destroyed people and country, lived by damage, and promoted cruelty' (Rose, 2004, p. 4).

The majority of white/Pākehā citizens in both countries remain largely oblivious of the history of their nations, of how this has been based on the erroneous assumption of white superiority and of the multiplicitous entangled trajectories of economic marginalisation, of intergenerational trauma, of the obliteration of histories, knowledges, languages and lives, that continue to negatively impact the lives of Indigenous peoples in their countries and elsewhere. These limited understandings of colonisation relieve the settler descendants of any sense of responsibility in relation to either historical or ongoing injustices:

> They think of colonization as something that happened in the distant past, as perhaps the unfortunate birthpangs of a new nation. They do not consider the fact that they live on land that has been stolen, or ceded through broken treaties, or to which Indigenous peoples claim a pre-existing ontological and cosmological relationship. They do not consider themselves to be implicated in the continued settlement and occupation of unceded Indigenous land.
>
> *(Tuck, McKenzie & McCoy, 2014, p. 7)*

By working collectively, a group of Indigenous and non-Indigenous colleagues, we have created this book to enhance awareness of the ongoing impact of colonisation on Indigenous peoples and settler descendant responsibility in relation to these lived experiences and to listen and learn from Indigenous wisdom on negotiating co-existence.

New Zealand writer Maurice Shadbolt (1999) identified a national syndrome of historical amnesia which he associated with a deep-seated guilt or unwillingness to acknowledge the tensions and treachery of our past. This amnesia and concomitant lack of inclusion of historical and local Indigenous knowledges in our education systems contributes to an unspoken hegemonic complacency of the dominant culture, and thus to the lack of understanding or empathy towards Māori regarding the negative effects of colonisation. In Australia, the amnesia or readiness to move and forget is embedded in the 'she'll be right' expression which moves to 'amnesia and the illusion of progress' along with 'a seduction ... that somehow it is all going to be okay' (Rose, 2004, p. 46). Rose continues that:

> The problem for memory is this: if we are to forget all things that make us uneasy, then we have to forget even to think about the places where uncomfortable

things happen. If we were able to do that, then we would find ourselves forgetting the losses for which we are ultimately accountable, and insulating ourselves against the absences that surround us.

(p. 47)

To counter this deliberate amnesia, white people need to interrogate their whiteness. As Liza Mazzei (2011) has highlighted:

> Because whiteness has historically gone unnamed and unnoticed as the hegemonic norm, a failure to voice whiteness, or put differently, the choice to articulate one's white identity by not doing so, is another strategy for maintaining power through a move to maintain the normative (and unspoken) presence of whiteness, hence, 'desiring silence'.
>
> *(p. 659)*

White educators need to make that choice and feel uncomfortable and awaken consciousness of their own amnesia and notice the historical amnesia that relates to the communities in which we live and work. Education offers a site for stirring awareness to feed great intercultural relationality and privileging Indigenous voices, knowledges and rights. Education systems should include such histories to avoid the ongoing cultural amnesia and 'desiring silence' that enables this assumption of superiority to persist.

Students at all levels, and in particular, teacher education students, require opportunities to study the history of their countries in order to contextualise their contemporary understandings (Siraj-Blatchford & Siraj-Blatchford, 1999). Recently, the New Zealand Minister of Education has agreed that schools need more support with regard to strengthening the teaching of New Zealand history, stating that 'New Zealand's history, extending back to the earliest Polynesian settlers, is of significant importance to us' (as cited in McLachlan, 2018, p. 1), yet the racist attitudes of teachers continue to obfuscate this objective.

Steps to mandate and assert the inclusion of Indigenous experiences of colonisation and nation-building in Australia and New Zealand are never immune to counter assertions, reductions and deletions by white superiority. Following Rhonda Craven's (1996a, 1996b) call for teacher education programmes to include Indigenous Australian studies in their programmes from the *Teaching the Teachers: Indigenous Australian Studies* project, many Australian universities included core Indigenous Australian knowledges courses in their teacher education programmes, though not all (Craven, Halse, Marsh, Mooney & Wilson-Miller, 2005). The establishment of the Australian Professional Standards for Teachers (Australian Institute for Teaching and School Leadership, 2011) and national accreditation of initial teacher education programmes (Australian Institute for Teaching and School Leadership, 2015) has since mandated inclusion of knowledge of Aboriginal and Torres Strait Islander histories, cultures and languages. And one of the six guiding principles of the National Quality Standard for Early Childhood Education and

Care (Australian Children's Education and Care Quality Authority, 2017) is 'Australia's Aboriginal and Torres Strait Islander cultures are valued' (p. 8).

With the introduction of Australia's first national curriculum for schools, Aboriginal and Torres Islander experience of colonisation was included in the original versions and reinforced through Aboriginal and Torres Islander Histories and Cultures defined as one of the cross-curricular priorities. Much of the content embedded in History and English was then removed following the review of the Curriculum by two white male conservative education commentators (see Donnelly & Wiltshire, 2014) (as discussed in Chapter 2). They referred to a submission from the Institute of Public Affairs that claimed that the Australian Curriculum is 'unbalanced, ideologically biased and systematically hostile to the legacy of Western Civilisation' as it privileges the cross-curricular priorities of Aboriginal and Torres Islander Histories and Cultures, Sustainability and Australia's engagement with Asia. These deletions can clearly be seen on pages 107–112 and 142 of the tracked changes to F-10 Australian Curriculum (Australian Curriculum and Assessment Reporting Authority, 2015). The *Queensland Kindergarten Learning Guideline* (Queensland Studies Authority, 2010) included foregrounding Aboriginal and Torres Strait Islander ways of knowing, being and learning, yet the revised *Queensland Kindergarten Learning Guideline* (The State of Queensland, 2018) removed such assertion and inclusion (as previously discussed in Chapter Two) in response to white feedback that Aboriginal and Torres Islander cultures were being privileged.

Respecting and re-invigorating Indigenous languages is key to challenging the hegemonic dominance of English, the language of the colonisers. Despite its recently proclaimed 'superdiverse' status (Royal Society of New Zealand 2013), New Zealand due to colonisation has been a nation steadfastly monolingual in English (Waite, 1992) and the Māori language is severely endangered. Fewer than a quarter (21.3%) of Māori people and only 3.7% of the total population of Aotearoa speak enough te reo Māori to hold a conversation in that language (Statistics NZ, 2013). The commitment of the Katoa teachers to the inclusion of te reo Māori and tikanga (values and cultural practices) as per the Ministry of Education and Education Council documents, of Pacific Islands' languages and dispositions (see for example, Luafutu-Simpson, 2011), and of the home languages of the specific children attending, was constantly visible, integrated throughout their pedagogies and documentation. Gundoo educators also sought ways to revitalise remaining fragments of Wakka Wakka and Gubbi Gubbi languages through songs, naming games and wall charts, along with speaking in the community language of Aboriginal English. Most of the educators are from the community, so they are speaking their language. Cultural knowledges are foregrounded and embedded into daily practices. And the introduction of the Queensland *Foundations for Success* (State of Queensland (Department of Education), 2016) curriculum for Aboriginal and Torres Strait Islander children now offers resources to further support foregrounding cultural pride, relationality and freedom.

Western superiority has a long legacy of silencing and ignoring Indigenous ways of being, knowing and relating with regard to citizenship (co-existence with others), civil rights and civilisation. Through this book we invite readers to notice the wisdom that Indigenous cultures and children bring to construction of concepts and practices that facilitate co-existence with others, which we refer to as community building. From the Gundoo community we learnt:

- Pride in community membership is foundational
- Kinship ties run deep – you relate to others as they are a part of you
- Everyone looks out for each other
- Elders are respected and young are cared for
- Collectivist ontology is felt and communicated through embodied knowledge
- Co-existence with others is with all entities (humans, fauna, flora, geoforms)
- By seeing others as they are a part of you, enacts empathic and inclusive relations
- Physical restraints are worked around, through and under and
- Aboriginal lore of kinship relations and responsibilities imbue all knowing, being and relating.

From the Katoa community we learnt about ways in which a collective of teachers can work from a deeply embedded ethic of respect for children, families and the environment, an ethics of relationality, which enabled them to inclusively reflect core Māori values throughout their planning, teaching and ongoing reflection. As Bob Jickling has pointed out: 'Our epistemologies, our systems of knowledge, rest on ethical choices whether these are made consciously or not' (2005, p. 239). He critiques western cultural frameworks for organizing knowledge for 'our tendency to separate ethical, emotional, and spiritual knowledge from "hard" science' (p. 40). We consider that teacher education programmes should reflect this concern to develop in future teachers a commitment to ongoing critique of the foundational ethical premises on which they base their praxis.

Challenging the injustices of racism, intergenerational trauma and social class

Racism encourages a 'blame the victim' attitude with regard to the disparities that result from long-term institutional discrimination (see Figure 7.1). It perpetuates the invisibility of intergenerational trauma that scars and impedes the lives of Indigenous peoples (Pihama et al., 2014). This means that in order to intervene rather than perpetuate this situation, a constant awareness of racism and intergenerational trauma as well as a sensitivity in relation to the implications should be at the forefront of teachers' work.

Racism utilises the imposition of labels which serve as carriers of racist discourses. These discourses also mask the hegemony of institutional policies and practices that are designed by and for the dominant cultural group, whereby the 'norms' are normed to those of the coloniser, excluding the priorities and values of the colonised. Drawing on the work of Gaile Cannella and Radhika Viruru (2004),

FIGURE 7.1 Tom Scott cartoon (1991, p. 61) reproduced with permission of author

Mathias Urban explains that in both 'colonial and neocolonial contexts, representation has been, and continues to be, employed as a powerful "methodology of contemporary colonization"' (2018, p. 9). Racism is enacted in the representations imposed by the colonisers:

> 'Māori' is a construction of colonisation. Prior to contact with Europeans, 'māori' meant simply 'ordinary' and Māori individuals identified not as Māori, but with their hapū and iwi [sub-tribe and tribe] (Kawharu, 1992). It is ironic that as a result of colonisation, to be 'ordinary' or 'normal' in this country now means to be part of the dominant Pākehā mainstream (Mead, 1996).
>
> *(Ritchie, 2002, p. 24)*

Linda Mead [Smith] (1996) called for being Māori to be repositioned as normal. An anti-racist, counter-colonial approach therefore involves the renormalisation of being Indigenous as normal.

Racism operates against respectful relationality and, in tandem with complex overlays of ideological impacts of colonialism, class and gender, negatively influences the identities and life experiences of Indigenous peoples on an ongoing daily basis (Poata-Smith, 2013). Colonialist policies having disenfranchised Indigenous peoples from exercising political influence then proceeded to alienate them from their lands and thus their economic base, along with denying them equitable educational opportunities, resulting in the original peoples being relegated to marginalised corners of society in their own country. Meanwhile, Pākeha/white citizens who have benefitted from both colonisation and the current socioeconomic and political arrangements live 'in a bubble of blissful ignorance' of the ongoing impacts of racism, inadvertently (if not blatantly) perpetuating it and frequently denying its existence (McConnell, 2018). For them, acknowledging racism is optional. Maintaining a state of ignorance enables the avoidance of empathising with the pain carried intergenerationally by Indigenous peoples of the trauma of seeing both human and more-than-human kin mistreated and massacred (Rose, 2008).

As discussed in the previous chapter, for Bena the meaning and use of the label 'Aboriginal' *is* abnormal. It is a generic term that has been imposed by the colonisers; it is not a term that comes from her own history, her own languages, her own genealogical connectedness to her people and places. 'Aboriginal' is an anthropological term that has been used to distinguish Indigenous Australians' otherness, as well as homogenise a diverse collection of hundreds of cultural groups who live across vastly variant landscapes (Kowal, 2015). Such classification has fuelled constructions of Australian First Nations Peoples as less than, and produced intergenerational lived inequities and merged diverse identities. Better informed understanding of past and present Indigenous inequities is necessary before healing begins (Burridge, 1999) and mythologies of inequities dissipate. Bodkin-Andrews and Carlson (2016) argue that the most substantial obstructions to overcoming the inequities suffered by Aboriginal Australians is the compounded assault of ignorance and racism that perpetuates, and the continued personal attacks on identity. We need to recognise and name racism and the daily lived obstructions racism imposes on Australian First Nations Peoples to enable visibility of their strengths and wisdom (Bodkin-Andrews & Carlson, 2016).

It is concerning that there seems to have been a political 'blanding' of the recently 'refreshed' *Te Whāriki 2017*, regarding serious issues related to the ongoing legacy of colonisation, and our responsibility as educators to intervene in the perpetuation of racist injustices. The curriculum no longer contains the reflective question from the original *Te Whāriki*: 'In what ways do the environment and programme reflect the values embodied in Te Tiriti o Waitangi, and what impact does this have on adults and children?' (1996, p. 56). Nor has it retained the expectation that: 'The early childhood curriculum actively contributes towards countering racism and other forms of prejudice' (1996, p. 18). Interestingly, *Te Whāriki 2017* does not mention racism at all and mentions challenging prejudice just once. Miles Ferris, the president of the Māori school principals' association Te Akatea, has recently pointed out that 'There's a high level of racial bias, discrimination throughout our system that's not often talked about. And it's not till we address those issues that I think we're going to see long-term and effective change' (as cited in Radio New Zealand News, 2 May, 2018). Whilst white/ Pākehā educators may only 'unconsciously' perpetuate racism (see discussion of 'unconscious bias' in Chapter Two) and when witnessing instances of racism can choose whether or not to confront it, Indigenous people have no option but to be on the receiving end of racist acts and aggressions on a daily basis. We believe that it is a core responsibility (response-ability) of all educators to challenge the ongoing prevalence of racism and a key challenge for teacher education providers to activate commitment towards this.

In Chapter Four, following our thread of the barriers and confinement enforced through physical and metaphoric fences, Kerryn wrote of how her experience as an Aboriginal Australian person is always political, always questioned. And though we have policy mechanisms such as cultural capability frameworks to cultivate a better-informed citizenry (a strategy to reduce racism), racism is once again not named. In the politics and discourses of niceness (which early childhood education is particularly well known for – see Stonehouse, 1994) and diplomacy, acknowledgement of racism is avoided in early childhood education and education policies generally in Australian and New Zealand. To wholly work towards the civic learning of coexistence with others in colonised nations, the violence and wounding in Indigenous peoples' lived daily reality of racism needs to be recognised, felt and redressed. As Margaret Sims (2014) has advocated: 'Understanding that none of us is free of racism, and accepting the challenge to improve is the foundation for change. Early childhood professionals can make a difference. It is up to us to ensure that we do' (p. 93).

Collectivist challenges to individualism

Aboriginal Australian and Māori worldviews are collectivist ontologies as discussed in Chapter One. Aboriginal Australian worldviews are based on collective good rather than individualism (Martin, 2008) and this was illustrated in the stories provided in Chapter Four. Kinship ties weave the threads for collective rights, responsibilities and actions with all entities. To relate to an other as they are part of you, as Aunty Margaret Kemarre Turner (2010) expressed, is a resonant aphorism of Aboriginal Australian ways of knowing, being, doing and relating. In a Māori worldview, 'a person is always relationally connected' (Salmond, 2017, p. 407). For Māori and Aboriginal Australian worldviews, this relationality includes the more-than-human and spiritual realms, and is not hierarchically arranged. In Aotearoa supernatural beings such as taniwhā, that inhabit oceans and seas, are kaitiaki, guardians, who look out for people and vice versa. 'In this networked world, a person is constantly negotiating their relationships with others, striving to keep them in balance and good heart' (Salmond, 2017, p. 407). However, colonisation has imposed hierarchical, gendered, stratified social orderings, prioritising the rights of the individual above that of the collective. For example, laws were passed that individualised collective land title, thus making it easier for settlers to purchase lands from Māori. In te ao Māori (Māori worldview), the Earth Mother, Papatūa-nuku, and the whenua (land/placenta) were ancestral sources of nurture, not a commodity to be sold. Since the rapid introduction of neoliberal economic and social policies that have been embraced by New Zealand governments from the mid-1980s onwards:

> the neo-liberal conception of the cost-benefit calculating individual has become commonplace, eroding shared values and collective institutions from

families to the state. Such an understanding of the self runs contrary to ancestral Māori ideas of a person as defined by their relationships with others, past
and present, and values such as utu (reciprocity and balanced exchange); aroha
(fellow feeling), manaakitanga (hospitality, care for others) and tino rangatiratanga (chiefly leadership) in which mana is exhibited in acts of generosity.

(Salmond, 2017, p. 409)

Thus individual greed and profiteering has sought to replace Māori values, threa-
tening the capacity to maintain the sense of collective responsibility that enables
care for both social and environmental wellbeing.

In the study we saw young children's enactment of their sense of responsibility,
held and done by and for the benefit of the collective. This was often not adult
provoked nor explicitly encouraged and was expressed through shared identity and
communal and familial obligations for collective interest or will. At Gundoo, children caring for each other was particularly resonant, with this by far being the most
frequently observed practice contributing to young children's community building.
Collective interests, rights and responsibilities were readily demonstrated by the
children, nurtured by the community cultural value of thinking of your 'mob'
(your kin and community). Recognition and pride in community and tribal
membership is foundational to identity building and now reinforced by the Foundations for Success (State of Queensland (Department of Education), 2016) learning area Being proud and strong, at Gundoo. From this base, collectivism is
enacted through a strong embodied ethos of everyone caring for each other and
sharing. Knowledge of kinship relations and responsibilities holds and forms collective empathic and inclusive relations, actions and responsibilities with all entities
(humans, fauna, flora, geoforms).

Collective responsibility is a core value in te ao Māori, the Māori worldview, and
was evident at Katoa through expression of whanaungatanga (relationships), kotahitanga (collectivity), manaakitanga (caring, responsibility for others) and rangatiratanga
(leadership in service of the collective). It was also evident in expression of tuakana/
teina relationships, whereby older children support younger siblings/cousins. During
the data collection period there were 10 pairs of siblings attending the research centre,
and a further number who were cousins. The encouragement of tuakana (older siblings) to enact their responsibilities to teina (younger siblings) was an expression of
collective responsibility. Collective responsibility was reinforced by the consistent
articulation by the teachers of these core Māori values. Teachers at Katoa recognised
that they have a responsibility to support these bonds and enable young children to
demonstrate and practise their roles as carers, nurturers and responsible community
members (Leaupepe, 2018; Rameka & Glasgow, 2017).

Collectivist ontologies offer a very different frame from individualist, neoliberal,
nuclear family ontologies on which national education policies are based, and also
blinkered to seeing other ontologies. Indigenous ways of thinking have sustained
thousands of years, providing an extraordinary legacy of wisdom to listen to. Indigenous value systems provide a strong context for collectivist approaches to civic

action. Not only can western policy makers pay greater heed to ensuring that local Indigenous values are embedded within curriculum and pedagogies, they also need to ensure that teachers receive appropriate professional learning to enable the fostering of these values within their educational settings.

Challenges for early childhood discourses and policies

> How we create or recreate the world counts. We can no longer be aloof or disinterested observers. Ethics-based epistemologies are concerned with right relationships
>
> (Jickling, 2005, p. 41).

Following on from the previous section, we ask the following questions: to what extent do we, and our discourses, policies and practices, position infants and young children as autonomous individuals, or alternatively, as embedded, contributing members of their extended families and communities? And, to what extent are we able to critique the normativising, controlling and inherently violent doctrines of developmentalism and behaviourism as promoted in the adultist patronisation of children embedded in western discourses? (Cannella & Viruru, 2004). And how can we as a community of early childhood education teachers and scholars resist universalising, normativising globalised discourses that impose 'generic' western standards and measurement on children from diverse communities?

In recent years we have seen a turn towards globalised measurement of educational attainment, which has now reached the early childhood care and education sector in the form of the International Early Learning and Child Wellbeing Study (IELS), an initiative of the Organisation for Economic Co-operation and Development (OECD). These have been critiqued as being a form of hegemonic neocolonialism (Urban, 2018), and of neoliberal governmentality that generates a form of internal policing via normative expectations generated by datafication (Roberts-Holmes, 2019). It is hard to see how such decontextualised assessments might have any relevance for teachers, children and families in such diverse settings as Gundoo and Katoa.

Discourses create their own truths and thus normalise practices (Ingleby, 1986; Inglis & Thorpe, 2015), so if we conceive of children as egocentric, autonomous, incapable of sharing or empathising, and if we fail to notice and affirm their acts of caring and concern for others, their efforts to 'act in concert' with others on collaborative endeavours, then the latter capacities will likely wither. Yet if we view children as capable of acting in concert to (re)create their social worlds and to deeply respect and care for their environment, we will see a different set of 'outcomes'. As early childhood teachers, scholars and researchers, we can critique the ways in which we are seduced by universalised values and aspirations for children and endeavour in order to explore the extent to which we have deeply engaged understandings of particular families' histories, values, aspirations for their children and grandchildren. We can consider the ways in which we seek to come to know familial interests and dispositions. We can reflect on how, as a 'caring' profession, we extend our caring to the families and communities in which we work and on the ways in which we model this caring and foster this with the infants and young children who attend our services.

Universal policy implementation without recognition of community context and cultural values and practices works to denounce Indigeneity and enforce assimilation. This was illustrated in Chapter Four through the discussion of universalisation of national and state policies on separate spaces for separate age groups, fencing, sleeping and dogs are in conflict with cultural values and practices and do not take into account the community context. Gundoo implements pedagogy and delivery of practice that meets the national legislated early learning framework, regulations and standards, enduring historical and current government provisions, whist recognising and honouring the strengths and cultural agency of each child. This is not an easy path to tread and requires ongoing code-switching, negotiation and sacrifices.

Challenges for pedagogies

Pedagogies that support and enable children as citizens of the here and now – community builders of today – require educators to step back and down from their adultist positionings. To no longer see their classroom as their domain that they rule, but rather to flatten the hierarchy and be with the children, place and community. This requires teachers to critically examine such deeply embedded cultural constructs, such as their role as teachers, their cultural values and priorities. This might include questioning our allegiances to western lineality of time, of development, of evolutionist and futurist orientation, including 'stages of development', and hierarchies of knowledge. This in turn leads us to reject the inadequacy of child-centred individualistic pedagogies, seeing the child in isolation from their collective identities, places, histories and genealogy. We identified four key pedagogical principles at play at Gundoo and Katoa that supported children's community building: foregrounding cultural identity and wisdom; pedagogies of silence; real community contributions; and more-than-human relational pedagogy. These approaches challenge us to relinquish our sense of knowing what is best for others, to see instead the complexity of children's reciprocally attuned embodied responses.

Foregrounding cultural identity and wisdom

In Chapter Six, we recognised that cultural pride was a resonant theme in the pedagogical practices at Gundoo and Katoa. At Gundoo, this is evident in the practice of kinship relationality, the resources and materials selected and used, such as Aboriginal and Torres Strait Islander children's picture books and posters, use of Aboriginal English and languages, and celebrating Aboriginal and Torres Strait Islander days of importance. From Katoa Kindergarten we saw how overarching themes based on the core Māori values of kotahitanga, whanaungatanga and rangatiratanga engendered recognising, acknowledging and affirming the entanglement of histories, colonisation, identities and complexities of multiple cultural affiliations, the teachers' careful research and responsiveness aimed at including home languages of every child. This is seen in the responsive and thoughtful learning stories that contribute to the overall planning story at Katoa, whereby 'Figurations have agency, history, and a life of their own' (Lakind & Adsit-Morris, 2018, p. 32) rather than hegemonic treatment of universalised dispositions as has become common practice in early childhood education in Aotearoa New Zealand.

At both Gundoo and Katoa Kindergarten, we saw enactment of a deep respect for the knowledges and wisdom of Elders, and recognition of the importance of seeking permission from Elders. At Gundoo, their position alongside the aged care home provided an ideal opportunity for daily intergenerational exchanges, valuing each other as precious members of community. Community artists and Elders would visit and children would visit local museum to foreground Aboriginal knowledge sharing. The Katoa teachers consistently worked at building and maintaining a relationship with the local marae and Elders associated with that community. The input of all attending families/whānau was regularly sought and an integral part of the teachers' planning process was to research key Māori content to include in their daily teaching interactions, documentation and pedagogical reflection. We advocate for the specificity of such knowledges to be forefronted in teachers' work.

Pedagogies of silence

A default western understanding of teachers is that they talk, that they fill the class-room with talk, commanding silence from the children in order that the teacher's voice prevails. The western construct is of an explicit teacher of content and skills. At Gundoo, the educators were present, providing resources and comfort and care as needed, but they rarely intervened with questions or commentary, only reminders of safety cautions, creating a reassuring space for the children to initiate, negotiate and act together. Others have observed this aspect of Aboriginal pedagogies, in which children are freely permitted to explore and engage with others and the learning environment, in real-life situations that involve risks (Fasoli, Wunungmurra, Ecenarro & Fleet, 2010; Sumsion, Harrison, Letsch, Bradley & Stapleton, 2018). As discussed in Chapter Six, we saw freedom to choose and move as a consistent principle that informed the ped-agogies employed. Such is enacted through pedagogies of silence. Through a western lens this practice may be read as lazy or slack, but in fact the practice is intentional and is very much about being present. Physical watchful presence communicates encour-agement and assurance. Choice of positionality in a room or outdoor area is inten-tional in the watchful presence. Relationality is nurtured through doing together, a practice not filled with words, but doing and being with children. As Kerryn shares 'Words are special. Don't fill in time with just words.' Much is instead communicated through eyes, nods and gentle touch. Katoa educators noticed this quietness in the Gundoo day video.

Words are not the only way of expressing wisdom, connection, empathy and trust. Teachers at Katoa would often observe children struggling with an individual or collective task, not intervening to assist or suggest a resolution, trusting that the children would eventually work things out. There were also many instances observed of children's wordless community building, whereby even very young children assisted one another or attended to an injury in silence, their embodied physical presence resonating empathy and concern, the reading of another's feelings and needs not requiring verbal expression.

Real community contributions

Through Gundoo and Katoa both being recognised by family and community members as a community hub, family and community members would visit and contribute to the daily life of the children's centres without a need to be nudged and organised by educators. Intergenerational family membership was particularly visible in the nurturing acceptance story shared from the babies room at Gundoo in Chapter Four. As mentioned before, Gundoo is a community hub, through being governed and staffed by Aboriginal and Torres Strait Islander people, it is recognised as a culturally safe place. So community member contributions were just part of being a community member, such as family members of all ages (including school age children) visiting kin, community members cooking echidna to share, community artists sharing stories and their arts. At Katoa, the grandfather of two attending sisters, Papa Barry, visited the kindergarten every day around lunchtime. Whānau members could use the kitchen to prepare food, such as when they cooked pork supplied by Papa Barry as described in Chapter Five. Also very noticeable was the deep connection and warm relationships of the teachers with families, teachers often taking considerable time just chatting and being alongside parents at the centre.

The process that was led by the Katoa head teacher Trinity required teachers' intentionality in building these relationships with families, backed by clear systems for planning, reflection, which required reaching out for whānau voice. The supportive nature of the teaching team involved modelling the teachers' own collaboration, and shared values of whanaungatanga, kotahitanga, empathy, concern, respect. In the 'Ko wai ahau?' planning story example, there were multiple levels of focus which included individual and family/whānau identity as well as a sense of community, the centre's relationship with the local tribe Ngāti Toa Rangatira, and regular visits to marae. Trinity and the other teachers encouraged the children's seeing themselves as part of the community, the inward and outward flow included inviting various people in such as the regular visits by a local band and a dancer, as well as going out into the community, walks to marae, up to the bush out the back, and down to the shop to get baking supplies or Easter eggs. Trinity spoke of how as a team they intentionally worked as a collective to bring in the values of the community. She mentioned as an example how Sonya had brought in from her relationships with the teachers of Toru Fetu, a nearby centre that features three different Pacific Island cultures (Cook Island Māori, Tuvalu and Niuean), a list of Samoan dispositions (Luafutu-Simpson, 2011) and these went up on the planning wall and were incorporated into the planning work. Community presence and contribution is highlighted here as integral to culturally responsive early childhood care and education.

More-than-human relational pedagogy

The study highlighted the importance of pedagogies recognising, respecting and making connections to the Country upon it is situated. As shared in Chapter One, both Aboriginal Australian worldviews and Māori worldviews are relational, inclusive of all entities of water, land, animals, flora, weather, sky and spirits.

KERRYN: It's about being embodied to connect to the country and living things from the stars to the earth, from horizon to horizon, not separating the people from land. The land is a part of our kin and even a small rock has its home and the language of the county can sing its ancient songs if we listen.

The Aboriginal notion of connection to country and protocols of Welcome to Country and of the Acknowledgement of Country speak of this consciousness of being entangled with all other matter. Māori cosmologies view all entities within the biosphere as descendants of Papatūānuku (Earth Mother) and Ranginui (Sky Father). Māori ontology is underpinned by a relational ethics, based in respect for mauri, the life force in both living and inanimate things, for wairuatanga, spiritual interconnectedness, and for hau, the spiritual power of obligatory reciprocity (Henare, 2001). In recent times, post-humanism and new-materialism has also proposed an awareness of being entangled with all other matter. Viewed from Indigenous ontological perspectives, this is not new but rather is ancient wisdom and deeply held spirituality. This requires attunement to the rhythms of other entities to align co-existence for the good of all.

The children at Gundoo and Katoa were very much interested in building communities with all entities. As illustrated in our stories, they included dogs, insects, cats, rocks, mud, puddles, trees, roots, plants, compost and gardens. And the pedagogies applied at Gundoo and Katoa welcomed these broad communities. Pedagogically this requires acknowledgement and acceptance and a broadening of language to de-centre humans from communities. To draw from Aboriginal lore and government, which according to Pascoe (2014) is the most democratic model of all the systems humans have devised, is to recognise and relate to another as if they are a part of you (Turner, 2010). And as an effort to reconcile the troubled times we live in (Harraway, 2016), this requires awareness of the responsibility to all others, 'facing our responsibility to the infinitude of the other, welcoming the stranger whose very existence is the possibility of touching and being touched, who gifts us with both the ability to respond and the longing for justice-to-come' (Barad, 2012, p. 219). We acknowledge the work of the Common Worlds Research Collective (2019) in contributing to recognition of more-than-human relations and pedagogies and argue that such pedagogies with

Indigenous wisdom may offer hope 'that response-ability to the infinitude of the other is contagious and spreads and heals the vast injuries of human privilege' (Phillips, 2018, p. 18).

Challenges to conceptualisations and practices of citizenship

Through being with children in Indigenous communities, relationality with all others was foregrounded in the early childhood centres: children's entre into a polis – a more public sphere – where they can build communities. As Moss (2014) proposed in *Transformative change and real utopias in early childhood education* 'early childhood centres are public spaces and public resources, open to all citizens as of right. They are places of realising potentiality, the potentiality of citizens and of early childhood education' (p. 81). They offer a wealth of relationships and resource for those in the neighbourhood:

> A place of infinite possibilities, giving constant rise to wonder and surprise, magic moments and goose bumps, and a source of hope and renewed belief in the world; a place, too, where 'freedom, democracy and solidarity are practiced and where the value of peace is promoted'.
>
> *(Moss, 2014, p. 82).*

As a western construct, citizenship is about human relations but children's and Indigenous worldviews see the necessity for relations beyond human – we are invited to conceptualise citizenship as co-existing with more-than-human others – with bees, with rocks, with trees, dirt and roots, with stick insects, with cats and dogs, with magpies, with fences, with mud and puddles.

We alert readers to the elitism of citizenship as property ownership from the historical foundations of citizenship and the resurgence in neoliberal times, where we witness the elite predominantly holding ruling power and the majority being denied power. And that rather than seeing land to be owned as giving further right to a voice in the ruling, that land is one of the many entities with which we co-exist. Building peaceful communities involves relations with all entities of the locale, so connection to place runs deep. We see that citizenship as obedience and compliance, which often dominates civic education curricula, in which students learn about formal civic institutions, limits or denies children and young people's civic agency and ignores Indigenous wisdom. This mode of citizenship operates in denial of the inherent democracy of Indigenous models. In the communities of Gundoo and Katoa, we witnessed community membership as foundational to civic identity. This shifts western definitions of citizenship as nation state membership, to one of membership of cultural communities, of located communities (place/country), children's communities and communities of self-choosing. As Hannah Arendt argued back in 1958, 'the polis ... is not the city-state in its physical location; it is the organisation of the people as it arises out of acting and speaking together ... no matter where they happen to be' (p. 198).

Though we often translated the focus of the study to educators and community members as being about children's rights, as a means to make the ambiguous concept of citizenship more focussed to our interests in active citizen participation, citizenship as rights possession did not come to the fore in our readings of children's actions. As noted by Yuval-Davis (1997) in Chapter One, a rights focus comes from a construction of citizens as strangers to each other. So Indigenous Peoples' rights are more asserted and formed in relation to their co-existence and negotiations with colonisers. In amidst Aboriginal Australian and Māori societies, relationship to another is foregrounded, as we witnessed in children's enactment of kinship roles and responsibilities at Gundoo and at Katoa. Citizenship or community building is not something you think, it is something you do. It is embodied – it is bodily known in Indigenous communities where cultural values are instilled from before birth.

We recognise and argue for cultural agency and cultural identity as inherent sources of citizenship and sites for community building. Cultural agency and identity provide solid foundations of security and belonging to shield the daily onslaught of racism violating Indigenous peoples' civic agency.

KERRYN: The notion of children's civic agency, in particular first nations' children's engagement and rights relating to an identity in Australian citizenship requires ongoing analysis to ensure its development within education systems. This study highlighted the importance of ongoing analysis of curriculum decision-making to respectfully reflect the voices of Aboriginal and Torres Strait Islander children and the children seeing their identity with agency in Australian citizenship. The national conversation is ongoing in this nation regarding citizenship and agency for Aboriginal and Torres Strait Islander people. And we ask: are we hearing children's voices in this conversation? How can we engage children in conversations that focus on enhancing their participation in civic rights? Gundoo demonstrated civil resilience to maintain strong community connections and social participation within a highly structured civic space. We have created this book to support the role and place for ongoing dialogue in this nation that strategically focuses on First Nations' worldviews and children's participation and rights to be considered as contributors for agents of future civic change.

We argue that there is much to learn (and much hope for sustainable peaceful communities) from citizenship conceptualised as embodied, emplaced and relational with all entities.

Taking up these challenges

From this study we hope to contribute to conversations challenging notions of 'civilisation'. We hope readers of this work will be encouraged to adopt an ongoing stance of critiquing the pervasive complacency with hegemonic discourses privileging western superiority, racism and modernism. Learning from local Indigenous knowledges, histories, ecologies and relationalities requires building and sustaining committed, long-term relationships. Embracing these ways of knowing, being, doing and relating as pedagogical frames enables recognition of children's community building as a relational, embodied, emplaced reciprocal engagement. As our planet faces the onslaught of Anthropogenic climate change, the wisdom of the sustainable philosophies of Indigenous peoples becomes even more salient.

Walk together.

References

Arendt, H. (1958/1998). *The Human Condition* (2nd edn). Chicago: The University of Chicago Press.

Australian Children's Education and Care Quality Authority (2017). *Guide to the National Quality Standard*. Retrieved from http://files.acecqa.gov.au/files/National-Quality-Framework-Resources-Kit/NQF-Resource-03-Guide-to-NQS.pdf

Australian Curriculum and Assessment Reporting Authority, (2015, September). *Tracked changes to F-10 Australian Curriculum*. Retrieved from https://acaraweb.blob.core.windows.net/resources/Changes_to_the_F-10_Australian_Curriculum.pdf

Australian Institute for Teaching and School Leadership (2011). *Australian Professional Standards for Teachers*. Retrieved from https://www.aitsl.edu.au/docs/default-source/general/australian-professional-standands-for-teachers-20171006.pdf?sfvrsn=399ae83c_12

Australian Institute for Teaching and School Leadership (2015). *Accreditation of initial teacher education programs in Australia: Standards and procedures*. Retrieved from https://www.aitsl.edu.au/docs/default-source/initial-teacher-education-resources/accreditation-of-ite-programs-in-australia.pdf

Barad, K. (2012). On touching – The inhuman that therefore I am. *Differences: A Journal of Feminist Cultural Studies*, 23(3), 206–223.

Bodkin-Andrews, G. & Carlson, B. (2016). The legacy of racism and Indigenous Australian identity within education. *Race Ethnicity and Education*, 19(4), 784–807.

Burridge, N. (1999). Reconciliation: bringing the nation together. In R. Craven (Ed.), *Teaching Indigenous Studies* (pp. 1–12). St Leonards: Allen and Unwin.

Cannella, G. S. & Viruru, R. (2004). *Childhood and Postcolonization. Power, Education and Contemporary Practice*. New York: RoutledgeFalmer.

Chesterman, J. H. & Galligan, B. (2009). *Citizens Without Rights: Aborigines and Australian Citizenship*. Cambridge: Cambridge University Press.

Common Worlds Research Collective (2019). *Common Worlds Research Collective*. Retrieved from http://commonworlds.net/

Craven, R. G. (Ed.) (1996a). *Teaching the Teachers: Indigenous Australian Studies for Primary Pre-Service Teacher Education. Model Core Subject Manual for Teacher Educators*. Vol. 1. Sydney: School of Teacher Education, University of New South Wales in association with the Council for Aboriginal Reconciliation.

Craven, R. G. (ed.) (1996b). *Teaching the Teachers: Indigenous Australian Studies for Primary Pre-Service Teacher Education. Model Core Subject Manual for Teacher Educators*. Vol. 2. Sydney: School of Teacher Education, University of New South Wales in association with the Council for Aboriginal Reconciliation.

Craven, R., Halse, C., Marsh, H., Mooney, J. & Wilson-Miller, J. (2005). *Teaching the teachers mandatory Aboriginal Studies: recent successful strategies*. Retrieved from http://www.

dest.gov.au/NR/rdonlyres/CF5C2704- 9DD6–4E02-B6B7- AD5A334E83C1/7431/
TeachingtheteachersVOLUME1PDF.pdf.

Donnelly, K. & Wiltshire, K. (2014). *Review of the Australian Curriculum: Final Report*.
Retrieved from https://docs.education.gov.au/system/files/doc/other/review_of_the_na
tional_curriculum_final_report.pdf

Fasoli, L., Wunungmurra, A., Ecenarro, V. & Fleet, A. (2010). Playing as becoming: sharing
Australian Aboriginal voices on play. In M. Ebbeck & M. Waniganayake (Eds), *Play in
Early Childhood Education: Learning in Diverse Contexts* (pp. 215–232). South Melbourne,
Vic.: Oxford.

Haraway, D. (2016). *Staying with the Trouble: Making Kin in the Chthulucene*. Durham, NC/
London, England: Duke Press.

Harper, D. (2019). Civil. *Online Etymology Dictionary*. Retrieved from https://www.etym
online.com/search?q=civil

Henare, M. (2001). Tapu, mana, mauri, hau, wairua: a Māori philosophy of vitalism and
cosmos. In J. A. Grim (Ed.), *Indigenous Traditions and Ecology. The Interbeing of Cosmology
and Community* (pp. 197–221). Cambridge, MA: Harvard University Press.

Ingleby, D. (1986). Development in social context. In M. Richards & P. Light (Eds), *Children of Social Worlds* (pp. 297–317). Cambridge: Polity Press.

Inglis, D. & Thorpe, C. (2015). *An Invitation to Social Theory*. Cambridge: Polity.

Jickling, B. (2005). 'The wolf must not be made a fool of': reflections on education, ethics,
and epistemology. In P. Tripp & L. Muzzin (Eds), *Teaching as Activism Equity Meets
Environmentalism* (pp. 35–46). Montréal: McGill-Queen's University Press.

Kawharu, S. H. (1992). The Treaty of Waitangi: a Maori point of view. *British Review of
New Zealand Studies*, 5, 23–36.

Khan Academy (2019). *Early civilizations*. Retrieved from https://www.khanacademy.org/huma
nities/world-history/world-history-beginnings/birth-agriculture-neolithic-revolution/a/intro
duction-what-is-civilization

Kowal, E. (2015). Time, indigeneity and white anti-racism in Australia. *The Australian Journal
of Anthropology*, 26, 94–111.

Lakind, A. & Adsit-Morris, C. (2018). Future child: pedagogy and the Post-Anthropocene.
Journal of Childhood Studies, 43(1), 30–43.

Leaupepe, M. (2018). Culturally responsive and relational pedagogy. Insights to sibling
relationships. The First Years: Ngā Tau Tuatahi. *New Zealand Journal of Infant and Toddler
Education*, 20(1), 31–34.

Luafutu-Simpson, P. (2011). *Exploring the Teaching of Effective Approaches for Assessing Young
Samoan Children's Learning in Early Childhood Centres: Developing an Authentic Samoan Lens*.
Wellington: Ako Aotearoa. Retrieved from https://akoaotearoa.ac.nz/knowledge-centre/
developing-an-authentic-samoan-lens/effective-approaches-for-assessing-young-samoa
n-childrens-learning/

McConnell, G. (2018, 9 April). *Taika Waititi's right, New Zealand really is a racist place*. Retrieved
from https://www.stuff.co.nz/entertainment/celebrities/102948539/taika-waititis- right-
new-zealand-really-is-a-racist-place

McLachlan, L.-M. (2018). *Concerns over how NZ history is taught: 'You Māori are lucky'*.
Retrieved from https://www.radionz.co.nz/news/te-manu-korihi/362800/concerns-
over-how-nz-history-is-taught-you-maori-are-lucky

Martin, K. (2008). Targeting the divide. *Koori Mail*, 424, 44.

Mazzei, L. (2011). Desiring silence: gender, race and pedagogy in education. *British Educational Research Journal*, 37(4), 657–669.

Mead, L. T. T. R. (1996). *Ngā Aho o te Kākahu Mātauranga: The Multiple Layers of Struggle by
Maori in Education*. (D.Phil Thesis), University of Auckland, Auckland.

Moss, P. (2014). *Transformative Change and Real Utopias in Early Childhood Education. A Story of Democracy, Experimentation and Potentiality*. Abingdon, OX: Routledge.

Oxford Dictionary. (2019a). *Civilization*. Retrieved from https://en.oxforddictionaries.com/definition/civilization

Oxford Dictionary. (2019b). *Uncivilized*. Retrieved from https://en.oxforddictionaries.com/definition/uncivilized

Pascoe, B. (2014). *Dark Emu Black Seeds: Agriculture or Accident*. Broome, WA: Magabala Books.

Phillips, L. G. (2018). Sticky: childhoodnature touch encounters. In A. Cutter-Mackenzie, K. Malone & E. Barratt Hacking (Eds), *Research Handbook on Childhoodnature: Assemblages of Childhood and Nature Research*. Living Reference online. Retrieved from https://link-springer-com.ezproxy.library.uq.edu.au/content/pdf/10.1007%2F978-3-319-51949-4_90-1.pdf

Pihama, L., Reynolds, P., Smith, C., Reid, J., Smith, L. T. & Te Nana, R. (2014). Positioning historical trauma theory within Aotearoa New Zealand. *AlterNative: An International Journal of Indigenous Peoples*, 10(3), 248–262.

Poata-Smith, E. S. (2013). Emergent identities: the changing contours of Indigenous identities in Aotearoa/New Zealand. In M. Nakata, M. Harris and B. Carlson (Eds), *The Politics of Identity: Emerging Indigeneity* (pp. 24–59). Sydney: University of Technology Sydney E-Press.

Queensland Studies Authority (2010). *Queensland Kindergarten Learning Guideline*. Brisbane: QSA.

Radio New Zealand News. (2018, 2 May). *Ministry urges 'bold step' for Māori education*. Retrieved from https://www.radionz.co.nz/news/te-manu-korihi/356413/ministry-urges-bold-step-for-maori-education

Rameka, L. & Glasgow, A. (2017). Tuākana/tēina agency in early childhood education. *Early Childhood Folio*, 21(1), 27–32.

Ritchie, J. (2002). *'It's Becoming Part of Their Knowing': A Study of Bicultural Development in an Early Childhood Teacher Education Setting in Aotearoa/New Zealand*. (PhD thesis), University of Waikato, Hamilton.

Roberts-Holmes, G. (2019). Governing and commercialising early childhood education: profiting from The International Early Learning and Well-being Study (IELS)? *Policy Futures in Education*. doi:10.1177/1478210318821761

Rose, D. B. (2004). *Reports from a Wild Country: Ethics for Decolonisation*. Sydney: University of New South Wales Press.

Rose, D. B. (2008). On history, trees, and ethical proximity. *Postcolonial Studies*, 11(2), 157–167.

Royal Society of New Zealand. (2013). *Languages in Aotearoa New Zealand*. Retrieved from https://royalsociety.org.nz/what-we-do/our-expert-advice/all-expert-advice-papers/languages-in-aotearoa-new-zealand/

Sabbioni, J. (1998). Preface. In J. Sabbioni, K. Schaffer & S. Smith (Eds) *Indigenous Australian Voices: A Reader* (pp. xxv). Piscataway: Rutgers University Press.

Salmond, A. (2017). *Tears of Rangi. Experiments Across Worlds*. Auckland: Auckland University Press.

Scott, T. (1991). *In a Jugular Vein: A Collection of Cartoons and Comments*. Wellington, NZ: Daphne Brasell Associates Press.

Shadbolt, M. (1999). *From the Edge of the Sky. A Memoir*. Auckland: David Ling Publishing.

Sims, M. (2014). Racism. Surely not? *Australasian Journal of Early Childhood*, 39(1), 89–93.

Siraj-Blatchford, I. & Siraj-Blatchford, J. (1999). 'Race', Research and Reform: the impact of the three Rs on anti-racist preschool and primary education in the U.K. *Race, Ethnicity and Education, 2*(1), 127–148.

Skerrett, M. & Ritchie, J. (forthcoming). Frayed and fragmented: Te Whāriki unwoven. In J. Nuttall and A. Gunn (Eds) *Weaving Te Whariki 3*. Wellington: NZCER Press.

State of Queensland (Department of Education). (2016). *Foundations for Success*. Retrieved from http://www.foundationsforsuccess.qld.edu.au

State of Queensland (Queensland Curriculum and Assessment Authority) (2018). *Queensland Kindergarten Learning Guideline*. Brisbane: QCAA. Retrieved from https://www.qcaa.qld.edu.au/downloads/p_10/qklg_2019.pdf

Statistics New Zealand. (2013). *New Zealand Social Indicators. Māori Language Speakers*. Retrieved from http://archive.stats.govt.nz/browse_for_stats/snapshots-of-nz/nz-social-indicators/Home/Culture%20and%20identity/maori-lang-speakers.aspx

Stonehouse, A. (1994). *Not Just Nice Ladies: A Book of Readings on Early Childhood Care and Education*. Castle Hill, NSW: Pademelon Press.

Sumsion, J., Harrison, L., Letsch, K., Bradley, B. S. & Stapleton, M. (2018). 'Belonging' in Australian early childhood education and care curriculum and quality assurance: Opportunities and risks. *Contemporary Issues in Early Childhood*, 19 (4), 340–355.

Tuck, E. & Gaztambide-Fernández, R. A. (2013). Curriculum, replacement, and settler futurity. *Journal of Curriculum Theorizing*, 29(1), 72–89.

Tuck, E., McKenzie, M. & McCoy, K. (2014). Land education: Indigenous, post-colonial, and decolonizing perspectives on place and environmental education research. *Environmental Education Research*, 20(1), 1–23. doi:10.1080/13504622.2013.877708

Turner, M. K., with McDonald, B. & Dobson, V. P. (Trans.) (2010). *Iwenhe Tyerrtye: What it Means to be an Aboriginal Person*. Alice Springs: IAD Press.

Urban, M. (2018). The shape of things to come and what to do about Tom and Mia: interrogating the OECD's International Early Learning and Child Well-Being Study from an anti-colonialist perspective. *Policy Futures in Education*. doi:10.1177/1478210318819177

Waite, J. (1992). *Aoteareo: Speaking for Ourselves. A Discussion on the Development of a New Zealand Languages Policy*. Wellington: Learning Media.

Wolfe, P. (2006). Settler colonialism and the elimination of the native. *Journal of Genocide Research*, 8(4), 387–409. doi:10.1080/14623520601056240

Yuval-Davis, N. (1997). *Gender and Nation*. Thousand Oaks, CA: Sage Publications.

INDEX